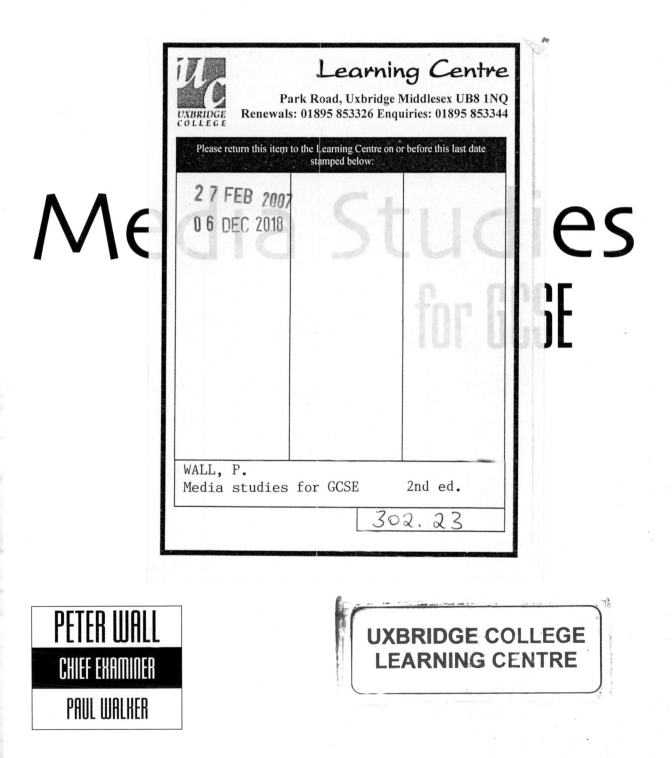

Media Studies for GCSE

PETER WALL
CHIEF EXAMINER
PAUL WALKER

Published by HarperCollins*Publishers* Limited
77-85 Fulham Palace Rd
Hammersmith
London W6 8JB

www.**Collins**Education.com
Online support for schools and colleges

An imprint of HarperCollins*Publishers*

©HarperCollins*Publishers* 2002

First published 2002

10 9 8 7 6 5 4

ISBN 0-00-713391-X

Peter Wall asserts the moral right to be identified as the author of this work.

British Library Cataloguing in Publication Data

A catalogue record for this publication is available from the British Library

Internal design: Ken Vail Graphic Design, Cambridge
Cover design: Caroline Grimshaw
Commissioning Editor: Helen Clark
Project Management: Charlie Evans
Cover photo: Getty images
Edited by Charlie Evans and Charlie Rundall
Permissions cleared by Gavin Jones
Production: Katie Morris

Printed by Printing Express Ltd., Hong Kong

Acknowledgements

Realia: © Philips, pp2, 82; © TiVo, pp2 (bottom right), 96 (left); Advertising Archive, pp3 (top left), 11, 12, (bottom left), 36, 77, 82 (bottom left), 161, 167, 171; Dixons, p3 (bottom right); ITV Digital, p4 (top); Sky Broadcasting, pp4 (bottom), 46, 50-51, 94 (top), 103, 105, 192, 194-5, 197, 201-2; Siemens, p5; Conde Nast Publications Ltd, p6 (top); She, p6; Cameron/Arenaimages.com, p35; When Saturday Comes, p44; Guardian Newspapers Ltd, p46; The Sun (for supplying text), p52; More, p60; British Board of Film Classification, p61; Advertising Standards Authority, p62; Broadcasters Audience Research Board Ltd, p67; Radio Joint Audience Research Limited, p67; National Readership Surveys Ltd, p67 (bottom right); The Mirror, pp70, 124; City Screen, p80; Blockbuster, p81; Heat, p88; Splash News (photo), p88; Sight and Sound, p91; Empire, p92; Hotdog, p93; Ryanair.com, p94 (top); Tesco.com, p94 (middle); Askjeeves.co.uk, p94 (bottom); Amazon.com, p95 (top); Cheapholidays.com, p95 (middle); Mp3grandcentral.com, p95 (bottom); Homechoice, p96 (right); © Digital Radio, p97; Lycos.co.uk, p99; Yahoo.co.uk, p100; © Guardian Unlimited, p101 (text); FHM.com, p102; Esquire.co.uk, p102; Company.co.uk, p102; Elle.com, p102,; ZenADSL, p104; Angelfire.com, p107 (middle); Smart.co.uk, p107 (bottom); The Online Gooner, p107 (top); BBC Online, p108 (top left); Getaforecast.com, p108 (top right); Howletts.net, p108 (bottom right); Camcentral.com, p108 (bottom left); Big Brother Web-site, p109 (top right); Channel 4.com, p109 (top left); Reprinted by kind permission of Atlantic Syndication, p112 (top); Yorkshire Evening Post, p112; Metro, p112; East Anglian Daily Times, p112; The Star (Sheffield), p126; Glory Glory Man United, p128; Hello Magazine, p130; OK! Magazine, p130; Heat, p130; Reproduced by kind permission of D.C. Thomson & Co. Ltd., pp133, 136; Panini Publishing, pp134 (left), 137 (right); Dark Horse Comics, Inc., pp134 (right), 137 (left); Published by kind permission of NME/IPC Media, p148; Smash!Hits, p156; Mojo, p156; Classic FM, pp156, 186; Kerrang, p157; Q, p157; Jockey Slut, p157; Premier Resorts Ltd, p162; Fujifilm Ltd, p169 (bottom); Dolce and Gabbana Sunglasses, p169; Diadora, p169; New Zealand Tourist Board, p170; Sony UK Ltd, pp170, 176, 211; Lever-Faberge, p171 (right); Capital Radio, p177 (top); Foreverbroadcasting.com, p177; Radio Authority, p185; Virgin Radio, p186; talkSPORT FM, p186; Viz, p205; Time Out Magazine Ltd, p207.

Photos: PA Photos, pp8-9, 24, 32, 38-9, 48-9, 52, 55, 89, 90, 101, 119, 122, 123, 158, 160, 180, 182; The Ronald Grant Archive, pp12 (bottom right), 22, 27 (bottom), 35 (Tomb Raider), 83, 85, 86, 138-9, 165, 234; HarperCollins*Publishers*, pp12 (top); Redferns Picture Library, pp13 (bottom left), 145-7, 150, 154; COTY Inc., p14; BBC, pp17, 46, 183, 184; Freemantle Media Stills Library, p23; Corbis, pp25, 59 (top left), 176 (right), 188, 218; Hulton Getty, pp27 (top), 142, 78, 116, 140; © Apple Computer Inc, pp30, 215; Tony Stone, pp40, 58-9; Cineworld, p79; Roberts, p98; Ericsson, p106; The British Library, p114; © Steve Lumb, pp155, 195; Radio Caroline, p185.

Illustrations: Tom Gauld, pp33, 56, 63, 74, 110, 129, 174, 187, 219, 223, 229, 231; Janek Matysiak, pp10, 18-19, 41, 47, 209, 213, 220-1.

Contents

Why Media Studies?

The media: monster or angel?

There is a powerful force sending its messages to virtually everyone on earth. It is using every form of communication tool available. It is in your sitting room, your bedroom, maybe even your bathroom. It is in shops, cinemas, libraries and churches. It travels in cars, on buses, trains, planes and ships. Even if you blast off into space, it is out there waiting for you. No matter how hard you try, you cannot escape it.

The name of this force is 'the media', and whether you like it or not, to a large extent it defines your life and the way you think. 'The media' is the name given to channels of communication a society uses to speak for itself. It includes television, cinema, video, radio, newspapers, magazines, books and the Internet. Really it is a mass of individual contact points between communication tools and human beings.

It is difficult to visualise this, however, and most people speak about the media as if it were a single being with a personality of its own. It has been portrayed more as a monster than as an angel. Television has been criticised for luring schoolchildren away from their homework; videos have been accused of encouraging violence and drug abuse; newspapers and magazines of filling our heads with gossip; and computer games of turning us into goggle-eyed morons. Whatever the problem, it seems the media is in part to blame.

Television has, however, brought information and learning to millions of people, with satellite broadcasting allowing us to experience history as it happens. Videos are widely used as teaching aids in schools and colleges. Radio supplies a lifeline for those cut off from the outside world. Magazines and newspapers provide knowledge as well as entertainment, while computers provide us with an 'information superhighway' that facilitates world-wide communication.

Is the media a good thing or a bad thing? As we have seen, the media is not one 'thing', but a large number of interactions between individual receivers and specific media products, or texts; so really, the question is meaningless. Also, judgements about what is 'good' or 'bad' tend to differ between individuals, groups and societies over time. A more helpful approach is to examine media products and ask how they are made, what they contain and what receivers make of them. In doing this, we can begin to understand the part media products play in modern life.

Press clippings

Collect stories from the press that focus on the positive and negative roles that the media is seen to play in our society. What views of the media can be seen in these 'clippings'? Do you agree with the views that are put forward in them?

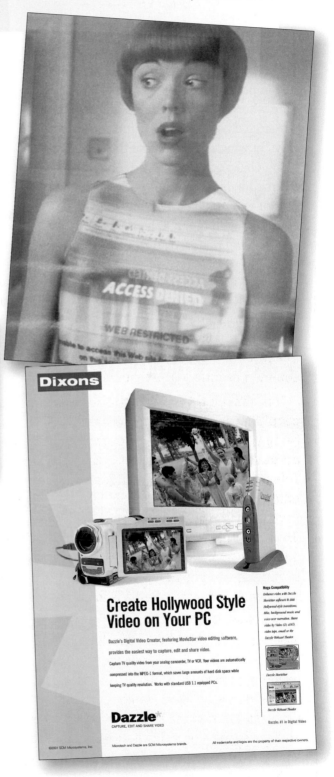

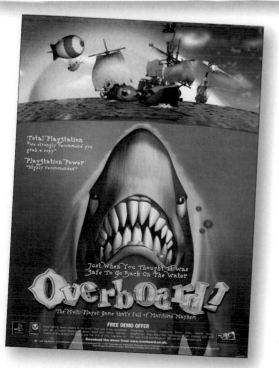

An ever-increasing range of media services and technology is available to the consumer.

The changing world of the media

It is important to realise that we live at a time when the media itself is undergoing dynamic change. Many of the traditional ways in which we consume the media are being changed by the new technologies the media uses to deliver its products to us. For example, many homes are now equipped with digital televisions capable of receiving hundreds of television channels and radio stations beamed to us via satellites. Similarly many homes have powerful personal computers connected to the Internet.

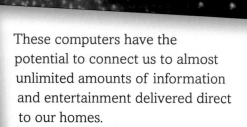

These computers have the potential to connect us to almost unlimited amounts of information and entertainment delivered direct to our homes.

A key aspect of this new technology is that it is interactive. This means that we can influence and even change the nature of the media products we receive. Not only can we select a specific programme to watch, we can even choose the camera angle from which we see it. So, when you watch a football match using digital technology, you have the power to direct the programme from your own armchair. The advent of DVD (Digital

Video Disc) offers audiences the choice of selecting a whole range of extras when they buy or rent a film. Such extras might include the option of replacing the original soundtrack with a commentary by the director or the stars.

You can use your digital television to shop or to get access to your bank account. You can also use it to send and receive e-mails just like a personal computer. The technology of digital television and that of the personal computer are now coming even closer together. This is called convergence. It means that a world of information is potentially available to you through your television. With the simple click of a mouse, you are able to obtain just about anything you want. Recently released films can be piped to you on demand. When you consider too the improved quality of television pictures and sound, with large, wide-screen, surround-sound sets, it becomes clear that many of us no longer need to leave the house to go to the cinema, to a football match or even to the shops. Most newspapers and magazines, even, are available to us in on-line editions, which means we can read them on our computer screens.

It is not only in the home that these technological changes are affecting the way we consume the media. Much of the information and entertainment available at home is becoming accessible through the mobile phone, too. This means that people are able to enjoy these benefits while on the move.

One of the important concerns of Media Studies is to consider just how these technological changes are likely to influence our lives. It is clear that as you begin your study of the media you are doing so at a time when some important and exciting changes are taking place.

Discussion

Do you think young people will soon be hanging round street corners watching the latest movies on the screen of a WAP phone?

Key concepts

At GCSE you are going to have to get to grips with what we call 'key concepts' for studying the media. These concepts are language, representation, institution and audience. By looking at these you can begin to understand how the media works and the part it plays in our lives. Look at the magazine covers on this page, and let us see what we mean by each of these concepts.

Language The covers of magazines use both words and images to communicate with us. These words and images are put together in very much the same way as any other magazines. Certain conventions have been followed so that we recognise the covers as belonging to magazines. The covers are media messages that have been encoded, and we decode them. This process of communication requires the use of 'media language'. As media students you will be looking at the way in which media products are put together, or constructed. You will learn terminology that will help you to analyse media products.

Representation The magazine covers are presenting us with information about the world. *GQ* is telling us, for example, the 100 best things in the world, which they have selected. In giving us this information, someone has selected and shaped what we see. The woman on the front cover of *She* is not, in some senses, a real woman, but an image used to represent a woman. This process of presenting information about the world to us is called 'representation'. In looking at this key concept we will be assessing just how accurate media representations are.

Institution The magazines have been produced by a media organisation, or 'institution'. This institution has arranged for the magazines to be written, illustrated, put together, printed, advertised and distributed to your local newsagent. This process is called media production. In the section on media institutions, we will be looking at how these work, and at how the way they work can influence the media products they create.

Audience The people who buy and read the magazine are usually called the 'audience'. We use the word 'audience' to describe consumers of all media products, not just film, television and radio. The audience is important because this is where media products are targeted. Without an audience a media product serves little purpose. In considering the key concept of audience, we will be looking at the nature of media audiences. We will also look at how audiences consume the media and what effect the media has upon the lives of its audiences.

Activity

Now look at the magazine covers again on p6. They are both taken from 'lifestyle' magazines. Write down briefly what you think are the main characteristics of these covers. Working in pairs, make a list of the sort of features you would expect to find in a lifestyle magazine aimed at:

Men	Women	Men and Women

Describe the sort of person you think might buy a lifestyle magazine. You need to consider:

1 their age
2 their job and income
3 the family life
4 their hobbies and interests
5 where they live

From your experience of looking at lifestyle magazines, are there any features missing that you think would interest readers?

You and the media

Now you can look at your own involvement with the media by having a go at the tasks below.

1 Media journal

So, how big a part does the media play in your life? Over the next week keep a diary of when, where and for how long you come into contact with media products. Note down:

- what you watch on television or video
- which radio stations you listen to
- what tapes and CDs you play
- which newspapers and magazines you read
- any computer packages you use

Record not only the media products that you choose to use, but also those that you see and hear around you, for example:

- adverts on billboards, buses and trains
- music in shops
- videos in shopping centres
- magazines in waiting rooms

How much time in total have you spent in contact with the media during the week?

2 Analysis

After completing your diary, compare it with those of other students and note the differences.

- What is your reaction to the amount of time you spend in contact with the media?
- Why do you use the media in the way you do?

3 Who does what?

Make a note of the electrical media products you have at home, such as:

- televisions
- video recorders
- radios
- CD and tape players
- computers

In pairs, discuss the following questions:

- Who are the main users of each product?
- Who controls their use?
- Do conflicts arise over their use?

2 Language

Aspects of language

Visual language

When you hear the word 'language', you will probably automatically think of words, either spoken or written. Words are an important means of communication between human beings. But the media does not communicate with words alone. It can also use pictures and sounds to convey meaning. Indeed, some media can work purely in a visual language, through pictures that you understand in the same way as words.

Photography is an example of a visual medium, or one that relies for its impact on images. Film and television are also visual media, although both use words and sounds as well to communicate information. Print-based media, such as newspapers, magazines and comics, employ a combination of printed words and pictures, such as photographs, drawings and graphics, to give you information.

Radio, on the other hand, is obviously a medium that relies on the spoken word and other sounds to communicate: it is an aural medium. Pop music, which makes up a large part of many radio stations' output, conversely carries with it a lot of visual images such as pictures of the bands and CD cover designs.

You sometimes hear people say that we live in a media-saturated society. They mean that everywhere you look, words and images are fighting for your attention and bombarding you with messages. But with so much 'information overload', how much do you really take in?

As small children you learn how to use language. For one thing, it helps you let other people know what you want. Of course, the vocabulary that you learn will depend on the culture in which you grow up. The words learnt by French children for describing the world are different from those learnt by children in the UK. As you grow up, you also learn to understand visual signs. No one sits down with you and explains how to watch television. Simply by repeatedly watching TV, you learn to make sense of the various short cuts that a visual medium, such as TV, uses to tell you a story more quickly. For example, if a character is shown leaving a room and is seen in the next shot driving a car, the viewer fills in the missing sequence in their imagination and understands that the character has left the house, got into the car and set off.

In the same way that you learn to read words on a page, so you learn to read visual language. The idea of 'reading' is important in Media Studies. When you read a book, you use your imagination to create pictures in your head; you bring something of yourself to the book by working it out in your mind. Similarly, if you apply the idea of reading to television, it suggests that you are active in bringing something of yourself to it. Just as you use your imagination to fill in the missing parts of a visual narrative to make sense of what has happened, you learn to read other elements of visual language. The way in which you read an image or set of images may well be decided by your upbringing and previous experiences.

Not everyone who watches a set of images on the television will take from them the same meaning. For example, an advertisement that uses an attractive young woman to sell a product may well have a positive impact on many men in the audience. Female viewers with strong opinions about the ways in which women's bodies are exploited by the media are likely to read the advertisement very differently. Similarly a

You learn to fill in the missing information needed to make sense of the narrative.

cookery programme featuring recipes for cooking pork chops would have little appeal to vegetarians or members of certain religious groups. In fact many of them will turn of the programme on the grounds that it is offensive.

In most media, words and pictures work together to create meaning. Very often, words can be used to limit or anchor the meaning of a visual image. In newspapers, photographs have captions to tell the reader how to interpret the images. On news bulletins, newsreaders or reporters talk over images to explain what is happening, which guides the viewers' interpretation of the meaning of the images they see. This process is called 'anchorage'. Just as the anchor of a ship is used to hold it in one place, so the words in a caption or commentary are used to hold or limit the meaning of an image.

Group discussion

AS A GROUP

Are men offended if their bodies are used to sell products?

Caption competition

ON YR. OWN

Choose some images from newspapers and magazines, complete with their original captions. Think up new captions for these images, which will change their meaning as much as possible.

- Is it more difficult to change the meaning of some images than others?
- If so, why is this?

Connotation and denotation

Both words and images, it is argued, work on at least two levels:

Denotation The common-sense or everyday meaning of a sign. A red rose, for example, is a garden plant. That is its denotational meaning.

Connotation The additional or associated meaning that an image or word carries with it, over and above its ordinary, everyday meaning. A red rose is a symbol of love. If you give someone a red rose, they are unlikely to think you are simply handing over a garden plant; for someone who lives in Lancashire, it is also the symbol that represents their county.

When you 'read' a TV programme, magazine or film, your understanding of these texts relies on your ability to respond to both these layers of meaning at the same time.

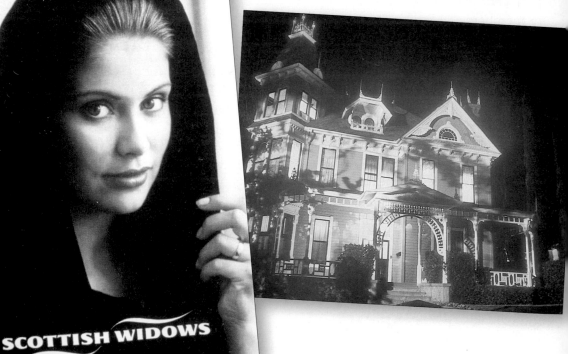

Meanings

IN PAIRS

Working in pairs, look carefully at each image. What is its:

- denotational meaning?
- connotational meaning?

Use each pair's work as the basis for a class discussion on the meanings of the images. Does everyone think they mean the same thing?

Media language

Look at the image on p14. It is an advertisement for a women's perfume that appeared in a magazine called *She*. The magazine describes itself as being 'for busy modern women'.

The image, in the form of a photograph, shows a man and woman embracing. They are clearly the main focus of the image as they are placed in the foreground and occupy most of the image, with the woman herself at the centre. There is writing in French and more writing in English with what appears to be a perfume bottle also in the frame. In the background there are other people, probably a man and a woman. The setting looks like a railway station. We can say that this is the denotational meaning of the image. Most of what is stated refers to what we can see in the advertisement. We have not yet considered any of the associated meanings, or connotations, that it may contain.

So let us look a little more deeply at how the text is put together, or constructed. Firstly we should mention that the image is almost wholly in black and white, apart from the perfume bottle and the name of the perfume, L'Aimant. Not only is it a black-and-white photograph, it is a grainy black-and-white photograph. Look closely at the faces and you can see the grainy quality of the image. This makes it look rather like a newspaper photograph taken using the type of film to take photos in difficult lighting conditions. Notice how the two central figures are in high contrast, with strong blacks and whites, compared to the background, which looks paler and bleached out. They are also more sharply in focus than the background, which looks blurred. These qualities, along with the figures' size and position, make them stand out and become the focus of our attention.

Look at how they are embracing. Their body language says they belong together. They are holding one another closely in the way that lovers do. The man's hands are holding the woman round her waist. She is holding his head in her hands. Their faces are touching. Both are smiling. They are clearly comfortable and do not feel awkward, holding one another in this way.

Toujours
L'AIMANT

LOVE & BE LOVED

François Coty

the edge of the picture. This places the woman at the centre, suggesting she is the most important element in the picture.

Now look at the background. Although it is comparatively less distinct, it is still possible to make out the detail. The couple have been photographed in a railway station. You can see the tracks behind the woman's shoulder next to the other figures standing on the platform. On the opposite platform we can see buildings with a sign which reads 'Metropolitain'. The name and the typeface, or the way in which it is printed, refer to the Paris underground, placing the station in that city. Paris is a city with connotations of romance.

Some of the words too are in French. The name of the perfume is L'Aimant, the French word for a magnet. Again there is an association working here. Magnets attract. Presumably it is being suggested that a woman who wears this perfume will attract men. But look again at the figures. The couple are attractive, but they do not seem to be the sort of young and gorgeous couple normally featured in advertisements for perfume. The image may not be of a young couple falling in love. Indeed the other French word is giving us a clue to the meaning of the image. It says

Indeed they are so wrapped up in one another that they do not even notice that they are being photographed. They are dressed conventionally, almost formally, as though they have been to work or on a business trip. We could describe the shot as a mid shot, as we see just the top half of their bodies. This allows us to look closely at the two figures while still seeing what is going on in the background. Notice how the photographer has taken the shot with the man's back disappearing out of 'toujours' which means 'always'. The words are being used to anchor the meaning of the image, suggesting that this perfume not only attracts a man, but makes sure he remains attracted. Perhaps the image is telling us that the couple are reunited at the railway station after being apart. The perfume is one of the attractions that holds them together.

The photograph is a single moment of a narrative frozen in time. It could be a single frame or a still from a film. What we do not know is what happens before or after this moment. We call upon our own experiences to guess at these details. We do not know if they are married. We do not know if they are having an affair. The location suggests they are reunited after one of them has been on a journey. The perfume ensures that they will be drawn back together again. Certainly their expressions show they are pleased to be together.

So what does the advertisement represent? It has been created by an advertising agency to sell the perfume. It does not, however, tell us anything about what the perfume smells like, but suggests how using it might influence our lives. It is intended to appeal to the lifestyle of the audience, in this case women who read *She* magazine. The message seems to be: Wear this perfume and your man will always want to hold you in his arms. 'Love and be loved', the audience is told.

Of course, many among the female audience looking at the advertisement may be sceptical of the claims being made. Many may try the perfume while shopping and decide they do not even like the smell. Some women, and men for that matter, might also be concerned at the message contained in this advertisement. Like many similar ones aimed at women, it is

suggesting that a women's role in society is to attract and keep a man – that being attractive and appealing to the opposite sex is an important duty for a woman and that happiness and security are to be found in the arms of a man. Perfume and similar products will help her in this function.

So what seems a fairly straightforward text on a denotational level, has some complex meanings when we dig a little deeper. It is also a text, along with many similar texts, that has the potential to influence the way in which we live our lives and the roles we play in our society.

Activity

ON YR. OWN

Choose a similar product aimed at men. Does it have any similarities with the advertisement we have just looked at? What are the differences? What do you think it says about the role of men in our society?

Texts

The term 'media text' refers to any product of the media – a magazine article or quiz show, for example. The word 'text' has important connotations when it's used in an educational context. Because English literature has been such an important part of the curriculum for so many years, the word 'text' is often associated with literary texts. Texts are the books you may study as part of your English course. Often these will be classics of English literature, representing high levels of achievement by great writers. *Hamlet*, *Pride and Prejudice*, *Wuthering Heights* and *Great Expectations* are texts in this sense. Because of this connotation of the word 'text', calling a quiz show a text may seem a little strange. Some people may argue that a quiz show is trivial compared to the great classics of English literature. But this concept of texts is important. Just as the classics of English literature are studied, so you study and analyse a soap opera in order to learn about the society in which you live. If that idea seems a little silly, then remember that in his lifetime Shakespeare's plays would have been performed in pubs, with all social classes crowding in to watch them. It is now a common idea that Shakespeare is of interest only to an elite, but that was certainly not true when the plays were first written. This is not to suggest that *Coronation Street* or *Neighbours* will one day have the importance of *Othello* or *Silas Marner*. The argument is that by studying these texts, we can learn a lot about the lives and culture of the people who consume them.

This argument can be taken one step further: the more texts you study, the better you become at reading them. For example, if you were to go to the ballet for the first time, you might find it hard to understand what it was all about. People who go to the ballet regularly would have learned the codes and conventions that ballet uses and, in most cases, would easily follow what was going on. The same is true of people who go to the cinema regularly: they are likely to be very good at reading films. They may spot jokes, for instance, in the references that one film makes to another, that those who go to the cinema less often would probably miss.

As you can see, the words 'read' and 'text' themselves have important connotations. In the chapter on audience (see pages 58–75) the way the media affects people is discussed. The word 'read' implies a reader who is actively involved in the text. Just like the reader of a book, readers of other media texts are contributing to the meaning that the text makes, by means of their involvement with it. This is obviously a long way from the common picture of the passive TV viewer, who mindlessly consumes whatever images are displayed on the screen.

Class discussion

AS A CLASS

Imagine you are in a Media Studies class at your school or college in the year 2500. Your teacher brings in an episode of *Neighbours* and the front page of the *Sun* from 2001.

- What do you think the class would make of it?
- What impression would the class get of life at the beginning of the 21st century?
- Do you think it would be an accurate impression?

Codes

To most people, the word 'code' stands for a secret method of communicating, which must be cracked or decoded so that the hidden message can be understood. Numbers or symbols, for example, may be used instead of letters of the alphabet; until you work out how to decipher the code, the message will have no meaning. Language itself is a code; the words in a particular language have meanings because everyone who speaks that language uses them in roughly the same way to mean roughly the same thing.

Each medium has its own code. Once you have learned the code, you can understand the meaning. For example, the music that is played at the beginning of a news bulletin is part of a code. It is serious music that sounds important and calls the viewer to the TV set, in just the same way that a town crier used to ring a bell and shout 'Oyez' to summon an audience to hear an important announcement. There are other codes at work in a news bulletin. Well-spoken, well-dressed people sit behind a desk in a studio and tell viewers about the world. They introduce other people, tell the viewers what is happening and show them pictures of events that have taken place. Sometimes the viewer can hear only the presenter's or reporter's

voice, while at other times he or she talks directly to the viewer. All these are codes that TV uses to communicate with viewers. These codes come to form a convention, or an accepted way of doing things that people are used to and have learned to recognise. There is a convention that the news appears at fixed times every day and that certain people will present it in a specific way. Because of these conventions, if you switch on your TV set halfway through the news, you don't think you're watching a quiz show. We will look further at these concepts later in this chapter under the heading of 'Genre' (see pages 27–29).

Weather charts, such as you see in a newspaper or on TV, are good examples of a code. If you don't understand how to read its symbols, the chart makes little sense.

Class discussion

- What codes are used in radio?
- When you switch on your radio, can you tell what sort of programme you are listening to?
- Is it easy to tell by listening what sort of station you have tuned to?
- If so, what is it that gives you this information?

Image analysis

Making an image

The study of how images are put together, and how the audience takes meaning from them, is called image analysis. The factors that affect 'still' photographs also apply to moving images on film or television. Imagine that a friend has asked you to take their photograph. Before you take the photo, there are a number of decisions you will make – consciously or otherwise.

Shots One important decision is how large you want the subject to be relative to the frame. The size of an image within the frame has various technical names according to how close the camera is to the subject:

The long shot (LS) shows the subject in their environment or context. The subject only takes up a small amount of the frame. In film and TV this is sometimes called an establishing shot, because it establishes where a character is. An establishing shot is often used at the beginning of a sequence to give the audience an idea of the setting or context the character is in.

The medium shot (MS) usually shows the top half of someone's body. A roughly equal amount of the frame is given to the subject and the setting. This shot is commonly used when TV reporters are speaking to the camera – outside 10 Downing Street, for example – so that both the reporter and setting are noticeable.

The close-up shot (CU) shows head and shoulders. The subject fills most of the screen and you can see a great deal of detail in his or her face. This is a good shot for showing emotion and creating a strong feeling of intimacy with the subject.

The big close-up (BCU) shows the face of the subject filling the whole of the frame. This is a powerful shot for showing strong feelings, such as someone in tears.

Point-of-view shot – see the section on point of view (pages 23–24)

Point-of-view shot – see the section on point of view (pages 23–24)

On your own
ON YR. OWN

Collect some examples of photographs from newspapers and magazines, or maybe a photo of yourself on holiday. For each photo, identify what type of shot is being used and the angle from which it was taken. Try to work out why the photographer has chosen to shoot the image in this way.

Long shot

Medium shot

Angle Another decision you will make before you take your photograph is the angle at which you will hold the camera.

- You may have noticed that images are usually shot at eye-level, so that the camera and the subject are on the same level. This creates a feeling that the viewer is equal with the subject.
- A high-angle shot allows the viewer to look down on the subject, which gives a sense of superiority.
- A low-angle shot has the opposite effect. The viewer is invited to look up at the subject, which may make the viewer feel uncomfortable or dominated.

Other factors Several other factors will also influence each shot:

Setting Where will the photograph be taken – in a back garden, in the street or in a studio? The setting of the photograph will influence how it is interpreted. In film-making, it is very important to sort out the setting, decide what will take place in front of the camera and how it will be shot. These considerations are known as the 'mise-en-scène'.

Framing Once you have decided on the setting, the next job is to frame the shot. This means that you have to decide how your subject will be positioned within the photograph. You do this by looking through the viewfinder until you get the best image for your purpose.

Focus Is everything sharply in focus, or are some parts of the image blurred? If so, is the blurring deliberate?

Colour Is the photograph in colour or black and white? Are there reasons for this choice? If the photo is in colour, what sort of colours are most obvious: bright colours or duller ones? Do the colours blend well together?

Close-up shot

Big close-up shot

Point-of-view shot

On storyboards, the names of these shots are usually abbreviated.

Lighting How is the image lit? Is natural lighting used, or artificial light, such as from a flashgun? Backlighting, where the chief source of light is from behind the central figure, can have a strong impact on the sidelighting.

Pose and body language How are the figures displayed within the frame? Are they posed or do they look natural? Have they been caught in action, or lined up for the camera?

Composition How have the different elements that make up the photograph been put together? When you look at a photo, think about where you look first. Where is your eye led? Is it drawn to the most important detail in the photograph? If there is a group of people, who seems to be the most important one?

The movie camera is often regarded as an all-seeing eye, which observes without being observed. It is able to follow the action wherever it takes place. It can stalk people, following them without their knowledge, and it can peep through windows. The fact that the camera as well as the subject can move allows the creation of images that are more complex and dynamic than still photographs. Two shots that enable it to do this are:

The pan, in which the camera moves horizontally, either following a piece of action or shifting across from one image to another, as though making a survey of the scene.

The zoom, where the camera zooms in from a long shot to a big close-up, moving in to inspect what is going on.

These effects show the power of the camera to control the action within the frame, either by holding an image as it moves, or by seeking out subjects that are part of the action.

Editing

If you are making a film or a video, another series of decisions has to be made once the images have been recorded. This is called editing, which is the process of putting the images together in a logical sequence. An editor links the scenes by using a range of devices intended to shift the viewer's attention from one scene to another.

The cut is where one scene ends and another begins immediately. This is probably the most frequently used of all the edits. An audience is likely to read this device to mean that all the action is taking place in a normal time sequence, or that one scene follows logically from another.

The fade is where the picture slowly disappears until the screen is blank (usually black). After a fade, a new scene may be started by fading up, which is when an image slowly appears from a blank screen. The audience might read this device to mean that a period of time has passed in between the two scenes. A shot that finishes in the evening, for example, will often be followed by one that fades up the next morning.

The dissolve is where one scene gradually fades out as a new scene fades in. It is possible to freeze these images on a video recorder and see both scenes mixed into a single frame in the middle of a dissolve. This device is another method of showing that time has passed, or that people have moved on – in a journey, say. The dissolve is also commonly used when landscape images, such as a misty morning, are set to music to give gentle, romantic views of the countryside, for example.

The wipe is where a new scene wipes over an existing scene from one side of the screen to the other. This kind of edit sharply shifts the viewers attention from one scene to another. It is especially effective at suggesting that parallel action is taking place elsewhere. Technology has enabled film and TV programme makers to produce a whole range of more elaborate methods of switching scenes, many of which are based on the wipe – for example, a scene folding up and disappearing into the ear of a character in the next scene.

Another job that an editor performs is the linking together of sound and images. Moving images are usually accompanied by sounds. These may be in the form of music to create atmosphere; they may be sounds related to what we see on the screen, such as people speaking to each other, which is known as dialogue; or they may be sound effects, such as explosions. Alternatively the soundtrack may take the form of an off-screen commentary, known as a voice-over.

This section has concentrated on how photographs and moving images have codes and conventions, which the viewer learns to read in order to make sense of them. Obviously this is also true of other media forms. The case study on newspapers (see pages 110–126) looks at how page layout works as a code that suggests to the reader how to read the page.

ON YR. OWN

Activity

Look carefully at the first two or three minutes of any film, video or television programme. Write down your responses to the following questions:

- How long does each shot last before an edit changes it to another shot?
- What effect do you think the time between edits has on the way you react to the sequence?
- What is on the soundtrack during the sequence?
- Does the soundtrack match the visuals and the way they are edited?

Narratives

Words and pictures are often combined in media texts in order to create narratives. Narratives are basically stories. From our earliest years, we enjoy narratives, whether in the form of a story told at bedtime to send us off to sleep, or a story told to our class at the end of a hard day at primary school. These stories are sometimes offered as a reward for good behaviour or are withheld as a punishment for being naughty. As we grow up, the link between stories and behaviour is therefore mixed in our minds. Narratives themselves are often about rewards or punishments for the ways that people behave.

Narratives are important to people. One reason is that they help to make sense of the world. Religious books, for example, are full of stories that attempt to explain the disasters that afflict the human race. The actual number of possible narratives is, however, limited.

New stories are uncommon: most narratives are variations on a limited number of timeless themes. The characters and settings may vary, but the structure remains the same.

Class discussion

AS A CLASS

- What are the first narratives you remember?
- Where did you hear them?
- How did they affect you?

In groups

AS A GROUP

Think about the following structure for a narrative:

1 boy meets girl and falls in love;

2 boy loses girl through misunderstanding;

3 boy gets girl back again.

- Now think of examples of how this narrative appears in different forms across a range of media, such as films, soap operas, magazines, tabloid newspapers and pop songs.

- What other narratives are common to many stories? Make a list of the narratives that occur most frequently.

- Do some narratives work better in one particular medium than in others?

Suspense

If stories occur so frequently, why don't people get bored with them? One reason is that narratives take different forms according to their settings and the characters used to tell the story. They do not simply retell a story that has been told many times before: their effects are more complex. An important element in any narrative is suspense, which is the feeling of excitement or anxiety that you have as you wait for something to happen. Suspense is an example of what is called a 'narrative code'. This is a way of describing the conventions or elements that an audience expects to be included in a story. Suspense works by means of a device called an enigma, which is a puzzle or a riddle. A good narrative teases the audience by giving clues about what will happen next, or making the audience try to

An old-fashioned cliff-hanger.

work out the answer to the puzzle. Murder mysteries and detective stories are popular across a range of media (such as films, TV, comics and magazines) because they work by teasing their audience. Cliff-hangers, likewise, are a key element of soaps. Originally the term 'cliff-hanger' described a situation when, at the end of an episode, a character was left dangling – either literally or metaphorically – over the edge of a cliff. Cliff-hangers keep the audience guessing what will happen in the next episode.

Enigmas also play an important role in non-fiction texts. For example, the news begins with headlines, which tease the viewer with information to get them to stay tuned to find out more. Newspaper headlines whet the reader's appetite for the story: they contain teasing clues about the narrative to follow.

Headlines

Each member of the class should find a headline from a newspaper or magazine. The rest of the class then guesses what the story is about, or makes up a story to fit the headline.

Martians turned my son into an olive

Pop star arrested in drugs probe

Is there life out there? **GOTCHA!**

Body found in burnt-out car **Just one for the road**

Terror on the 5.04 **King Rat**

Point of view

Another aspect of narrative structure is the point of view from which the audience sees the story. Many films and television programmes are about the eternal battle between good and evil. The audience is usually encouraged to identify with the good characters, and wants them to win. In a police series, for example, the viewer is invited to watch the action from the point of view of the police officer, who is trying to solve a crime and put a criminal behind bars for the protection of society.

Scenes may be shot in such a way that the viewer sees the same things as one of the characters.

Narratives are constructed to ensure that most of the audience will respond in a certain way. One way of placing the viewer alongside the hero or good character is to let the audience see what the hero sees. The viewer shares information with the hero. The hero may even speak directly to you through a voice-over, which allows you to share his or her thoughts and feelings.

A photo taken from behind police lines. What point of view does it give?

As you watch a film or TV programme, note how often the camera shows you what the hero sees. The camera becomes the hero's eyes and gives the audience the same privileged view as that of the hero. This shot is called the 'point-of-view' shot and is a very important way of 'positioning' the audience alongside a specific character. A device called a Steadicam has been developed which allows a camera operator to film while walking or even running and yet keep the shot steady. Steadicams and lightweight video equipment have increased the opportunities for using 'point-of-view' shots. A programme such as *The Bill* places the audience right alongside the police as they raid houses or chase suspects.

Needless to say, it is not only fictional programmes that tell their story from the viewpoint of one character. When conflict is taking place between the police and the community, for example, the news often shows pictures shot from behind a line of police officers.

Points of view

ON YR. OWN

Can you think of any films or TV programmes that show the action from the viewpoint of a character who is operating outside the law?

Class discussion

AS A CLASS

Notice that in the caption for image shown above the word 'riot' was not used to describe the conflict between the police and the community. If it had been, would it have made a difference to your opinion of the incident? If the police had been described as dealing with a 'mob', would it necessarily be an accurate description of what took place? Before trying to answer this question, you might like to look at the section on visual language on pages 8–17, which covers the concept of anchorage.

Conflict

The idea of conflict is important in narratives. Many stories are framed as a fight between two people or two groups. In fiction this is often depicted as a conflict between good and evil. In Westerns, peace-loving communities are frequently threatened by outlaws. The conflict is often resolved by a gunman. Gangster films present a conflict between society and those who flout its laws and values. Narratives based on conflict are found in many unlikely places. Many wildlife programmes are structured as narratives. The plot may rely on conflict between animals that hunt and those that are hunted. The side that the audience supports is often determined by the viewpoint of the group of animals that is 'starring' in the show. In this way, even natural born killers can be presented in a sympathetic light.

In a wildlife programme, an animal can be a hero or a villain, depending on the narrative structure of the film.

The audience is invited to take sides in the conflict, usually supporting the forces of good against those of evil. In the media's coverage of the news, this has important effects, especially in the presentation of stories about politics or international relations. It is often said that the news on television and radio should be unbiased. This means that it should avoid taking sides in a dispute and should simply present the different viewpoints, allowing the audience to form its own opinion. In reality, however, the coverage of such events as major football games on television or in the press may encourage the audience to support one side against the other. In the same way, in responding to the manner in which the news is presented, most people will inevitably take up a position in favour of one viewpoint.

When the UK is at war or in conflict with other countries, the narrative is often told from the viewpoint that the UK is right and its opponents are wrong. Battles are seen from behind British lines, looking towards the enemy (see the chapter on audience, pages 58–75). Some people argue that the same is true of industrial disputes: strikers may form part of a narrative in which they are pictured as disruptive forces trying to stop peace-loving people getting on with their lives.

On your own

ON YR. OWN

Make a list of examples from the media in which conflict is a key element in the narrative. For each example, explain the position that you think the audience is being invited to take up in relation to each side involved in the conflict.

Motivation

Characters and their motivation are extremely important in narratives. As we have already seen, the audience is often invited to see the action through the eyes of one particular character. This character is identified as the hero.

Class discussion

AS A CLASS

How do you know who the main characters in a film or TV programme are? What sort of clues are given at the beginning of a film or television programme about which characters will be important and which will be unimportant? Now write down a list of the clues you look for in deciding whether a character is going to be important.

All the main characters will have a motivation, a reason for doing something that drives them to achieve their aim. This motivation may take the form of a goal they set out to achieve. It may be to catch a criminal, to win a person they have fallen for, or maybe just to have a good time. Some characters go in search of themselves, or on a similar quest. These goals may bring them into conflict with other characters, whose goals are in opposition to theirs – a criminal who doesn't want to get caught, for example, or a man or a woman who doesn't want to be won, or a person who doesn't want the hero to have a good time. The viewer's interest in this narrative is, of course, to discover whether or not the hero manages to achieve his or her goal.

Ideology

We experience narrative from childhood onwards. Narrative also plays a key role in forming our social behaviour and attitudes in later life. There is much debate about the ideas of good and evil, and especially about the question of whose job it is to teach young people about right and wrong. The concepts of good and evil, right and wrong, are key elements of television programmes, newspapers and even pop music. It is argued that people learn their value systems from these media; they present an ideology, a system of beliefs by which people organise their lives.

An important part of growing up is learning to see narrative as both a reward and a way of teaching good behaviour. For example, you may learn to believe that if you work hard and don't argue with people in authority, then you will be rewarded; bad behaviour will be punished. The problem lies in who decides what is good and bad. Many people in authority have a strong interest in encouraging the belief that obedience and respect for people in superior positions is good behaviour. Can you trust the people who control the media to work in your best interests?

In Nazi Germany in the 1930s, the media was used as a powerful instrument of propaganda. Among other devices, it used narratives to persuade ordinary people that those from different ethnic backgrounds were the cause of evil in the world. Sadly, many people were taken in by these lies. In other words, narrative is a powerful means of getting over ideas that can have an impact on people's behaviour. One reason for examining narrative in Media Studies is to make you more aware of its effects and so perhaps less easily influenced by it.

An image of Nazi Germany.

Disaster films bring people together, for instance on a ship or in a burning building, so that conflicts and ambitions can be played out against a dramatic backdrop. Soaps present a series of neighbourhood locations in which the characters meet, and the narrative can develop through the reactions of the characters to each other. The pub is a popular meeting place in soaps – far more so than in real life!

In other words, narrative can take different forms according to the type of film, TV series or news report in which it appears. Each form has its own conventions, or common practices, and different types of programme can be identified by looking at the conventions used. The types or categories into which different texts can be fitted are known as genres. The idea of genres allows you to group texts together so that you

Genre

In order to hold the narrative of a film or television programme together, a scriptwriter will often seek a device that allows the characters to explore their ambitions. The road movie is an ideal form for a journey of self-exploration, an adventure in which the characters can find their true identity.

On your own

Choose an issue – the use of illegal drugs, for instance – that you think is of concern to people of your age group. Collect some examples of how this issue is presented in the media, including the newspapers, magazines, television, the radio and perhaps in popular music. Look carefully at the examples. Do you think you are being given the opportunity to make up your own mind about the issue? Or do you think you are being persuaded to adopt a particular point of view?

The Western traditionally gave Hollywood's view of how the West was won.

can study them and develop ideas about how they work. For example, the Western has already been mentioned as a particular genre of film. A list can be drawn up of the distinctive features of the Western: the use of guns and horses, for example, distinguishes this genre from that of, say, the musical; also, the setting of most Westerns can be identified as the Wild West; conflict with the American Indian is another feature of the genre; and many films show the American Indians as savages who threaten the white man's attempt to bring civilisation to the West.

The examples of genre you have analysed show that it is a useful device for examining media texts and identifying characteristics that are common to groups of them. Of course, it is a useful concept not only to students of media texts, but also to institutions and consumers of the texts – the audience. It allows the producer to identify a formula that the audience will find attractive and want to consume. If a film or a TV programme has been successful, then there is a reasonable chance that one made to a similar formula will also be successful. Of course this isn't always true: the cinema and TV are littered with unsuccessful sequels and rip-offs of blockbusters.

For the audience, the advantage of identifying a text as belonging to a certain genre is that it highlights it as something they are likely to find enjoyable. For example, films are often advertised as being similar to or even better than another film of the same type. This draws the attention of the audience to similarities and gives them certain expectations about the style and content of the text. It also provides a short cut for audiences, because they have already learnt the conventions by which a genre works. The character types may be familiar and predictable, as may many of the storylines. Viewing within a recognised genre, therefore, will not be such hard work as learning the rules of a new one. This is probably one reason why common forms of TV genre, such as soaps and sitcoms, prove so lastingly popular.

Clearly genre is a concept that can be used more widely than simply putting media texts in groups or categories. It is important to realise

Activity

AS A CLASS

As a class, think of as many different genres as you can. Next, on your own, draw up a chart similar to the one below. Choose six different genres from either television or film and fill in the boxes on the grid with details of typical settings, stock characters, props and narratives of each genre.

Genre	Setting	Stock characters	Props	Narrative
Western	Wild West, desert, cacti, hot	Cowboys, Indians, beautiful female settler	Guns, lassoes, horses, cattle	Conflict between American Indians and settlers, resolved by a lone gunman
Soap				
Detective story				
Etc.				

that genre is not fixed. The characteristics of a genre are likely to change over a period of time. If you compare an episode of an early police series such as *Dixon of Dock Green*, first broadcast in 1955, with a contemporary series such as *The Bill* or *Cops*, the differences may well be greater than the similarities.

Activity

Watch a television programme that was first shown 30 years ago. Which of its qualities make it seem old-fashioned or out of date? Are there any aspects of it that you might still find in an up-to-date example of the genre?

One other important quality of genre is that new genres evolve and old genres become less popular and even disappear. The variety show, typified by *Sunday Night at the London Palladium*, popular throughout the 1960s, has disappeared from prime-time television viewing. New genres are often created by the fusing together of existing genres. These are called hybrids, after the botanical term to describe the cross-breeding of plants. A typical hybrid is the docu-soap. This new genre is based on elements of the documentary, such as the realistic recording of the events in people's lives. It also contains qualities we expect to find in a soap opera. These include the focus on individual characters across several episodes, ongoing narratives, and a location that has a sense of community in which people live or work together.

As a means of analysing media texts, the idea of genre has its limitations. One problem is that you can easily go round in a circle; soaps belong to the soap genre because they have the qualities that soaps have. This tells you neither why soaps are so popular, nor what you can expect to learn from studying them. Another problem with the concept of genre is that it does not acknowledge the individual's contribution to a text. This is especially a problem with films, where a director may have a distinctive style of making films in the same way that a novelist has a distinctive style of writing books. For example, Alfred Hitchcock made many thrillers, but in some ways, they are more distinctive as films made by Alfred Hitchcock than they are as thrillers. Other well-known film directors, such as Jane Campion, Francis Ford Coppola, Spike Lee, David Lynch and Quentin Tarantino all bring their own personal signatures to the genres in which they have worked.

Class discussion

Are there any people whose names you recognise who work 'behind the scenes' of radio, film or television rather than appearing on it? You might like to consider, for example, writers, directors and producers. Choose one of these people and write down two or three examples of their work. Describe some of the features that you think might make their work recognisable.

However, media texts are more generally the products of people working together in teams for an organisation – for instance, a newspaper or radio station – rather than the creation of an individual. Even a book such as this one relies on a team of editors, designers, artists, photographers and production staff to work on the words that the writers have produced before it is ready to be sold. The organisations that these people work for are called media institutions.

Representation

Representation is the act of communicating by using symbols, for example using a stick-man to stand for a person. Usually representation takes the form of words, images or symbols. If I give you an apple, I have given you an apple; if I give you a picture of an apple, I have given you a representation of an apple. The difference between reality and representation of reality is not difficult to understand. What is not so obvious is that representation is an act or process in which reality is transformed. The picture I give you might be a photograph, a painting or even a drawing of an apple. The drawing might be a detailed still-life, or it could be a simple outline. Or I might convey the idea of the fruit by using the word 'apple'. The message you get in each case will be 'apple'. What you think about the apple, however, depends to a large degree on how I represent it. If I want to sell you an apple, I might give you a photograph of the best apple I can find and use computer techniques to make it look even better. If I were an artist and wished to suggest the idea of sickness, I might paint a rotting apple. If I were a journalist, I might use an apple as an image to represent a corrupt organisation by describing it as 'rotten to the core'. In each case, the idea of 'apple' will have been worked on to help it convey a meaning. This process of working on an idea or image to convey a specific meaning is called mediation, and it is central to our understanding of media messages.

Selecting and structuring representations

On your way home, you see a car crash. A car and a van have collided. There is steam coming from the engines. The van driver is sitting at the side of the road and has blood pouring from his head. Another person is being helped into an ambulance. Traffic in both directions has been stopped by the police. A fire engine arrives and you assume there must be a person trapped in the wreckage. You hear someone say that the car-driver pulled out in front of the van without looking. But someone else says that the car had priority. Everywhere you look there is something going on.

When you get home you tell your family what you saw. But do you? If you told them everything you saw it would take a long time and they would probably get bored. So what you do is select the most interesting facts and tell them. If you told these facts in the order you experienced them, you would also run the risk of losing your audience. You are more likely to say 'as I was walking up the road I noticed the police had stopped the traffic. As I got closer I saw an ambulance and what looked like steam rising into the air. Eventually I saw a van and a car had crashed.' In other words you reorganize and edit the information so that it has more impact. You might also take a stand on the cause of the accident: 'I thought it was the car-driver's fault.' What you have done is to give your own representation of the events you witnessed.

The process you have carried out can be illustrated by the diagram below.

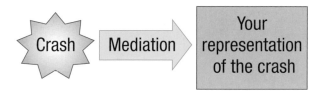

Now imagine you were a journalist reporting the same crash. The process you would go through to produce your report would be very similar. You would select what you saw as the most relevant or interesting aspects of the event, and arrange them into a story that would hopefully attract the attention of your audience.

Group activity

AS A GROUP

Get some members of the group to perform a short drama. It could be about an accident, a robbery or an argument.

The rest of the group act as reporters and produce individual reports about the event.

Compare the different reports.

Activity

ON YR. OWN

Find two eyewitnesses to an event that has taken place in school. It might be a sporting event, someone getting into trouble, or a prize-giving. Write down a list of questions to ask each eyewitness as though you were a reporter. Now use their answers to write two different accounts of what took place. Compare these two versions and make a list of:

1 What is the same? 2 What is different?

Versions of reality

It is important to understand that every report of an event, be it a conversation or a media report, is a representation (or RE-presentation) of the event, not a 'presentation' of reality. If we think in terms of the media, reading a newspaper story is equivalent to reading a letter about an event. Listening to a radio report is like receiving a phone call about the event. In both cases, it is easy to see how what you learn about the event is largely controlled by the person writing the letter or making the call – it is their representation of the happening. In the case of television, you may think it is possible to give a direct presentation of the event being reported; after all, the camera records events as they happen. This is not the case, however. All television reports are edited packages. In TV newsrooms, staff take the raw footage shot at an event and edit it. They select what they consider to be the best images and arrange or reorder them into a sequence they hope will be of interest to the viewer. They also write a commentary to accompany the visual images, which tells the story of what has happened. The story makes sense of the images, informing the viewer about what is happening. Unlike your report of the accident to your family, there is a time limit on the amount of information a television report can convey. The average news report lasts no more than a few minutes, so newsroom staff have to cut film and commentary. A lot of the film footage recorded at events is never broadcast. Commentaries are never complete: they do not tell you everything that could be said. What the viewer gets is a version of an event, according to the television newsroom.

TV interviews may be edited rather than broadcast in full.

Even in the broadcast of live events, such as football matches, the coverage is 'edited'. You are shown only what is within the camera shot, which is directed by the camera operator. The camera operator decides to film one part of the action rather than another and controls what the viewer will see. Most sporting events, however, are presented in the form of highlights, and, as many football fans who attend games will know, it is very easy to make one side look superior to another by careful selection of film footage. When you consider the selection and reordering that goes into all forms of representation, it becomes obvious that representations are 'versions' of events, not events in themselves.

A representation of an event, an issue, a group or an individual is only one of many possible versions. So it is clear that there must be other versions of the same event and other ways of representing it. The person viewing the representation has a problem, therefore: is the version they are viewing the true one? In fact, when analysing the media, is it possible to talk about a 'true' representation? A television documentary, for example, appears to offer us a representation of the world as it exists. We call this 'realism'. But we also look upon soap

Group activity

If you have access to a video camera, film a role-play of, for example, a family argument, or street interviews about a proposed shopping-complex development, or a sporting triumph for a local team. Play back the footage.

- Each person in the group makes two lists. On one list, put what you would include in a short report and, on the other, put what you would leave out.
- Each person then writes a commentary to accompany the video, giving the viewer the story.
- Back in the group, compare your lists and commentaries. How are they different?
- Try to reach an agreement on what should be included or said in the report. You will have to negotiate between different versions of the event.
- If you have editing facilities available, you could actually produce a report.

operas as examples of realism, although they are works of fiction performed by actors. To find out if it is possible to talk about a 'true' representation, the factors that influence the production of representations must be studied.

Whose truth?

Imagine your family photograph album. It is full of pictures of you at different stages of your life. Each picture is a representation of you and gives anyone looking at it information on which to base ideas about the type of person you are. Suppose you had to choose one photograph from the album to represent the image of you that you would like a stranger to have. It is a fair bet that you would choose one that shows you as a really cool character, wearing your most fashionable clothes. One thing is certain: the photograph you would pick

of yourself would be different from the one your parents would choose to show to a stranger. They would undoubtedly select one of you looking smart and sensible to create what they would see as a 'good impression'. You would probably reject their choice as embarrassing and not a 'true' representation of yourself. Who would be right?

In analysing the media, the issue is not so much who is right, but rather what makes people choose to represent events, issues, groups and individuals in certain ways. Think about you and your family: it is clear that you both have an interest in how you are portrayed to a stranger. Your family would doubtless wish strangers to see a pleasant, well-brought-up person, who is a credit to them. You, on the other hand, would probably want strangers to see you as a street-wise individual with obvious character.

On your own

ON YR. OWN

Find or take three photographs showing different representations of yourself or another person you know well. For example, the pictures might show you at school, at a party or with your family. How 'true' is each one? Write a paragraph about each one and how it represents the truth.

What if you were a politician and your parents were the owners of a national newspaper that supported the opposition party? The interests that would influence the choice of representation in this case are obvious. It is in your interest to show yourself as a person who is in tune with the views of most voters. Your parents, however, as supporters of your opponents, would wish to portray you as someone who is out of step with most people; they might even try to depict you as a danger to the country, to persuade the readers of their newspaper not to vote for you.

This is an example of bias. Bias usually results from a person having some kind of relationship with the person or thing they are biased in favour of. For example, if you were selling a car, a potential buyer would probably not believe everything you said about it because you stand to make money by striking a deal; they would say your representation of the car was biased.

Virtually every area of the media has been criticised for the way it represents people and issues. It has been pointed out, for example, that heroes in action and adventure films have traditionally been male; only recently have films with women as the central characters begun to appear. This fact has been seen as a representation of the old-fashioned view that women were not as intelligent, brave and resourceful as men, and should concern themselves with children and housework. What is called sexism (or prejudice against people because of their sex) has also been pinpointed in the way women are represented in the national press and in advertising. A woman's dress sense and appearance tend to be given attention by the press regardless of why the woman is in the news. Some people say that this means that women are not taken as seriously by the press as men are, and that as a result their views are given less weight.

Activity

ON YR. OWN

Choose a political controversy that you have recently seen in a national newspaper. Write down briefly the main gist of the story. Then answer the following questions:

1 Do you think the newspaper is trying to show its readers both sides of the argument?

2 Do you think the newspaper is encouraging readers to take sides in the story?

3 If you do, what is the evidence of this?

Group activity

AS A GROUP

Look at some examples of the ways in which old people are represented in the media. You might like to consider the tabloid press, or television programmes such as soap operas or sitcoms.

• What do the representations have in common?

• How accurate do you think they are?

Tomb Raider *and* Charlie's Angels *were among the first action films to have female leads.*

Women have traditionally been used in advertising to sell products. This is especially the case when the product is aimed at men. Car adverts in magazines and on television have traditionally shown a man driving and have included images of an attractive young woman. The message is that if you are male, driving the car will make you attractive to females. Adverts for household goods, on the other hand, such as cleaning materials and food, have traditionally been aimed at women. This can be seen as a reflection of the old-fashioned view that a woman's place was in the home. It has generally been the case that in advertising women have been shown as passive, while men have been portrayed as active and adventurous.

Activity

Make a list of advertisements either in print or on television that you consider represent women in a negative way. Are there any advertisements currently appearing that show women in a positive light? If you are able to find examples of the latter, consider why you think advertisers have taken this approach.

Representations change with the times, however, and the move towards gender equality has had an effect on how men and women are represented in adverts. More women are now shown driving cars while men are sometimes shown working in the kitchen and taking care of children.

Recently, more car adverts have been aimed at women.

Content analysis

One method of examining how people are represented in the media is called 'content analysis'. This method measures the number of times a particular representation occurs and draws conclusions about it. For example, a content analyst might count the number of women police officers portrayed in crime dramas; if they were to discover that very few women are represented as police officers, they would ask why this is. Is it because the media is sexist and men are seen as more interesting than women? Or does it reflect the reality of the police force, where there are fewer women officers?

To carry out content analysis, it is very important to stick to a strict pattern of working, known as the experimental method. Most researchers carrying out content analysis use the following steps:

Statement. Select the area you are going to study. Draw up a statement of the idea that you wish to test – for instance, 'More men than women are shown driving in television adverts for cars.'

What will you count? In this case, you would count the numbers of male and female drivers in car adverts on television.

When will you count? Set the times you are going to watch adverts and for how long. You might choose to watch adverts between 6pm and 10pm on Tuesdays, Thursdays and Saturdays one week, and Mondays, Wednesdays and Sundays the next week. You might do this for two weeks, four weeks or six weeks, and so on.

Carry out the counting. Make sure that the people doing the research know exactly what they are counting and that they are all counting the same thing.

Compile the results. Add up all the figures gathered by the researchers and work out the total for each category counted.

Analyse the results. Calculate whether the figures the research has come up with support or disprove the original statement. In this case, are more men than women shown driving cars in adverts for cars on television?

Content-analysis exercise

ON YR. OWN

Design and carry out a content-analysis experiment on the portrayal of families in advertising. Use the experimental method outlined above to design your investigation.

- How are the men and women in families represented?

- How often are fathers shown carrying out DIY and tasks involving machines?

- How often are mothers seen carrying out domestic chores, such as cleaning, cooking and caring for children?

- Do adverts depict an accurate picture of the roles of men and women in families you know, or are the representations stereotyped?

- Does it matter if the representations are stereotyped?

Stereotypes

If a certain sort of person is represented in a similar way over and over again by the media, what is called a 'stereotype' of that kind of person develops. A stereotype is a fixed idea about the characteristics of a certain type of person or thing. Many characters in fairy-tales and pantomimes are stereotypes; the audience recognises them instantly and believes that they act in certain ways and have certain characteristics. For example, if a woman dressed in black with a pointed hat and a broomstick appears in a pantomime, the audience immediately assumes she is an evil witch and will hiss and boo to show disapproval. A similar process is at work when an old person is portrayed as grumpy or senile in a television soap opera. Other stereotypes include fat people being shown as funny, successful businesswomen as unemotional, and people who live in the country as less intelligent than those who live in cities.

Media stereotypes of some groups have been seen as particularly offensive. It is argued that they increase prejudice in society. This is often true of the representation of people from ethnic-minority backgrounds, homosexuals and members of certain religious groups. In extreme cases, the media can be used to encourage violence against certain groups. This happened in Nazi Germany, where Jews were the subject of vicious and twisted propaganda.

In pairs

What assumptions do you make about the people in these photographs?

Activity

Write down some of the assumptions that you think people are likely to make when they look at these photographs. Do you think any of these assumptions are likely to be true? Explain the reasons for your views.

Class discussion

`AS A CLASS`

List stereotypes you see frequently in the media. Are stereotypes ever true? Do you think these stereotypes have changed over time?

Role-play

`ON YR. OWN`

Rewrite a stereotypical media portrayal of a particular person, group or event to show it in a different light. For example, you could reverse the roles usually assigned to men and women in films or television shows. Try to imagine a female James Bond and a male Miss Moneypenny. How would the dialogue and action work?

Are you a stereotype?

Perhaps some of the strongest stereotypes portrayed in the media are those of young people. One that is easily recognisable is the youngster from a so-called 'broken home' who gets into trouble with the police. This portrayal has become so common that it is almost taken for granted that in TV programmes any teenager who breaks the law must have family problems. This stereotype ignores those young people from stable family backgrounds who get into trouble, and law-abiding teenagers from single-parent homes.

One of the major factors that helps build up a stereotype is the way people in the media dress. Whenever a young person is portrayed as being on the slippery slope to a life of drugs and crime, they are almost certain to be dressed in a way that goes against adult ideas about sensible clothes. If a teenage character in a TV programme is going off the rails, this is not signalled by the character going out and getting a smart haircut and an outfit suitable for an interview; the character is more likely to be dressed in the latest street fashion. Similarly, pop bands tend to use their clothes to present a rebellious image in order to attract fans. Once they are famous, their fans may well adopt the dress style of the band, helping to make the stereotype stronger.

The use of clothes to represent youthful rebellion has affected the way young people are perceived. Look at the picture on the right. It shows a young man in trendy clothes going through the bag of an old lady. Has he mugged her? Or perhaps the old lady suffers from a heart condition, or asthma, and has asked the man to get her medication from her handbag. Your view of what is going on is determined to a large degree by a stereotype presented to you by the media.

Some young people are stereotyped by the fact that they are hardly ever represented in the media. Young people with disabilities are rarely shown in films or on television. If they do appear, they are shown only to highlight the issue of disability, rather than as characters in their own right.

A stereotypical image of a 'problem' teenager.

On your own

ON YR. OWN

Examine popular television shows, such as soap operas and drama serials. How many people with disabilities are portrayed? How old are they? What story-lines are they involved in? What conclusions can you draw about the stereotyping of people with disabilities on these sorts of TV programmes?

Review

Representation is the key function of the media. You should, however, always ask yourself the following questions:

- Whose representation is it?
- What reason could the media have for representing the person, group, issue or event in this way?
- How else could the person, group, issue or event be represented?
- What is the effect of representing them in this way?

Imagine that you wake up one day and decide you would like to publish your own newspaper. Alternatively, your ambitions may be more limited: you might like to make a new quiz show for Channel 4, or set up a community radio station. The chances are that no matter how enthusiastic you are about your schemes, they are unlikely to get very far – at least not in the short term. This is because however talented or hardworking you may be, in order to do any of these things you will need access to technology and access to money to pay for the resources you need to get your idea off the ground. You will need these things because you are going to make a product or commodity that you want people to use, in just the same way that any other manufacturer makes a product to be sold.

Of course, you may be very rich, in which case your dreams could become a reality. Even so, there is no guarantee that your newspaper, quiz show or radio station would be a success and pay back the money invested in it. Media institutions are big business. They exist to make a profit. Just as car manufacturers or supermarket chains aim to earn money for their shareholders, so media institutions are owned by people who want them to make as much money as possible.

There are, of course, exceptions. For example, the BBC is funded through a licence fee, which everyone in the UK who uses a television has to pay. Even so, the BBC is expected to help fund itself through, for instance, the sales of programmes overseas and the publication of spin-off books and magazines.

A media institution is a money-making business, just like any other.

Class discussion

AS A CLASS

Much of the money made by commercial TV and radio stations is raised through advertising. Should BBC television and radio carry advertising, instead of depending on the licence fee? Does the BBC carry any advertising at the moment?

Types of institution

Multinationals

A car manufacturer has to invest money in land, buildings and equipment in order to make cars. In the same way, a media producer has to buy or rent such items as TV studios, printing presses or transmitters in order to deliver its product to the consumer. Car manufacturers maximise their profit by producing cars that are sold all over the world. Such firms with world-wide interests are called multinationals. Many media institutions are also multinationals, with interests in a wide range of media and cultural products. This book, for example, is produced by Collins Educational, which is part of the international company HarperCollins*Publishers*. HarperCollins is in turn owned by News International, Rupert Murdoch's vast media empire. Other media interests that are part of News International include the *Sun* and *The Times* newspapers, and Sky Television, as well as other media industries across the globe.

Such control of media output in the hands of one organisation, and ultimately one man, is a cause of great concern to many people. The *Sun*, for instance, has a circulation of 4 million daily and is read by one in four of the population in the UK. It is so influential in swaying political opinion in the UK that it has arguably decided the outcome of general elections. Many people feel that ownership of the media has become too unequal, especially where such corporations as News International control a variety of different media across the world. Too much power, they argue, is in the hands of too few people (see the section on controlling institutions, pages 55–57).

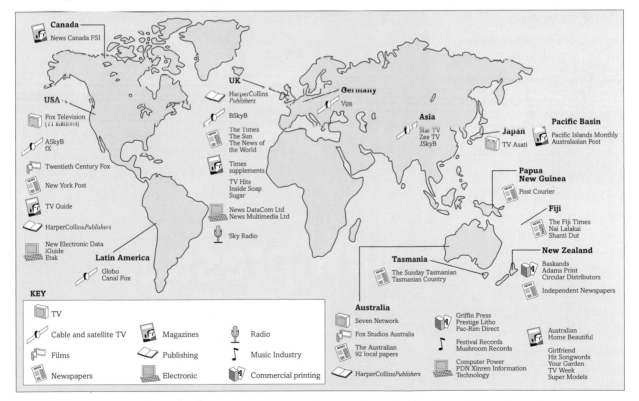

Some companies around the world that are owned or partly owned by News International.

Class discussion

It has been suggested that there should be strict controls on how much of the British media any one company or person should be allowed to own – no more than two national newspapers, for example, or one national newspaper and one television company.

- What do you think would happen under a system like this?
- Do you think there should be such controls?

Small institutions

Small institutions are at the opposite end of the spectrum to the multinational media corporations. They may use limited technology to produce alternative or community-based media products. Football supporters, for example, may buy a copy of a fanzine written by other fans of the same club. Such fanzines exist outside the established media and may offer more radical points of view. Music fans produce fanzines offering a different perspective on the music scene or on a specific type of music. In some cases, they become part of the mainstream of media institutions. *When Saturday Comes* started as a small-circulation fanzine but is now on sale throughout the country.

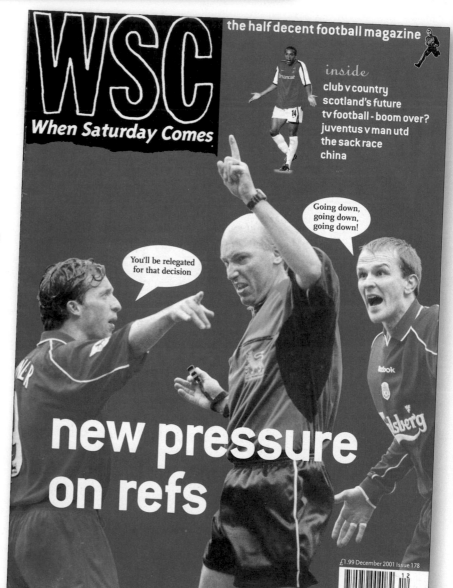

In the 1960s popular music was not well catered for by mainstream radio. Several pirate stations sprang up to fill the gap. These were sometimes housed on boats anchored off the coast just outside the control of the authorities. This practice went on until 1967, when the BBC launched Radio 1. Many of the presenters who had worked for these pirate stations were given shows on the new legitimate radio service.

Increasing use of the Internet has significantly changed the way in which many alternative media organisations operate. Rather than go to all the trouble of printing a magazine to reach an audience of a few hundred people, organisations can now create a website with a potential audience of millions. Potentially anyone with a fairly basic knowledge of information and computer technology can build a site and become a media institution. Try putting the name of your favourite band or team into a search engine and you will immediately discover a number of sites run by other fans wanting to share their enthusiasm.

Class discussion

Do fanzines offer the audience something that can't be found in mainstream products?

Value systems

Media institutions have so far been discussed in terms of being organisations made up of equipment, bricks and mortar. The word 'institution' carries with it another important connotation, though. The place where you are taking your Media Studies course is probably an institution. It is not simply a series of buildings in which people attend lessons, but a system of values and conventions by which people work and study together. Some of these conventions are written down, for instance, rules about smoking. Some conventions exist because people agree that they should, or because they have always existed. Most will make sense to everyone, while others will seem silly to some people.

A media institution will carry with it a similar value system, supported by conventions concerning the way things should be done. You sometimes hear it called 'professionalism', which implies that this is the way that people who are good at the job will do it. Professionalism means sticking to the standards and work practices that are the norm within a particular industry or institution. What makes a good news story is a matter of professional judgement. Which news story is the most important is another matter of professional judgement. In television news, presenters are always smartly dressed and speak directly and clearly to the audience in 'proper' English – they are professional.

These notions of professionalism, or the right way to do things, exist in all media. There is a 'right' way to write newspaper stories, take news photographs or introduce records on the radio. These are part of the conventions that were discussed in the chapter on media language (see pages 13–16). Anyone who gets a job in a media institution will be expected to adopt the same attitudes and approaches to the job as those who already work there. In fact, some people argue that recruitment into the media is limited to people of fairly restricted social backgrounds. Others argue that this is changing. Certainly organisations such as the BBC have equal-opportunities policies designed to ensure that people from under-represented minorities are positively encouraged to apply for jobs.

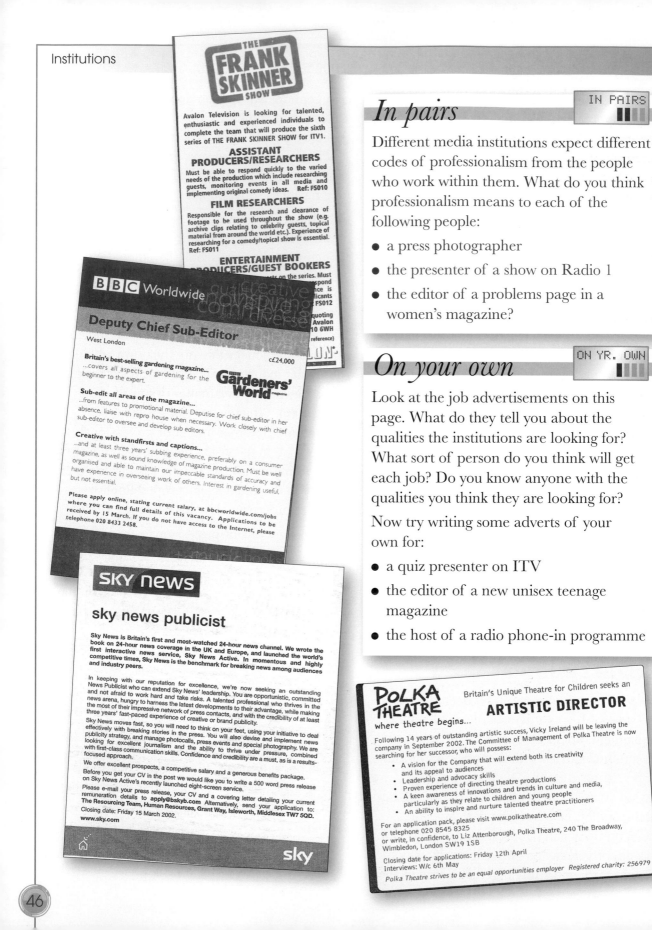

THE FRANK SKINNER SHOW

Avalon Television is looking for talented, enthusiastic and experienced individuals to complete the team that will produce the sixth series of THE FRANK SKINNER SHOW for ITV1.

ASSISTANT PRODUCERS/RESEARCHERS

Must be able to respond quickly to the varied needs of the production which include researching guests, monitoring events in all media and implementing original comedy ideas.   Ref: FS010

FILM RESEARCHERS

Responsible for the research and clearance of footage to be used throughout the show (e.g. archive clips relating to celebrity guests, topical material from around the world etc.). Experience of researching for a comedy/topical show is essential. Ref: FS011

ENTERTAINMENT PRODUCERS/GUEST BOOKERS

...cts on the series. Must ...spond ...ce is ...licants FS012 ...quoting ...Avalon ...10 6WH ...reference)

BBC Worldwide

Deputy Chief Sub-Editor

West London

c£24,000

Britain's best-selling gardening magazine...
...covers all aspects of gardening for the beginner to the expert.

Gardeners' World magazine

Sub-edit all areas of the magazine...
...from features to promotional material. Deputise for chief sub-editor in her absence, liaise with repro house when necessary. Work closely with chief sub-editor to oversee and develop sub editors.

Creative with standfirsts and captions...
...and at least three years' subbing experience, preferably on a consumer magazine, as well as sound knowledge of magazine production. Must be well organised and able to maintain our impeccable standards of accuracy and have experience in overseeing work of others. Interest in gardening useful, but not essential.

Please apply online, stating current salary, at bbcworldwide.com/jobs where you can find full details of this vacancy. Applications to be received by 15 March. If you do not have access to the Internet, please telephone 020 8433 2458.

sky news

sky news publicist

Sky News is Britain's first and most-watched 24-hour news channel. We wrote the book on 24-hour news coverage in the UK and Europe, and launched the world's first interactive news service, Sky News Active. In momentous and highly competitive times, Sky News is the benchmark for breaking news among audiences and industry peers.

In keeping with our reputation for excellence, we're now seeking an outstanding News Publicist who can extend Sky News' leadership. You are opportunistic, committed and not afraid to work hard and take risks. A talented professional who thrives in the news arena, hungry to harness the latest developments to their advantage, while making the most of their impressive network of press contacts, and with the credibility of at least three years' fast-paced experience of creative or brand publicity.

Sky News moves fast, so you will need to think on your feet, using your initiative to deal effectively with breaking stories in the press. You will also devise and implement news publicity strategy, and manage photocalls, press events and special photography. We are looking for excellent journalism and the ability to thrive under pressure, combined with first-class communication skills. Confidence and credibility are a must, as is a results-focused approach.

We offer excellent prospects, a competitive salary and a generous benefits package.

Before you get your CV in the post we would like you to write a 500 word press release on Sky News Active's recently launched eight-screen service.

Please e-mail your press release, your CV and a covering letter detailing your current remuneration details to apply@bskyb.com Alternatively, send your application to: The Resourcing Team, Human Resources, Grant Way, Isleworth, Middlesex TW7 5QD.

Closing date: Friday 15 March 2002.

www.sky.com

sky

POLKA THEATRE
where theatre begins...

Britain's Unique Theatre for Children seeks an

ARTISTIC DIRECTOR

Following 14 years of outstanding artistic success, Vicky Ireland will be leaving the company in September 2002. The Committee of Management of Polka Theatre is now searching for her successor, who will possess:

- A vision for the Company that will extend both its creativity and its appeal to audiences
- Leadership and advocacy skills
- Proven experience of directing theatre productions
- A keen awareness of innovations and trends in culture and media, particularly as they relate to children and young people
- An ability to inspire and nurture talented theatre practitioners

For an application pack, please visit www.polkatheatre.com or telephone 020 8545 8325 or write, in confidence, to Liz Attenborough, Polka Theatre, 240 The Broadway, Wimbledon, London SW19 1SB

Closing date for applications: Friday 12th April
Interviews: W/c 6th May

Polka Theatre strives to be an equal opportunities employer Registered charity: 256979

In pairs

IN PAIRS

Different media institutions expect different codes of professionalism from the people who work within them. What do you think professionalism means to each of the following people:

- a press photographer
- the presenter of a show on Radio 1
- the editor of a problems page in a women's magazine?

On your own

ON YR. OWN

Look at the job advertisements on this page. What do they tell you about the qualities the institutions are looking for? What sort of person do you think will get each job? Do you know anyone with the qualities you think they are looking for?

Now try writing some adverts of your own for:

- a quiz presenter on ITV
- the editor of a new unisex teenage magazine
- the host of a radio phone-in programme

Professional working practices can make anything that is different from them seem amateurish. If you look at one of your own attempts at practical production, you will probably compare it to a professional production and feel a little disappointed. It is difficult to produce anything that you can feel proud of if its value is going to be measured against the work of experienced professionals with vast resources at their disposal.

If you look at a home-produced fanzine or listen to pirate radio, however, it becomes clear that some people are not simply trying, and failing, to imitate what the professionals do. These alternative media may, in fact, have been created because the major media institutions themselves have failed to address the issues that the audience feel are relevant. Of course, the irony is that if the alternative media are too successful, they themselves will be swallowed into the mainstream and become part of the system they were opposing.

In pairs

ON YR. OWN

Imagine you have decided to set up your own fanzine or pirate radio station.

- Name three features you would include
- Explain why you would include them
- If these features do not already exist in mainstream media, explain why you think this is

Taking risks

Suppose you managed to find the money to set yourself up as a media institution. Many people would be quick to tell you that the media is a good place to lose your money. Your investment, as it is called, would be quite risky. This is one of the arguments that multinational media companies put forward in defence of their large and diverse interests. By spreading their risks over a wide range of different products, they stand less chance of losing out completely if they don't get it right.

The problem for media producers is the unpredictability of the audience. For example, most media products are designed to be consumed over a short period of time. The consumer who buys a car or a pair of socks will enjoy these products over a relatively long period of time, which makes them seem good value for money. A film, on the other hand, lasts for only a couple of hours, and consumers judge it on the pleasure they get during that time. This makes the success of a film difficult to predict. Even products that can give more lengthy enjoyment, such as magazines, rely heavily on an immediate appeal to and impact on the reader.

Unlike a car or a sock, a media product is rarely a standard item that can be mass-produced. Each television programme has to be different from every other television programme. But, as the chapter on language pointed out (see pages 8–29), it will probably contain many similarities with others of its genre. Media producers have to tread a very careful path between identifying and repeating a successful formula, and producing new and innovative products. If they get it wrong, their investment will probably turn into a loss.

Media producers are, however, able to take steps to cut this risk factor to a minimum. On television, one-off pilot programmes are often made to try out a formula before a full series of programmes is made. The pilots will be tested on the market, and only if audiences respond positively will a studio commit money to the full project.

Working within an established and successful genre is one means of reducing the risk. Another is to use well-known stars. This is especially true in the case of Hollywood films, where a star name is a big box-office draw and is likely to provide some guarantee of a film's popularity. Similarly in the music industry recording companies prefer to invest money in promoting stars who are already established, rather than risking it on new or up-and-coming talent. In fact, the media industry relies heavily on the concept of celebrity. The famous (and not-so-famous) fill the pages of newspapers and magazines, and appear on countless TV chat shows and radio programmes; some celebrities are even said to be famous just for being famous!

People may go to see a film just on the strength of the stars who are appearing in it.

Despite all efforts by the big institutions to make sure that they invest in winning formulas, the media is littered with products that audiences did not want, many of them quite spectacular failures. Each of these products represents an instance of a media producer who failed to guess correctly what the audience wanted.

Class discussion

Who sets the trend in popular music – the fans or the record companies?

In pairs

Make a list of media enterprises that have failed. These will include:

- magazines that folded after only a few issues
- television series that never got beyond the pilot stage
- blockbuster movies that disappeared after only a short time on general release
- bands and recording stars who disappeared after releasing one single

Can you think of any examples of spectacular success – for instance, low-budget movies that became box-office blockbusters?

Should we judge the success or failure of a media enterprise on the basis of the money it made or lost? What other standards can you use to judge a media text's success?

Write up your discussion as a report.

In pairs

Who are the big box-office draws at the moment? Make a list of stars – male and female – whom you think a Hollywood producer would expect to guarantee the success of a film.

- What are the most popular films at the moment? Who are the stars of these films?
- What makes a star or celebrity?
- How are stars useful?
- Do you think anyone you know will become a celebrity?
- Would you like to be one?

Competition between institutions

Market segmentation

In recent years, institutions have brought about an increasing segmentation of markets in their desire to sell to audiences (see the section on audience segmentation, page 64). Market segmentation is the breaking down of the market for media products into small units. For example, within the market for magazines, specialist magazines with a limited audience – and therefore a small circulation – can be said to have segmented the market. Instead of selling large amounts of a product that appeals to a mass audience, institutions sell products to much more specialised audiences. Changes in working practices and technology have made printing cheaper, which allows the production of magazines that can be profitable with just a small circulation. In fact, many of these small ventures are owned by large media institutions. Quite often titles on magazine racks competing with one another are owned by the same company.

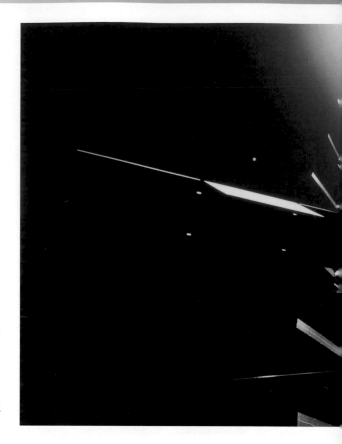

Niches

ON YR. OWN

Call in at a large newsagent's and look at the titles that cater for specialist audiences, such as:

- film and cinema enthusiasts
- computer buffs
- DIY freaks
- people who like nice food
- people who enjoy reading about the lives of celebrities

Try to find out by looking on the contents page the name of the company that owns each title.

The growth of satellite and cable broadcasting has led to an increasing segmentation in the television market. In urban areas especially, increasing numbers of viewers receive a package of programmes through their local cable operator. The cable operator downloads many of the programmes via satellite and feeds them by means of fibre-optic cable to individual homes. Many homes, however, still rely on a satellite dish to receive programmes. These receive a signal bounced off a satellite. The signal is fed from the dish to a combined receiver/decoder, which is able to unscramble the encrypted signal with the help of a smart-card supplied to subscribers. Programmes can then be received on a TV set and recorded on a video recorder, in the same way as is possible with a terrestrial channel.

Sky uses a group of four Astra satellites. The satellites are in the same geostationary orbit, which means that they move at the same speed as the earth rotates. Because of this, they stay in the same postion relative to the earth, so that a constant signal is maintained across the satellites' footprint (the area of the earth's surface covered by its signal). More satellites are planned in the future.

The advent of digital technologies means that there has been an increase in the number of different channels available, and also means that programmers are even more able to cater for niche markets of audiences with specialised interests. For example, channels aimed at people who like music are now segmented into more specific genres of music, such as pop, dance, hip-hop and indie. News and entertainment targeted at Asian viewers is available through the Star channels, offering Bollywood films and an Indian news channel.

Digital technology has also led to a rise in 'pay per view' programming. This means that subscribers can pay an additional sum of money to watch a specific programme. Commonly this is a major sporting event, broadcast live, or a recently released film.

Many people dislike the fact that these 'special' programmes are available only to those with the technology and who are able to pay. They argue that the free public-service channels can only offer less important and less attractive events, as the subscription-based channels outbid them for the rights to screen the major events.

Digital technology is also becoming more accessible for radio broadcasting. This is likely to have a similar effect to the one it has had on TV, increasing the choice of stations available to audiences and creating niche markets targeted at those with specific tastes and interests. (See the chapter on radio, pages 174–191.)

Class discussion

AS A CLASS

Nostalgia is an important concept for media producers in a segmented market. The concept of 'gold' as applied to a satellite channel such as UK Gold, as well as radio, allows producers to recycle texts from previous years or decades. What do you think is the main attraction of this for:

- producers?
- audiences?

Marketing the product

When a big car company launches a new model, most people get to know about it. Television, press and radio advertising, features in motoring supplements, billboard adverts and displays in car-dealers' showrooms announce and promote the new product. Similarly, the media industries have their own marketing ploys for ensuring that a product is likely to reach the audience at which it is aimed.

On TV we are constantly bombarded with trailers for programmes that will be shown later that night, that week or even that month. Continuity announcers tell the audience between programmes about other programmes they might enjoy. Media institutions promote other media institutions, television listings appear in all the national dailies. Television news magazines tell us what the papers say. Radio programmes discuss what is on television that night, or what you missed last night. Programmes such as soap operas, and reality TV such as *Big Brother*, regularly feature in the tabloid press as their stars become engaged in headline-grabbing scandals.

PAUL: I'LL WAIT FOR HELEN

Big Brother Romeo Paul revealed last night that he was "really, really close" to having sex with flirty Helen.

After being voted out of the house, he said he wanted to see the blonde beauty again. He added: "the girl is incredible".

And as he was evicted, tearful Helen mouthed to the remaining housemates: "I love him".

Big Brother presenter Davina McCall did her bit for the romance by giving Paul, 25, Helen's mobile phone number.

And Paul admitted he was glad Helen's ex-boyfriend Big G was not in the TV audience waiting for him.

He said: "I was relieved he wasn't there. I've seen him, he's huge."

Asked whether the cameras put him off having sex, Paul said: "I think things would have been different if she'd been single. I didn't want to do the wrong thing. I wanted to stay a gentleman in there." He added: "I'm looking forward to seeing Helen in the real world. I want to take her out for a drink."

Even his mum wants them to get together. Jen Clarke said: "She's a great girl. Who would not want to fall for someone like that?"

When asked how Helen would react when she found out she had been dumped by Big G, Paul said: "I think she'll be probably be very relieved."

He also told Davina that he wants Helen to win the £70,000 prize.

Paul and Helen's flirting, kissing and cuddling has gripped the nation.

You scratch my back

Collect examples of how the following pairs of media forms promote each other's texts:

- television and cinema
- radio and the record industry
- newspapers and satellite broadcasting

Does this mutual promotion ever raise any questions about common ownership?

Scheduling

Of course, despite common ownership, real competition exists between media institutions. Each one wants to obtain the largest share of the market so that it can charge advertisers large sums of money for the privilege of promoting their products. Even an institution like the BBC needs to attract large audiences for its programmes, even though it is committed to public-service broadcasting.

This competition for audiences can be seen across the media. For example, in the press, the *Sun* and the *Daily Mirror* are involved in the tabloid wars, a battle for the largest circulation. In our case study on radio, the competition between public service broadcasting and commercial stations is studied (see pages 177–180). The style-magazine market is another circulation battleground, with magazines competing for the prize of advertising revenue for products aimed at the stylish under-thirties.

The most obvious example of competition between media institutions is the battle for prime-time viewing audiences. This fight is mainly between BBC1 and ITV, with increasing competition from the satellite channels. Each channel wants to maximise the viewing

audience for its prime-time slots. Early-evening programming is very important to 'hook' the audience into watching a particular channel in the hope that they will stay with it throughout the evening. Australian soaps, popular especially with younger viewers, are scheduled in prime early-evening slots to grab the audience in preparation for programmes later that evening.

Group discussion

Many listeners are reluctant to retune their radios from one station to another. As a result, they are likely to listen at breakfast time to the station they listen to late at night. How do you think this affects the schedules for radio stations? When are minority-interest programmes likely to be scheduled?

Drive-time is an important concept in radio listening. Drivers tune in on their way to or from work for news and travel information, as well as for the companionship that the radio provides on a journey. Modern car radios can be programmed to retune automatically to the station that is giving out travel information or a news bulletin, even if the driver is listening to a cassette tape or CD at the time.

Television news programmes are an important part of an evening's scheduling. BBC1 and ITV used to schedule their main evening news to avoid clashing head to head with one another. Now they broadcast the news at the same time in direct competition. Both channels clearly like to have a fixed time slot for the news. In consequence, they have to schedule other programmes around these slots, which form a key element in shaping an evening's viewing for many family audiences.

Some commentators have made the important point that because news is part of an evening's entertainment, this has an effect on the way in which it is presented. While the news should inform, it must hold the attention of the viewer in competition with programmes that are made to entertain or amuse. In other words, the news is under pressure to compete with other programmes.

Another important aspect of scheduling is what broadcasters call the 'nine o'clock watershed'. This means the time after which more adult content – swearing, violence and sex – can be included in programmes, because (at least in theory) younger viewers for whom such material is deemed unsuitable will probably be in bed. In other words, scheduling is used to maximise a channel's audience, but there are factors that restrict the schedule. (The ways in which material is regulated are discussed in more detail in the chapter on audience, pages 58–62.)

Class discussion

AS A CLASS

Many households now have more than one TV set. Does this affect how the television is watched in many houses? How do schedulers think people watch TV at home? For instance, do they assume that all people watch television as part of a family? Do all people live in families?

8.00 EastEnders Ian jumps to some hasty conclusions following a visit from Mrs Davis, and a familiar face returns to the Square. (Txt) 7812
See Feature, page 6

8.30 Dalziel & Pascoe Secrets of the Dead: 3 of 4. Crime drama series starring Warren Clarke and Colin Buchanan. A solicitor is murdered in a Yorkshire village where Dalziel is attending the funeral of a close friend's wife. When Dalziel visits the murder scene, he discovers a letter addressed to him from the dead woman among the solicitor's possessions. With John Alderton. (Txt, W/S) 44676

10.00 News (Txt) 107102
10.25 Local News; Weather 874522

10.35 Living with Cancer 5 of 6: This week, three patients suffering from cancer of the mouth. (Txt, W/S) 357638
See Feature, page 80

11.15 The Unspoken Truth
FILM Fact-based drama. A woman takes the wrap for a murder committed by her abusive husband...
(95mins, 1995, Txt) Rating ✔✔
Starring: Lea Thompson, James Marshall, Patricia Kalember.
See Films, page 24 113947 **Weather View**

12.50 to 6.00 AM News 24 50853232

REGIONAL VARIATIONS
WALES: 6.30pm Wales Today; Weather. (Txt) 299 **7.00** X-Ray. (Txt) 8164; Children in Need. **7.30-8.00** Holiday: As England, 7.00pm. 183 **10.35** The Exchange with Huw Edwards: Topical debate. (Txt, W/S) 357638 **11.15** Living with Cancer: As England, 10.35pm. 607305 See Feature, page 80 **11.55** FILM: The Unspoken Truth. As England, 11.15pm. 173589; Weather; News. **1.35-6.00am** News 24. 95397394
NORTHERN IRELAND: 6.30pm Newsline; Weather. 299 **7.00-7.30** Fair Play: Consumer show. 8164 **10.35** Animals Undercover. 262725 **11.05** Living with Cancer: As England, 10.35pm. 678893 See Feature, page 80 **11.45** FILM: The Unspoken Truth. As England, 11.15pm. 333034; Weather View. **1.20-6.00am** News 24. 72038232

together, Ashley is determined to enjoy his 40th birthday party. Meanwhile, Zoe walks out of Home Farm. (Txt) 6560
7.30 Coronation Street Eve comes to Mike's rescue, and Toyah and Spider get reacquainted. (Txt) 251

8.00 Tonight with Trevor McDonald News and current affairs programme. (Txt) 2980

8.30 Shafted Big-money psychological game show hosted by Robert Kilroy-Silk (Txt, W/S) 1015

9.00 Twister
FILM Disaster movie. A meteorologist is on the verge of divorce from her former colleague, with whom she developed a prototype tornado-measuring device. But before the divorce papers can be signed, a wave of tornadoes sweep across the US compelling the pair to reunite to see if the device will work. Concludes after the News. (60mins, 1996, Txt) Rating ✔✔✔
Starring: Helen Hunt, Bill Paxton, Jami Gertz, Cary Elwes.
See Films, page 24 7909

10.00 News; Weather (Txt) 372589
10.20 FILM: Twister Conclusion. (65mins, Txt) 2442893

11.25 Local News; Weather 641744 **11.40 Champions League Weekly** Ian Payne and Trevor Harris preview the second group phase starting next week. 166638 **12.10 AM Nationwide League Extra** Matt Smith presents a goals round-up. Repeated tomorrow. 1273394 **12.55 Miss World – You Decide** The public vote for who they think should be the 10 semi-finalists. 7472290; News. **2.20 Young, Gifted and Broke** (Txt, Rpt) 5650348 **2.45 Trisha** (Txt, Rpt) 7189139 **3.40 The Web Review** (Txt, Rpt) 37093394 **4.05 Box Office America** (Rpt) 7759139; News. **4.30-5.30 AM Nightscreen** 38597

REGIONAL VARIATIONS
London except:
ANGLIA: 10-1.40pm Home Malone. 6.00-6.30pm glia News: Local magazine.
CARLTON/CENTRAL: 0-1.40pm Shortland Street: New
Zealand drama serial. 6.00-6.30 Central News. 4.30-5.30am Jobfinder.
■ **MERIDIAN:** 1.10-1.40pm Southern Steam: Today, a local steam engine enthusiast. 6.00-6.30 Meridian Tonight: Local magazine. 4.30am Nightscreen. 5.00-5.30am Freescreen.

Both the BBC and ITV have their main news programme at 10pm.

Not all programmes are aimed at a mass audience. On television, BBC2 and Channel 4 were both deliberately set up to attract minority audiences who were not well catered for by the mainstream channels. Ratings are important to them, too, although audiences are generally much smaller. Snooker, for example, on BBC2 and, to a lesser extent, racing on Channel 4, are examples of popular programmes attracting audiences who might otherwise be unaware of these channels and what they offer. Even minority-interest channels have to take account of the need to attract sizeable audiences.

Controlling institutions

It has been argued that in a democratic society we should have a media that is free from control and able to express opinions as it wishes, without interference from government. Other people argue that some elements of the media abuse that freedom and behave irresponsibly, for example by invading people's privacy, taking photographs of them when they are off guard.

In pairs

IN PAIRS

Christmas is a time when the major networks compete with each other for audiences.

- What factors will determine the type of programming shown on each channel from 3pm until 10pm on Christmas Day?
- Make a sample schedule for either BBC1 or ITV. Remember that you are trying to provide entertaining programmes that will appeal to all the family.
- What sort of programmes might audiences for Channel 4 and BBC2 want to see on Christmas Day?

Celebrities enduring unwanted press attention is not uncommon.

In many countries the media is censored.

The media is subject to a range of different regulations. Some of these are statutory, which means that they have the force of law behind them. Libel is an example of a statutory regulation. If a newspaper or news bulletin says something that is defamatory, or harmful to your reputation, you can take legal action to sue them for the damage they have done to you. Another example of control over what the media does is called self-regulation. This means that the industry itself punishes those who go beyond the bounds of what is acceptable. An example of self-regulation is the Press Complaints Commission, which deals with complaints about the newspaper industry. The work of the PCC is considered in more detail in the chapter on newspapers (pages 110–132). Most sections of the media industry are controlled in some way by regulatory bodies, such as the Independent Television Commission (ITC), which have varying powers to control what the media can and cannot do. These bodies are looked at in more detail in the chapter on audience (pages 58–75). A list of them, complete with the addresses and websites, is available in the resources section on page 238.

Governments throughout the world have an interest in who is controlling the flow of information. For many governments, controlling the media is an effective way of stifling the voices of people who do not agree with them. In many countries, there is censorship of the media, which means that the government decides what can and cannot be published or broadcast.

One method of international mass communication poses a real threat to efforts to control the information that passes between people across the globe – the Internet. The Internet was originally set up as a means of communication in the event of nuclear war, so that survivors throughout the world could communicate by computer. Because it crosses international boundaries and is made up largely of contributions from individuals, it is hard to police. Already the United States of America and several other countries have introduced legislation to control what people put on the Net. They argue that it is important to control access to material that is indecent or pornographic.

As we have seen, however, the Internet does allow ordinary people the opportunity to make their voices heard. Many argue that as the media is increasingly controlled by large multinational organisations, it is becoming more and more difficult for individuals with different points of view to get these across. By resisting attempts to control the Internet, they argue that they are fighting to preserve their freedom to express ideas without the interference of governments.

Class discussion

AS A CLASS

- Do you think there should be controls over what the media is allowed to publish or broadcast?
- Should the media have the right to tell people anything? If not, what sort of things should be censored?
- Can censorship be justified in some circumstances – when a country is at war, for example?

Review

ON YR. OWN

To help you remember what you have learned in this chapter, make notes to answer the following questions:

- What different types of institutions are there?
- Does the word 'institution' mean anything more than an organisation that makes media products?
- What have you learned about how media institutions market their products?
- Do you think we need to have tighter controls over what is published on the Internet?

5 Audience

Audience is the word used to describe people who consume media products. This includes viewers of television programmes, cinema-goers, radio listeners and readers of newspapers, magazines and comics. The importance of audience to the media is obvious. All the papers, broadcasts and recordings in the world would mean nothing if no one read, watched or listened to them. Without an audience, the media would be talking to itself. A question often asked in Media Studies, though, is, 'Who is in control?' Does the media control the audience, or the audience the media?

The media's effects on its audience

The evil empire

On one side of the debate are those who argue that the media is a very powerful force and that the effects it has on its audiences are largely bad. They believe that people, especially those who are easily influenced, tend to imitate what they see or read. There are many violent and sexual images in the media, which they say lead to more violence and sexual activity in society. Some people have also claimed that the portrayal of sex on TV has led to a decline in what are called 'moral standards'. They say that young people have copied characters in television dramas and become involved in sexual activity without considering its consequences.

Similar concerns have been expressed about the lyrics in popular music. Artists such as Eminem are said to have a bad influence on their young audiences because of the language they use and the attitudes they express in their

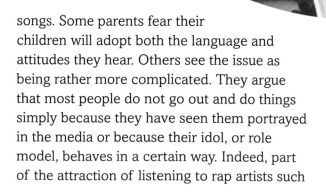

songs. Some parents fear their children will adopt both the language and attitudes they hear. Others see the issue as being rather more complicated. They argue that most people do not go out and do things simply because they have seen them portrayed in the media or because their idol, or role model, behaves in a certain way. Indeed, part of the attraction of listening to rap artists such

On your own

How much violence is there on television? Carry out a content-analysis experiment on an evening's viewing (see pages 36–37 for tips on how to do this). Count the number of violent acts shown. Consider:

- Are there different types of violence?

- Are some portrayals of violence worse than others? For example, compare the violence in dramas to that in cartoons.

- Do you think it is acceptable to show more explicit scenes of violence later at night when most young people are in bed?

as Eminem is arguably nothing more sinister than that it annoys or worries ones parents.

This argument surrounding the way in which the media influences our lives is called the 'effects debate'. No one knows for certain how the media does influence its audiences. What is clear is that the relationship is a complex one and that we should be wary of making simple judgements about how the media might impact upon people's behaviour.

Concern in Britain in the 1960s over the content of films and programmes on TV and radio led in 1965 to the creation of the National Viewers' and Listeners' Association. Its founder, Mary Whitehouse, became a national figure through her campaigns to clean up British television. The concerns expressed also led to what is known as the 'nine o'clock watershed' on terrestrial channels. This is an agreement not to show explicit sex or violence before 9pm, so that parents will know that they can let their children watch programmes before this time.

Newspapers and magazines have not escaped criticism. Explicit photography and the detailed descriptions of sex and violence in newspapers are believed by some to have a negative influence on readers. Magazines aimed at teenagers have been attacked for promoting sexual promiscuity by publishing material on contraception and physical relationships.

Music and fashion magazines have been slated for their 'glorification' of the bad behaviour of celebrities and stars. The National Lottery has been accused of encouraging people to gamble by leading them to believe that money and happiness are the same thing.

Group discussion

AS A GROUP

Do teenage magazines encourage their readers to think about sex?

The power of the media to influence, if not offend, is officially recognised by regulatory bodies set up to keep an eye on media output. The British Board of Film Classification (BBFC) gives each film and video a certificate stating whether it is suitable for children or young people to watch. The BBFC can also decide that a film or video is not suitable for public distribution and refuse to give it a certificate. All films and videos have to be certified by the BBFC if they are to be distributed legally to the public in Britain, although local councils have the final decision on whether a film should be shown in cinemas in their area. The BBFC started life as the British Board of Film Censors in 1912. It was set up to advise local councils on which films were suitable for public viewing. It became known as the British Board of Film Classification in 1985 when it was designated under the Video Recordings Act 1984 as the organisation that would carry out the classification of videos for sale or rent.

The BBFC classification symbols usually appear on videos and discs, although sometimes you see them on posters advertising films. Each film receives a certificate that states its category, which must be displayed before the film begins. 'Uc' is a category specially invented for videos. Videos that are exempt from classification are usually labelled 'E'; this applies to music and educational videos, for example.

Consumer advice is found on videos. It is in a form laid down by the BBFC.

British Board of Film Classification certification		
Film	Symbol	Video
Universal: suitable for viewers of all ages	U	Universal: suitable for all
	Uc	Particularly suitable for young children
Parental Guidance: whether children should watch the film is left for parents to decide	PG	Parental Guidance: suitable for general viewing, but some scenes may be unsuitable for younger children
Suitable only for viewers of 12 years and over	12	Suitable only for persons of 12 years and over. Not to be supplied to any person below that age
Suitable only for viewers of 15 years and over	15	Suitable only for persons of 15 years and over. Not to be supplied to any person below that age
Suitable only for viewers of 18 years and over. Contains scenes or language of an adult nature that are unsuitable for viewers under the age of 18	18	Suitable only for persons of 18 years and over. Not to be supplied to any person below that age
For restricted distribution only. To be viewed only at cinemas to which no one under the age of 18 is admitted	RESTRICTED 18	For restricted distribution only. To be supplied only in licensed sex shops to persons of not less than 18 years

Group discussion

The BBFC applies different standards of censorship and classification to films and videos. For example, a film may have more scenes of sex and violence cut when it is released on video than when it was shown at the cinema. Why do you think this is?

Video and computer games present new problems of classification. Many games are violent and use realistic graphics. Digital technology has developed, for instance, CD-ROMs (Compact Disc-Read Only Memory), CD-i (Compact Disc-interactive) and DVD (Digital Video Discs). These formats allow video images, including those showing extreme violence and explicit sex, to be stored on disc and played on computers. Some material of this sort is controlled under the Video Recordings Act (1984), and the BBFC is responsible for assessing it, via its video classification system. Many video and computer games, however, are exempt because they do not contain significant violence, sex and criminal techniques. In an attempt to deal with this situation, the computer games industry has designed its own voluntary system of categories for games not covered by the Video Recordings Act.

In 2003 a new regulatory body called Ofcom, or the Office of Communications, comes into existence. This combines the work of three main media regulators:

1 the Broadcasting Standards Commission, which is responsible for dealing with complaints made against all the radio and television broadcasters in the country, including satellite and cable as well as terrestrial;

2 the Independent Television Commission, which licenses and regulates all commercial television transmissions;

3 and the Radio Authority, which is responsible for licensing and regulating commercial radio stations, nationally and locally.

Brainwashing buyers

It is advertising that has provoked perhaps the most repeated attacks on the media's effect on audiences. Advertising is one of the major ways in which media producers make money. Manufacturers pay the media to promote images of their products, which they hope will encourage people to buy them. Many people say that the media's most important function is not to entertain audiences, but to deliver customers to advertisers. An enormous amount of advertising is carried in the media. Up to 60% of a newpaper's content is made up of advertisements. On commercial television, adverts appear on average four times an hour. On radio stations, too, they are played frequently. Even the non-commercial BBC broadcasts advertisements for its own merchandise, such as videos and books associated with its programmes.

Critics say that the way audiences are bombarded with advertising is little short of brainwashing. They believe that the sophisticated promotion of products in the media must lead viewers and listeners to buy things they don't need. The powerful effect of advertising on children causes particular disagreement and discussion. Parents complain about adverts for toys being shown during and around children's TV programmes. They say that advertisers – correctly – think that children will beg their parents for the toys they have seen advertised on television.

Children are not alone, however, in being deemed open to the effects of advertising. Success with the opposite sex, luxurious lifestyles, ultimate happiness and freedom from worry are all promised by advertisements for everything from chocolate to floor polish. The Advertising Standards Authority regulates the content of adverts in the media by monitoring such factors as taste, honesty and decency. (See the case study on advertising, pages 160–173.)

ASA

Television and computer zombies

The media has also been accused of having an even more sinister effect on its audience: it has been charged with turning people into virtual zombies, addicted to the glow of television and computer screens. A frightening picture is painted of people whose minds have been hijacked by the media. Children are seen as glued to the TV set instead of playing creatively. Teenagers are portrayed as living in a fantasy world of computer games. Adults are shown as being concerned only with soap operas, newspaper gossip and the latest product advertised on television. The media is charged with the break-up of family life, as adults gather round the television and children are hypnotised by the computer screen. This picture of the media's effect is known as the 'hypodermic model'. The idea is that the media injects its consumers with the messages and meanings it chooses and that the audience has no real power to resist. In support of this argument, it is pointed out that many people actually believe that what they see in soap operas is real. When a popular character dies,

it is common for wreaths to be sent to the studio by grief-stricken viewers. It is also noted that a good deal of space, especially in tabloid newspapers, is taken up with the news from soap operas, rather than from the real world.

Others believe, however, that this model seriously oversimplifies the complex relationship between media audiences and media texts. Yet evidence seems to exist that we should be concerned about the media having an effect on our behaviour. Advertising, for example, seeks to persuade audiences – with some success – to consume certain products. Indeed, the power of advertising is considered so great that some products, such as cigarettes, cannot be advertised on television.

Class discussion

Do you think the media can be held responsible for making people behave in antisocial ways?

Audience segmentation

It is important neither to overestimate the power of the audience nor to underestimate the ability of the media to take advantage of the audience's demands. Increasingly, media producers are cleverly identifying and splitting off ('segmenting') particular audiences in order to make money. Satellite and cable TV companies have been particularly good at this. If you look at the satellite and cable listings in any magazine you will see a host of channels aimed at minority or 'niche' markets. These will include pop music, sports, and specialist film and documentary channels. Such channels are clearly designed to appeal to specialist-interest groups. This allows advertisers to target audiences very precisely with goods and services that are likely to interest them.

This segmentation of audiences is likely to increase as technology allows people to demand what they want to see, when they want to see it. Linking television sets to the telephone network, for example, is likely to increase the opportunities for us to buy specific programmes, such as the latest video releases, to 'consume' at our convenience. Many people believe we are currently witnessing the end of the era of mass audiences, when millions of people all watch the same programme networked on national television. Instead we will use technology to demand the programmes we want to watch when it is most convenient to us.

Audience participation

One method the media has used to increase consumption of its products is audience participation. This means getting the audience involved in the media itself. Some television programmes depend on the audience providing most of the entertainment. These include shows made up of home videos sent in by viewers, or amateur talent contests, where, for example, people are auditioned by singing down the telephone.

A wide range of channels aimed at niche markets is available on cable and satellite.

More recent – and popular – forms of audience participation are docu-soaps and reality TV. Programmes such as *Big Brother* and *Airport* feature ordinary members of the public and in effect turn the audience into the stars of the show. The popularity of such shows has encouraged media producers to develop new series and to create other shows in the same genre. The appetite of the tabloid press for stories about the 'stars' seems insatiable. Many of the people featured in these shows fade back into the obscurity from which they emerged. Others, such as Jane McDonald, for example, build show-business careers on the strength of their original appearance.

Group discussion

What advantages does audience participation have for media producers?

AUDIENCE PARTICIPATION TECHNIQUES ● ● ● ● ●

- Talk shows
- Quiz programmes
- Phone votes
- Readers' letters, faxes and e-mails
- Open-access television
- Competition
- Community television programmes
- Right to reply

Class discussion

AS A CLASS

Think of some examples of 'ordinary' people becoming celebrities after appearing on television shows. For example, people featured in docu-soaps or reality television. Do you think the fame of these people will last or are they just famous for fifteen minutes? Do you think they deserve the celebrity status they are given by media such as the tabloid press? Would you like to be a celebrity overnight?

The audience's effects on the media

Are you a radio addict, a TV slave or a computer zombie? Do you live in a fantasy world peopled by characters who don't really exist? When you see something advertised, do you feel you must go out and buy it? Your answer to these questions will probably be, 'No'. The hypodermic model of the media's effect has been criticised for seeing audiences as too passive and stupid. After all, no one forces you to turn on the television or to buy a magazine. If the media was as much in control as the hypodermic model suggests, then people would watch, listen or read anything that was broadcast or published; this is clearly not the case. Some television shows are unsuccessful, and newspapers and magazines go out of business. Not all products advertised in the media sell, and some bands heralded as the 'next big thing' flop. These are examples of the power exercised by audiences.

Audience power has also led to the development of different forms of media. BBC Radio used to consist of just one station, the Home Service. This split into Radios 1, 2, 3 and 4 because it was recognised that there were different types of radio listeners; in other words, there were audiences with different tastes.

On TV, Channel 4's early success was based on catering for so-called 'minority audiences' through programmes on subjects that were largely ignored by the BBC and mainstream television stations. Classic FM, a national commercial radio station that plays nothing but classical music, was launched after it was realised that there was an audience for it – a different audience from the one that listened to classical music on Radio 3. All these developments point to the power of the audience to affect what the media produces.

To get a clear picture of how the media works in our society, we must consider how audiences can actually influence what it produces. It may be that many people enjoy watching soap operas. It is not the case, however, that people will mindlessly watch any soap opera that is screened. The TV graveyard is full of soap operas that failed to attract enough viewers. Pressure from viewers can also lead programme makers to change scripts, kill off unpopular characters and even bring others back from the dead.

Group discussion

AS A GROUP ▐▐▐

A number of pirate radio stations broadcast illegally in big cities, often targeting audiences from ethnic minority groups. What do you think is the appeal of these stations? Imagine you were to run a pirate station. Choose a name for it, and describe what sort of programmes and music it would contain.

Finding out about the audience

How does the audience use the media?

In order to study audiences, it is important to consider how people actually use media products. People might watch soap operas for amusement, treating them more like pantomimes than dramas in which they become emotionally involved. Some people use the radio for companionship. They put it on to hear a friendly voice and are not too concerned which friendly voice it is. Teenagers might like a certain type of music because it is good to dance to, not because of its rebellious lyrics. People might buy a newspaper not to find out about what is going on in the world but to check their horoscope, find out what is on television, or simply look at the girl on page three.

This way of looking at the relationship between the media and its audience is called the 'uses and gratifications' approach. It considers how people use media products and what they get out of them. They might use the media as part of their social lives. For example, going to the pictures can play a central role in the development of a relationship between two people. Friends might gather to watch a big match on television, or contact each other through requests or phone-ins on radio shows. For individuals, the media can fulfil personal and psychological needs. Viewers may see a reflection of themselves in characters on TV. They may watch detective shows to test their powers of reasoning in working out 'whodunnit'. Or they might enjoy the tension of seeing whether characters become romantically involved in a drama.

The term 'uses and gratifications' suggests that instead of sitting round soaking up media messages in a passive way, audiences actively select their media consumption and use it for their own purposes. Rather than being used by the media, people are actually using it to obtain gratification, or pleasure, in a variety of different ways.

> ### On your own
>
> Make a list of your favourite media products – television programmes, magazines, radio stations and so on. Write a few sentences about each one, saying:
> - how you use it
> - what you get out of it

What does the audience want from the media?

Media producers need to know what people think about their products in order to increase the size of their audiences. To discover what is popular and what is not, media organisations do a great deal of audience research. Commercial audience-research companies carry out these investigations for media producers. Additionally, organisations set up specifically to investigate audiences include:

The Broadcasters Audience Research Board (BARB), which produces information on television audiences for the BBC and ITV television companies. This information includes the numbers of people watching programmes, their reactions to them and their reasons for watching them.

BARB produces charts each week showing the top 30 most watched television programmes. Many newspapers publish charts showing the week's top 10 programmes, which are based on BARB's information. You can also look at the BARB website (www.barb.co.uk) to obtain up-to-date audience figures.

The Radio Joint Audience Research (RAJAR), which conducts research into radio audiences and the reasons why they tune in to particular stations and programmes.

The National Readership Surveys Ltd (NRS), which calculates the number of people reading newspapers and magazines.

Audience research

TECHNIQUES ● ● ● ● ●

- questionnaires

- interviews

- asking people to keep diaries of what they listen to or watch

- monitoring television sets to see which programmes are being watched.

These techniques generally produce two kinds of information…

DATA ● ● ● ● ● ● ● ● ●

- Quantitative data, or information in the form of numbers, such as how many people watched a particular programme or read a specific magazine.

- Qualitative data, or information on people's opinions about media products – whether they like them, for instance, and why or how they could be improved.

To make sense of information gathered through audience research, investigators group similar types of people into categories. This allows them to say which different kinds of people like or dislike particular media products. Measurements used to group people during research include age, sex, income, education and occupation. A very important measurement used in audience research is that of social class. A person's social class is determined by a combination of their income, education, lifestyle and other factors. Social classes in their broadest sense are split into upper, middle and lower or working classes. More complicated measurement scales split these three categories into smaller sections. The one used by many market-research organisations is based on the Registrar General's scale of social class set out as long ago as 1911. Newspaper and magazine publishers use this scale to judge what percentage of their readers comes from which group. The scale separates people into six groups, depending on the job of the head of the household (or main wage-earner).

Group activity

AS A GROUP ▐▐▐▐

Carry out a survey among the members of your class to find out which soap operas are the most popular. To do this you will have to produce a questionnaire and carry out interviews. Try to gather both quantitative and qualitative data.

Tip
Keep the questionnaire simple and the interviews short.

Group activity

AS A GROUP ▐▐▐▐

- How would you divide up members of an audience if you were doing research into the readership of a magazine?

- Make a list of the factors that would be important in helping you make sense of the information you gathered.

- How could the information gathered be used to make more money for the publisher of the magazine?

A COMMONLY USED CLASS-MEASUREMENT SCALE

Category	Description
A	**Upper middle class** People working in top-level management and professions
B	**Middle class** Middle-level managers and middle-ranking professionals
C1	**Lower middle class** Junior managers, supervisors, clerical workers and lower-ranking professionals
C2	**Skilled working class** Skilled manual workers
D	**Working class** Semi-skilled and unskilled manual workers
E	**People at lowest level income** For example, state pensioners and casual workers

Audience positioning

One of the ways in which the media is believed to inject its powerful effect into audiences is through what is known as audience positioning. Audience positioning refers to the relationship between the audience and the media product. It also refers to how a media product addresses, or talks to, its audience. A media text offers a position to an audience in the way in which it lets them see the people, issues and events it covers.

As the chapter on representation discusses (see pages 31–36), media texts are not direct records of reality, but 're-presentations' of it. Each media re-presentation is the product of a process of selection and editing of information, in the form of film shots, radio interviews or news stories. Because of this process, there will always be other possible re-presentations of the people, events, stories and issues appearing in the media. Crime dramas, for example, usually position the audience with the main detective character. The viewer follows the detective as if they were looking over his or her shoulder, gets the clues in the order the detective gets them, and sympathises with the detective's point of view. It is rare for a crime drama to position the audience with the criminal.

The position offered to audiences by media texts is not, however, the only possible one. Crime and police dramas could position the viewer with criminals, showing how they see the world and even encouraging viewers to sympathise with them. This does not usually happen, though. Why? Some say this is because it is in society's interests to promote 'good' behaviour and to discourage people from breaking the law. Others argue, however, that what is defined as 'good' behaviour is often biased. For example, people shown taking part in a demonstration in a police drama may be represented as nuisances, because the police may view them from the point of view of having to control such events. The right to demonstrate peacefully, though, is regarded as one of the basic rights of our society. The position offered to the audience in the police drama might therefore be seen as political, since it may influence viewers' opinions against the right to demonstrate.

Hordes of refugees see us as the softest touch in Europe

David Blunkett's take-it-or-leave it offer to asylum seekers is enlightened and long overdue.

Instead of being handed vouchers to use in the shops, they must stay at approved hostels – with three meals a day and some pocket money – or fend for themselves.

New arrivals may come and go but those who choose to leave must fend for themselves rather than rely on benefits at our expense.

Sounds like the essence of neighbourliness, doesn't it?

Yet the welfare industry is already screaming about a breach of "human rights". Britain is the No.1 destination for hundreds of thousands of refugees, both bogus and genuine.

They come because English is their second language, but mainly because they see the UK as the softest touch in Europe.

Abusing

Most – especially those with skills and talent – are more than welcome.

But some are abusing the system and disappearing into the black economy and taking on work while still claiming benefit.

Others, including well-organised and ruthless crime gangs, are taking full advantage of our tolerance.

Many are operating as part of an international criminal conspiracy.

And they are using the UK as a base for peddling drugs, vice and human bondage.

As a vivid example, the arrest of three families of asylum seekers has just cut pick-pocketing on the London Underground by HALF.

Refugees, political or economic, should be prepared to accommodate our genuine nervousness at a time of global crisis.

Arrivals

Mr Blunkett also wants applicants for British citizenship to learn English and show some understanding of the way we live.

These measures are long overdue.

As the long war against terrorism moves into its third month, we need to ensure our new arrivals are with us and not against us.

Point of view

Newspapers offer their audience a position on events, which influences who they sympathise with and who they criticise.

Who does this newspaper story position the reader with?

How does the story do this?

All media texts also have a way of talking to, or addressing, their users. The way a media text addresses its users also influences the position the user is offered. Television newsreaders address the viewer face to face, as if they were talking directly to them. They use a serious but sincere tone of voice, like that of a concerned friend. This, some argue, positions the viewer with the newsreader and encourages them to believe what he or she is saying. Remember, what the newsreader is saying is only a re-presentation of the news. However, because the newsreader appears to be friendly and worthy of trust, it is argued that viewers will tend to believe almost anything newsreaders say. This may be acceptable if news accounts are accurate, but what if they are biased or filled with lies?

Newspapers also position their readers through the way they address them. Stories in tabloid newspapers tend to be written as if the writer were having a conversation with the reader. It is assumed that the person reading the story will hold the same beliefs as those expressed in the paper. In fact, most tabloids claim that they do more than just report the news: they say they speak for their readers. Most tabloid newspapers did not, for example, support striking miners during their long industrial dispute in 1984. Many printed appeals for an end to the strike. The position they offered their readers was firmly against the strikers and they addressed their readers as if they agreed with that position.

Class discussion

AS A CLASS

During the Gulf War in 1991, BBC newsreaders referred to service personnel from this country as 'British forces'; ITN newsreaders called them 'our forces'.

- What difference does each term make to the audience's position?
- How does each description position the viewer in relation to each side in the conflict?

Typical audiences

Most media producers have a typical viewer in mind when they are putting together their products. This is someone whom the media producers believe to be typical of the audience for a particular product. Media producers mould their products to cater for the characteristics of this ideal consumer. For example, a men's lifestyle magazine may have a typical reader who is 35 years old, married with young children, works in an office, drives a car and takes foreign holidays. This is called an 'audience profile'. Most of the articles in the magazine will therefore be about topics that the publishers think a 35-year-old married man with children, a car and an office job will be interested in. This, then, will be the main audience position offered to the reader of the magazine.

In general, the presumed background and interests of the typical consumer will dictate the position given to the audience of a particular product. The audience position will determine such factors as:

The type of language used. A children's TV programme will not use adult words that its audience might not understand. A presenter on a rock-music programme will use the latest rock-world slang, rather than the 'correct' English used on BBC Radio 4.

The tone of voice used. Teenagers would be unlikely to watch or listen to television and radio programmes aimed at them if the presenters talked in dull, middle-aged voices. So presenters on youth programmes tend to speak in excited, breathless tones, to give the impression that something dynamic is always going on. Magazines and newspapers also adopt a particular tone in which they talk to the reader. The tone of such tabloid newspapers as the *Sun* is conversational, while that of such broadsheets as *The Times* is formal.

The subjects covered. A popular quiz show screened during the early evening is unlikely to ask in-depth questions about chemistry. However, University Challenge or Mastermind, screened mid-evening, may well ask questions on the subject.

Group discussion

- Why do you think different quiz shows cover different topics?
- What does the choice of subjects say about the audience that is expected to watch each quiz show?

On your own

Draw up a profile of the typical viewers or readers of the following:

- a television soap opera
- a tabloid newspaper
- a pop-music show on radio or television
- an action comic

Media producers would say that they tailor their programmes and publications to the needs of their audience by using these typical reader or viewer positions. Others argue that what the media producers really do is create viewers and readers who live their lives according to what they see on TV and read in magazines.

Media Studies audience research

Media producers are not the only ones interested in audience behaviour. Researchers in Media Studies devote much time and energy to finding out who watches, listens or reads what. They are particularly keen to discover how people of different ages, sex and social class use the media. They use techniques similar to those used by commercial researchers, and ask such questions as:

- Are some programmes watched more by men than women, and, if so, why?
- Do children take television dramas aimed at them seriously?
- Which social classes read which newspapers, and why?

The importance attached to certain types of programme by different people is also an area of key interest. Men, for example, may view documentaries as being of greater value than soap operas.

How and where do we become an audience?

One area of much interest to Media Studies research is what is called the viewing, listening or reading context, or where the audience consumes media products. The places in which the audience comes into contact with media products change over time, because of developments in media technology and social trends.

Before the introduction of television, most people relied on the radio as a source of information and entertainment. It became a habit in many homes for families to gather around the 'wireless set', as it was called. The tradition was carried on when TV sets became a common feature of most households.

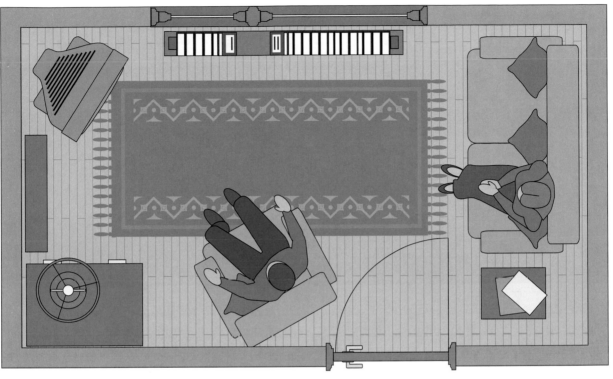

Most sitting-rooms are organised around the television set.

If you draw a map of most sitting-rooms, you will find that the television set is the central point around which the rest of the furniture is organised. This has implications for the way family life is structured. The television, rather than the other people in the room, becomes the focal point of attention. This, some say, leads to a breakdown in communication within families, as everyone is too busy watching TV to talk to each other. Others, however, argue that television promotes communication as it provides material for family members to talk about.

An interesting area of audience research looks at the issue of who has control over what is watched on the TV – father, mother or the children.

Class discussion

AS A CLASS

Does the central role of the television in most sitting-rooms encourage families to talk, or does it silence them?

The Royle Family is a sitcom about a family who spend most of their lives watching television together. Do you think they are a typical family? Do you think most families watch television in this way?

Who's in control?

ON YR. OWN

Monitor who controls what is watched on television in your house.
- Who keeps hold of the remote control?
- Does it depend on what time of day it is?
- Who has the final say over what is watched?

The replacement of radio with television led radio producers to look for other listening contexts. A major new listening context was offered by the development of in-car entertainment. Drive-time, or the hours when most people are driving to and from work, has become a peak period for radio consumption. Many radio stations have tailored their broadcast formats to meet the demands of the drive-time audience, providing a mix of music, traffic and weather reports. Another listening context targeted by radio producers is the workplace, with such features as 'office of the day', live coverage of community events and live outside broadcasts.

The introduction of the VCR (video cassette recorder) into people's homes led to a revolution in viewing habits. The VCR allowed viewers to:

Tape one programme while watching another. This increased the possible audience for a programme, as people did not have to make a choice between watching one programme or another.

Tape programmes while they were out. This again increased the possible audience for a programme, as people who would have missed it could now record it. Also, viewers were no longer tied to the scheduling of TV companies.

Buy or rent pre-recorded tapes and watch them at home. This could reduce the size of the possible audience for a programme, as viewers had a greater range of options from which to choose.

The launch of the VCR was also expected to have a major impact on the cinema. It was widely believed that if people were offered the choice between watching a film at the cinema or in the comfort of their home, they would opt to stay at home. As a result, it was predicted that cinemas would disappear from our towns and cities. To some extent this did happen, and many old independent picture houses closed because of a fall in customer numbers. The rise of the VCR also led to the development of the made-for-video film – a production that is not shown at cinemas and can be seen only on video. Although it went through a radical change, however, cinema did not disappear. The development of multi-screen cinema complexes attracted a new audience for films. The complexes owed much of their success to the fact that they made going to the cinema into an occasion. Surround-sound, luxury seats, fast food, drinks and special showings all contributed to this. In an interesting twist, video-rental shops then began to look more like cinema foyers, with pop-corn and ice-cream on sale.

Computer games have also affected the way people use the media. Many computer games run on television sets. This means that people use their television sets for playing games rather than for watching programmes, which reduces the audience for TV programmes. On the other hand, some people own more than one television set, so a spare one can of course be used to watch TV when a computer game is being played; this increases both the possible audience for TV programmes and the market for television sets. Other games and education systems run on computers with their own monitors, or on hand-held systems, a factor that again reduces the number of people available to watch television. This could, however, offer radio producers a new listening context: computer time.

The Internet, a large system of connected computers all round the world that people use to communicate with each other, has created a new audience that many media producers have tried to exploit. Newspapers and radio stations have set up their own home pages, which Internet users can visit via their computer screens. Advertisers have also put their own 'sites' on the Internet and sponsored others. This is not only exploitation of a new media

market, but also a response to a drop in TV viewing figures that is thought to be a result of the Internet.

Class activity

AS A CLASS

- Find out how many people in your class have a computer.
- How much leisure time do those who have a computer spend using it?
- How much time does each person in the class spend watching television? Keep two sets of figures, one for those with a computer and one for those without.
- Compare the two sets of results. Is there a difference between those who have a computer and those who don't?

Review — on your own

ON YR. OWN

When talking about audiences, it is easy to think of them as 'things' and to forget that they are actually made up of people like you. Everyone you know is part of an audience for at least one media product.

- Make a list of all the audiences of which you are a part.
- Do you accept without question everything that you see or hear as a member of each audience?
- Jot down how and why you became part of each audience.
- Do you consume the media? Or does it consume you?

6 Cinema

To watch a film at the cinema is to be part of a piece of trickery. Film is an optical illusion, a play of light onto a screen that the audience reads as a three-dimensional space in which the joys and fears of people's lives are acted out. In 2000, people in the UK made 142.5 million visits to the cinema, paying nearly £621 million for the privilege of being tricked, such is the popularity of the cinema today.

In this case study, we will be examining in detail the cinema as an industry, the making of films and their exhibition both at cinemas and at home, on video and television.

Class discussion

AS A CLASS ▮▮▮▮

- When did you last go to the cinema?
- What did you see?
- Was it good?
- How often do you go to the cinema?
- Are young people more likely to go to the cinema than older people?

Sound and vision

Film is able to weave its magic spell over us through a phenomenon called persistence of vision. Most of you will have seen a simple flick book, or even a device like a zoetrope, in which a series of still images is animated to create the illusion of movement. This happens because images remain within your vision after they have actually disappeared, which means that your brain will link a series of still images together to create continuous movement.

When we watch a film at a cinema, a strip of celluloid film is pulled through a projector, a machine that consists of a powerful light behind a lens. As each frame passes between the light and the lens, it is projected onto the screen for 1/24th of a second, before the next frame is pulled into the gate and appears on the screen. At the same time, a shutter opens and closes in synchronisation with the frame movement, so we don't see one frame replacing another.

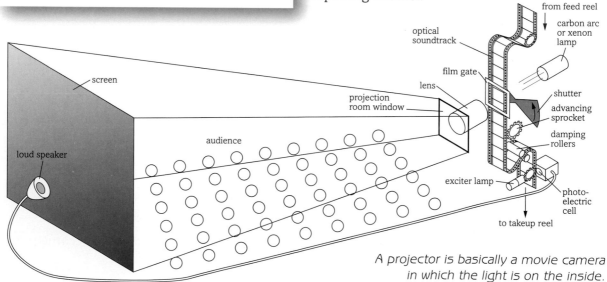

A projector is basically a movie camera in which the light is on the inside. A powerful bulb is needed to enlarge the 35 mm image of the frame to 300,000 times its size on screen.

What we are seeing is very like a slide show in which images are shown so quickly that we are deceived into believing we are watching a continuous sequence of events. If you watch early silent movies, you will notice that they flicker (the cinema used to be called the flicks) and that the movement of the characters is jerky. This is because they were shot and projected at 16 frames per second (fps), rather than the present-day 24 fps.

Sound first came to the cinema in the 1920s, when films were known as the 'talkies'. Today, sound plays a key role in the enjoyment audiences get from watching film. Film sound usually comes in the form of an optical soundtrack, as part of the 35 mm print (a positive copy of a film) on which most films are distributed. This track has a light shone through it by a small bulb called an exciter lamp. The beam of light is then picked up and read by a photoelectric cell, which converts light into electrical impulses. These impulses are then fed through an amplifier into the speakers, where they appear as sound.

When the first talkies began, a single loudspeaker behind the screen produced the sound for the audience. The auditorium of a modern cinema contains a number of strategically placed speakers to produce dramatic sound effects, including surround sound, whereby the audience can be made to feel a part of the action of the film. One of the earliest films to exploit the technological possibilities of surround sound was Francis Ford Coppola's *Apocalypse Now,* which was set during the Vietnam War. The director made the film to be projected with quintrophonic sound – three speakers at the front and two behind the audience. This gave the audience the impression that they were not just watching a war movie, they were in the midst of the fighting.

A poster for the film

A more recent innovation is digital sound, which comes either as part of the film print or as a separate CD, which is electronically synchronized with the film image. Digital technology can produce sound of a very high quality.

When a film arrives from the distributor for exhibition at the cinema, it comes in reels. On each side of the 35 mm print with its optical soundtrack are sprocket holes, which sprockets on the projector use to pull the film through the gate. The film slowly unwinds from a spool above the projector and winds back to one below it.

Going to the cinema

Going to the cinema has always been an exciting experience. In 1946, before the arrival of television, the British made a total of 1,640 million visits to the cinema. The popularity in the early 1980s of the mass-produced video recorder, together with the chance to rent the latest releases on video, reduced this grand number to 54 million in 1984, less than one visit to the cinema that year for each member of the population.

Today cinema has recovered much of its popularity, with audiences almost trebling to nearly 143 million in 2000, which means that on average we all go to the cinema at least twice a year. The apparent threat posed by video and DVD rental outlets and, more recently, satellite movie channels has, in fact, stimulated interest in film-going and led to an increased demand.

One of the reasons for this increase in cinema audiences in the past decade is the arrival of the multiplex (a cinema complex with numerous screens). The first multiplex cinema, based on an American concept, was opened in Milton Keynes, a town that previously did not have a cinema. Now there are over 1,700 screens across 186 multiplex sites throughout the UK, including the Warner Village in Birmingham which boasts 30 screens.

3D didn't catch on

A typical multiplex cinema is situated out of town, with good access by road. It is close to other amenities, such as shopping facilities and restaurants. It gives the cinema-goer access to around 10 screens, each offering a different programme. Shared projection rooms, box office and kiosks mean that the costs of running so many screens are comparatively small in terms of labour and capital. It also means it is more likely that audiences will find at least one film that they will want to see.

Multiplex cinemas

ON YR. OWN

- Is there a muliplex cinema near you?
- Why has it chosen the location that it has?
- How does it attract its audiences?

Persuading people to attend regularly is an important ploy in the marketing of cinemas. Of course, their out-of-town location, often at a major road junction, makes it almost essential to have or use a car to get to a multiplcx. This has an important bearing on the type of audience that multiplexes attract, as does the fairly high admission prices they charge.

In groups

AS A GROUP

There must be several films that you would like to see that you can't.

- Make a list of these films.
- List the reasons why you can't see them, and compare your list with those of the other groups.

There could be many reasons why you can't see a film, such as expense, difficulties of getting to the cinema or the age restriction of the certificate.

The multiplex is geared to showing mainstream commercial films, usually Hollywood products, which have been well hyped in the media. Occasionally, films that do not have a mass appeal are screened, but these are very much a minority. For example, some multiplexes regularly screen films that have a specific appeal to Asian audiences.

The timing of the release of films is quite important to distribution companies in their efforts to ensure a good financial return on a film. Most films have their première in London before going on general release and being shown across the country, usually a week or so later.

Increased interest in the cinema has also led to a more secure position for what are sometimes called art house, or independent, cinemas. These are cinemas committed to showing films that would not normally be on general release. They may be foreign films, or those made by independent production companies that may not have the mass appeal of Hollywood films. The finances of some independent cinemas are supported by organisations like the British Film Institute (BFI), which helps fund a network of regional film theatres committed to showing films that otherwise might not be commercially viable. There may be one in a town or city near you.

A guide for an independent cinema.

On your own

From a copy of your local newspaper or listings magazine, make a list of films that are on at your local cinemas.

- Which films on the list are showing for the first time in your area ?
- Which films have been shown previously, or have been retained by the cinema for another week ?
- Have any films been shown for more than a week ?
- Are any of the films on your list independent films ?

Films and TV on video

Of course, you don't have to go to the cinema to see a film. Films on television have always been popular and people in Britain are especially fond of the video recorder or more recently the DVD player, either rented or bought; in fact, three out of four homes now possess a video recorder. The British public spent a total of £408 million on video rental in 1999 and nearly £882 million on video retail sales, although this figure includes sales of tapes other than feature films. The rental market is slowly declining in the face of competition from cable and satellite, while the retail market is growing, having nearly doubled between 1990 and 1994. Much of this growth comes from videos targeted at young children, such as Disney films.

A Blockbuster video store.

In pairs

- What types other than Disney films are people likely to buy?
- What is the advantage of owning these titles, rather than renting them?
- Are there any DVDs or pre-recorded video tapes that people have bought in the house where you live? If so, name three or four of them. For each one, say why you think it was bought. How often do they get watched?
- If you had the chance to own just one DVD or video, which one would you choose? Give your reasons.

Films become available as video rentals only after being shown on general release, and perhaps after they have been replayed in one or two independent cinemas. Films available from video rental shops usually have a 'satellite hold-back' period of around six months, during which time the distribution company will not make them available for showing on the satellite channels. This means that the video rental shop has an opportunity to recover its outlay on the film before satellite audiences can watch it. Finally, the rights to a film are bought by one of the terrestrial channels to be shown across the network.

Films form part of the basic programming of the terrestrial TV channels. When a major film is shown for the first time on one of these channels, it is often accompanied by a similar hype to when it was first released at the cinema. In addition, satellite subscribers can have access to several movie channels, with some channels showing older films as part of the package.

Some people like to create in their own home the viewing conditions that cinema audiences enjoy. Terrestrial television broadcasts many films in NICAM or surround sound,which give stereophonic sound through a compatible TV or through a hi-fi system. Satellite also offers films in surround sound. Viewers must set up five speakers in the viewing area in order to enjoy the full benefits of this system.

Another innovation is the development of widescreen TV. The standard aspect ratio (see right) of a television is 4:3, roughly equivalent to academy ratio, the Hollywood standard before CinemaScope. Films shot for the cinema in widescreen have to be cropped or have part of their image selected for viewing on a standard TV, a technique called 'pan and scan'. Alternatively they can be shown in 'letterbox', with black spaces at the top and bottom of the screen. Widescreen TV, with a ratio of 16:9, allows almost all of the image of a CinemaScope film to fill the screen. After a slow start, widescreen is gaining popularity in this country, especially as more programmes are being transmitted in this format and the price of this hardware is gradually decreasing.

Aspect ratio

4

3

Aspect ratio means the relationship between the width of a screen or image and its height. An aspect ratio of 4:3 means that the screen looks like this.

Widescreen TV ads

Class discussion

As you can see, technology makes it possible to create a cinema in your living room. Do you as an audience watch a film in different ways according to the viewing conditions? Consider the following viewing conditions:

- At the cinema
- At home watching a rented video
- At home watching satellite TV
- At home watching terrestrial TV
- At home watching a recorded TV programme.

Among other things, you need to consider the extent to which you personally have control over the medium you are watching, as well as the amount of effort and cash you have invested in getting to see it.

You also need to think about the interaction between the film and the audience, such as the amount of discussion (or silence) that occurs in each viewing condition.

Hollywood and the film industry

Whether you watch a film at the cinema or at home, there is a good chance it was produced in the USA. Hollywood is almost the same thing as the film industry, and the majority of films on show at your local cinema are likely to have been made there.

There are, of course, other film industries. In India, films are in great demand, not only for the home market, but for export to Asian communities across the world. The Indian film industry is sometimes known as Bollywood (a mixture of the words 'Bombay' and 'Hollywood') and produces more than 900 films a year. In Europe, the French have always been active film producers ever since the first public showing of a film by the inventors of the 'cinematograph', the Lumière brothers, in Paris in 1895. Film is seen by many European countries as an important part of their cultural identity.

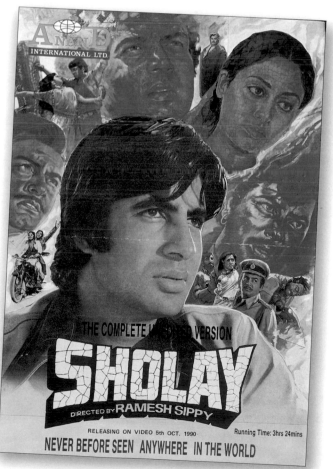

A poster advertising a product of 'Bollywood'.

83

All-time top 20 movies at the box office

	Released	Film Name	Director	Total Box Office
1	1997	Titanic	James Cameron	$600,788,188
2	1977	Star Wars	George Lucas	$460,998,007
3	1999	The Phantom Menace	George Lucas	$431,088,297
4	1982	ET: The Extra Terrestrial	Steven Spielberg	$399,804,539
5	1993	Jurassic Park	Steven Spielberg	$357,067,947
6	1994	Forrest Gump	Robert Zemeckis	$329,693,974
7	2001	Harry Potter and the Philosopher's Stone	Chris Columbus	$313,653,000
8	1994	The Lion King	Roger Allers	$312,855,561
9	1983	The Return of the Jedi	Richard Marquand	$309,205,079
10	1996	Independence Day	Roland Emerich	$306,169,255
11	1999	The Sixth Sense	M. Night Shyamalan	$293,501,675
12	1980	The Empire Strikes Back	Irvin Kershner	$290,271,960
13	1990	Home Alone	Chris Columbus	$285,761,243
14	2001	Lord of the Rings: The Fellowship of the Ring	Peter Jackson	$271,449,000
15	2001	Shrek	Larry Bafia	$267,652,016
16	2000	How The Grinch Stole Christmas	Ron Howard	$260,031,035
17	1975	Jaws	Steven Spielberg	$260,000,000
18	2001	Monsters Inc	Peter Doctor	$251,554,000
19	1989	Batman	Tim Burton	$251,188,924
20	1997	Men in Black	Barry Sonnenfield	$250,156,830

At the time of publication, three of these films were still on general release.

Group discussion

AS A GROUP

What does this information tell you about trends in cinema over the last four decades?

In the UK, many of the films made are financed by the US film industry with an eye for US box-office success. In 1994, 84 films were made in the UK at a total cost of £455.2 million, which means that the average budget for each film was £5.46 million. Of this figure, investment from the US represented £279 million, well over half. By contrast, the average Hollywood film costs £22 million. To this should be added £9 million of marketing costs by way of prints for distribution and advertising in the US alone.

The British film industry itself, however, is still capable of producing movies that make a lot of money on both sides of the Atlantic. Made for under £30 million, *Notting Hill* took this amount at the UK box office. It grossed a further £80 million in the USA and £125 million worldwide.

Every Hollywood producer dreams of producing a blockbuster – a film that will produce huge box-office receipts, like Steven Spielberg's *Jurassic Park,* for example. Increasingly, the box-office takings for such a film are only one part of its success story. Spin-offs from a film, including sweets, games, toys and, of course, such clothing as T-shirts, are a key ingredient in maximising profits. They also fulfill an important role in the marketing of the film, not only by drawing attention to it, but by holding the audience's interest for longer than success at the box office alone would normally manage to.

Films such as *Star Wars* and *Batman* have grossed more from their spin-off earnings than they actually took at the box office. (The 'gross' is the total revenue that a film brings in.) These are sometimes called event movies and are often accompanied by a huge amount of hype across the media before their nationwide release, which is often timed to coincide with school holidays, when families are most likely to go to the cinema.

How a film is made

The team

Wherever a film is made, the process is likely to be very similar. A key player at all stages of the production is the producer. Before any film is shot, a good deal of planning has to take place: with such vast sums of money at risk, pre-production – as the planning stages are called – is vitally important. The producer's job at this stage is to come up with an idea for a film, get it scripted and raise the money to make the picture. The idea may be the producer's own, or one bought from someone else. Wherever is comes from, a writer will be needed to turn the idea into a screenplay (script).

Once a producer has come up with or acquired an idea, commissioned a writer to produce a screenplay and found people to put up money for the film, then he or she must hire actors and technicians to work on the film.

The most important member of this team is the director. The director's job is to turn the screenplay into a motion picture. He or she is concerned mostly with the artistic qualities of

Directors will often let the actors know exactly what they want from the scene.

the film; in other words, the interpretation of the screenplay into a full-length movie. The artistic interpretation on the part of the director is likely to be one of the hallmarks of the film. Many directors give their films a personal stamp or signature, which makes it identifiable as their work.

Although a film may be seen as the personal vision of a director, he or she is only the head of a large team of people who are responsible for making the film. As the music plays over the end credits of a film at the cinema or on television, notice the long list of names and jobs that appears. Each person has contributed in some way to making the picture, right down to the vitally important function of providing food on set for the actors and technicians.

On your own

Obviously, some screenplays are produced specially for the cinema. Many, however, begin life in other forms.

- Think about where the ideas for films come from. For example, some films are based on real-life events. Write down the names of three films that are based on events that have actually taken place.

- Now write down a list of other sources of ideas for film. For each idea, name three films that have originated in this way.

Class discussion

AS A CLASS

- Who are the great film directors of the past and present?

- Are some directors as well known as stars?

- Are there directors whose films you would make a point of seeing?

People working on a film set.

What's in a name?

There are quite a lot of unusual names given to the jobs in the film industry. Here are some that you are likely to come across most frequently:

- **Gaffer:** chief electrician on the set, takes charge of the lighting
- **Best boy:** the gaffer's assistant (who can, of course, be a girl)
- **Focus puller:** assistant camera operator, whose chief job is to keep the shot in focus when the camera is moving
- **Key grip:** in charge of the grips, or stagehands, who look after the set and the props
- **Animal wrangler:** trains and looks after the animals.

Shooting

Once the producer has got a team together, work can start on the shooting of the film. A schedule has to be drawn up that makes the best use of all available resources, locations, the stars and other actors and technicians.

Things like stunts, which take a lot of organising, are built into the schedule. Obviously, it makes sense to shoot all the scenes that take place in one location together, regardless of the order in which they appear in the finished film.

The film footage shot each day is called the rushes. These are processed quickly so that the director and other key members of the crew can view them before the next day's shooting.

Film is generally shot on 35 mm film (this figure measures the width of the frame), which is the same size that is used in many still cameras. Formats such as 16 mm and 8 mm are also available. Eight mm film in the form of Super 8 was very popular with amateur film-makers, but has been largely superseded by video. Occasionally film-makers use Super 8 to give a home-made quality to a sequence in a film. Sound is recorded separately. The clapperboard, on which are chalked details of each take (that is, each uninterrupted sequence between edits), is used to ensure that at the editing stage sound and vision will be in perfect 'sync'. This is especially important for dialogue: audiences quickly spot the slightest error in lip sync, when an actor's lips move in different time to the words spoken.

Many films are dubbed into a different language. This means that the original pictures are used, but other actors speak the words translated into a different language. Of course, it is immediately obvious that the lip sync is completely out in this situation, as the movement of the actors' lips does not match the words that are being spoken.

The process in which everything is arranged in front of the camera is called the mise-en-scène, as we explained in the chapter on language (see page 18-21). Each shot at this stage has to be carefully planned to ensure, for example, that continuity will be achieved at the editing stage (see below). Continuity means that all details in a shot will match the details in the next one, even though they may be filmed several weeks apart. An actor who is seen to board a plane in Los Angeles will need to look the same when he or she leaves the plane in New York. If their clothes and hair length are different, for example, an audience will notice the lack of continuity between the two shots.

In pairs

IN PAIRS

Look at the photo on the page opposite of a film crew on location. Can you identify some of the personnel and see what they are doing?

Editing

Once a film has been shot, then the business of editing can begin. Modern techniques of editing film involve the use of computers and video equipment. Film is transferred to video tape and edited electronically, with a computer coding each frame of the original film. Many of the traditional skills are still used by the film editor. Much of the time, film is literally cut and stuck together with tape to join scenes. This is called splicing.

An editor's first job is to choose which of a series of takes to use. One scene may have been shot a number of times in different ways. Some of these takes may be unusable for technical reasons, for instance a problem with lighting or sound. In others, actors may have forgotten or fluffed their lines. (Takes that go wrong and are not used are called out-takes and are very much in demand as the source of such programmes as *It'll Be All Right on the Night*.) The editor's other main job is to join the chosen shots together into a logical and coherent narrative. In addition, sound has to be added from a separate magnetic sound source; this has to synchronise perfectly with the movement of an actor's lips on screen.

The kindest cut

- It is said that if an editor has done a good job, the audience won't even know it has been done at all. When you watch a film, can you tell where the edits come?

- Some films use long takes, whereas others use edits in quick succession. What does the style of editing tell you about these films?

Again, continuity is also an important element in the editing process. If a character is seen to walk in opposite directions when two scenes are edited together, it can be hard for the viewer to make sense of the action.

The edited version of a film is called a cut because the film has literally been cut into its final shape. This may not, however, be the cut that you see in the cinema. Different countries have different attitudes to censorship, and this is one reason why the version you see in the cinema in this country may be different from that shown elsewhere in the world. Equally, there is a growing fashion in different cuts, in the same way that there are different mixes of sound recordings. A video release version may even contain scenes not shown in the cinema. A DVD allows a host of extras to be included such as alternative cuts, documentaries showing the production process and interviews with the stars and director.

A page from Heat magazine.

Marketing the film

The star system

In the chapter on institutions, we looked at the importance of stars as a means of helping a producer ensure the success of a media product (pages 48–49). Nowhere is the system more powerful than in the film industry based in Hollywood. The stars are the public face of the film industry; they are the people with whom the audiences are most familiar. As such, their key function is to get people to the cinema. Audiences will go to see a film because of the star.

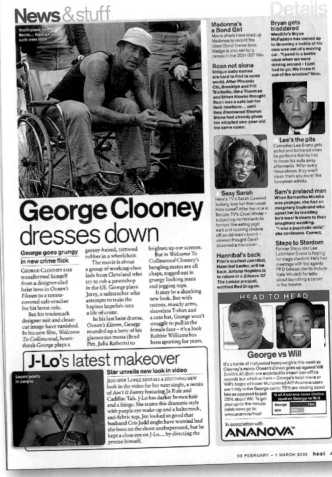

Class discussion

AS A CLASS

Are there any films that you would like to recut yourself? A sad film that you would like to have a happy ending, for example?

The film industry has always been clever at promoting itself and its products. Such events as the Oscar ceremonies, and film festivals such as Cannes, held each May in the south of France, attract a vast amount of media attention from across the globe.

What stars do off-screen is often as important or even more important than their performance on screen. Gossip is an age-old method of keeping stars in the public gaze. Stories of stars' private lives, whether true or not, are a way of ensuring constant media coverage and speculation among their fans.

Your stars

ON YR. OWN

Collect newspaper cuttings, or make a diary of TV and radio stories over a period of a month about a star who is in the news.

- What sort of stories appear?
- How is the star represented in the media?
- Does this publicity, including such events as chat show appearances, coincide with the release of a film in this country?

Stars attract fans, who will not only want to watch their films, but are interested in their lives. Some may even try to be like them. Stars, therefore, are a powerful force in the marketing

of a picture; they are often at the forefront of fashion and lifestyle, introducing the public to new ways of doing things. As trendsetters, stars often become associated with products that they are seen to endorse. Equally, the manufacturers of luxury goods such as cars and clothing are keen to have their products associated with the glamorous lifestyles of the stars. You will often see these items used as props in films. This is known as 'product placement'. It is an effective method of advertising, especially if the film is a huge box-office success.

Awards ceremonies are often very glamorous affairs, which receive a high level of press attention.

The more important a star, the more power he or she has. Stars like Clint Eastwood, for example, are able to set up their own companies and direct their own films. This is a far cry from the days of the studio system, where all the major stars were under contract to make a certain number of films to studios such as Warner Bros, MGM and Paramount. Stars who were not co-operative in fitting in with the demands of the studio bosses would find their careers in ruins.

Reviews

The film industry relies heavily on publicity in the other media, such as radio, television, magazines and newspapers. Reviews are an important source of information about films. They appear in a number of forms, for example on TV programmes where experts or members of the public offer their opinion of a film. Many magazines carry reviews of films released each month at the cinema, as well as video rental and retail releases. Specialist film magazines, such as *Empire* and *Premiere*, try to cover all the feature films that are released.

Newspapers provide similar information, some of it more detailed and considered than others, and radio stations often have slots in programmes in which newly released films are discussed.

A good film review should be more than just the reviewer's opinion of the film. It should provide potential viewers with information about the film that will allow them to decide whether it is worth seeing or not. For some people, the decision whether or not to see a film at the cinema may rest on the opinion of a reviewer whom they trust.

SIGHT AND SOUND

NOVEMBER 2001/£2.95

You will be scared:
'The Others'
Surviving terrorism:
Japan's epic 'Eureka'
Allen Smithee:
the wilderness years
Plus the London Film
Festival preview

EVERY NEW
FILM
REVIEWED

'Apocalypse Now Redux'
Brando reborn

On your own

ON YR. OWN

Earlier in this chapter you were asked to find out which films were showing at your local cinema. Now try to find out about each of these films.

- Where did you get your information about these films from?
- How reliable is the information?
- Do you trust the judgement of some reviewers more than others? If so, Why?
- Did you find any sources of information about the films other than reviews?

Film review

Choose a film that has just been released at the cinema. Collect as much information as you can about the film in the form of reviews from newspapers and magazines and information from TV and radio.

- Do all the reviewers agree about the film, or is there a difference of opinion about it? If so, why do you think this is?

- Now go to see the film. Which review, in your opinion, gave the most accurate evaluation of the film?

NEW FILMS

HARRY POTTER AND THE PHILOSOPHER'S STONE

SPECIAL PREVIEW

As we went to press, Chris Columbus was still beavering away on the final cut of Harry Potter and working in John Williams' original score. "We'll probably be running into the theatres cutting shots," he

RELEASED: NOVEMBER 16
CERTIFICATE: TBC

CAST
Daniel Radcliffe Harry Potter
Rupert Grint Ron Weasley
Emma Watson Hermione Granger
Richard Harris Albus Dumbledore

Director Chris Columbus
Producer David Heyman
Screenplay J.K. Rowling, Steve Kloves
Running time tbc
Distributor Warner Bros

IN A NUTSHELL
Harry is the only living person to have survived an encounter with evil Lord Voldemort. On his 11th birthday, he finds he's been accepted to Hogwarts School Of Witchcraft and Wizardry, where he discovers Quidditch and learns about the scar on his forehead.

Ron and Harry were standing for Double Maths no longer.

confessed when *Empire* asked him whether he'd have all the magical touches ready in time for the worldwide release in November. And, with an audience of over 100 million avid Potter book fans to please, you can't blame the

filmmakers for taking their time.
So far *Empire* has seen about 15 minutes of footage, mostly effects-free, and, there's no doubting that the casting is impressive. As well as the leads, there are roles for Julie Walters (Mrs. Weasley), John Cleese

(Nearly Headless Nick), Rik Mayall (Poltergeist Peeves), Leslie Phillips (the voice of the Sorting Hat at Hogwarts) and Verne Troyer (as, presumably, a mini-ghoul). But the real turn-ups are the three leading kids. Anyone expecting a Macaulay Culkin brat in the role of Harry will be pleasantly surprised by Daniel Radcliffe's mature performance, while Emma Watson and Rupert Grint are also spot-on. This trio provide a true heart to the movie and fans of the books won't be disappointed by the realisation of their heroes. Add to that some stunning sets and deliciously dark-toned cinematography, and we've got high hopes for this being a winner.

Inevitably, die-hard Potterists will be slightly disappointed by what is missing. The print doing the test screening rounds in the States has come in at 2 hrs. 32 mins. — lengthy for a 'kids' film', but the only complaint so far is that it's not long enough! Indeed, it would be great to see a finished article that's on the two-hour side rather than 90 minutes.
Emma Cochrane

Raging Bull ★★★★

US   1980   119m   bw/colour
UA/Chartoff-Winkler

The rise to fame of an unlikeable middle-weight boxer, based on the autobiography of Jake La Motta.

Tough, compelling, powerfully made ringside melodrama. A poll of American critics voted it the best movie of the 1980s.

w Paul Schrader, Mardik Martin d *Martin Scorsese* ph Michael Chapman m from library sources pd Gene Rudolf

☆ Robert DeNiro, Cathy Moriarty, Joe Pesci, Frank Vincent, Nicholas Colasanto

'Scorsese makes pictures about the kind of people you wouldn't want to know.' – *Variety*
'A bravura display of cinematic skill.' – *Daily Mail*

🏆 editing (Thelma Schoonmaker); Robert DeNiro

🎬 best film; best direction; Cathy Moriarty; Joe Pesci; Michael Chapman

📺 editing

The Raging Moon ★

GB   1970   111m   Technicolor
EMI (Bruce Cohn Curtis)

aka: *Long Ago Tomorrow*

A love affair develops between two inmates of a home for the physically handicapped.

Appealing romantic drama which nearly became a big commercial success.

wd Bryan Forbes, novel Peter Marshall ph Tony Imi m Stanley Myers

☆ Malcolm McDowell, *Nanette Newman*, Georgia Brown, Bernard Lee, Gerald Sim, Michael Flanders

The Raging Tide

US   1951   93m   bw
U-I (Aaron Rosenberg)

A San Francisco gangster stows away on a fishing trawler and redeems himself when he perishes saving the life of a fisherman.

Fearfully old-fashioned seafaring melodrama, rather well made.

w Ernest K. Gann novel *Fiddler's Green* by Ernest K. Gann d George Sherman ph Russell Metty

---

Newman ad John Graysmark, Patrizia von Brandenstein, Anthony Reading

☆ James Olson, Mary Steenburgen, James Cagney, Pat O'Brien, Elizabeth McGovern, Howard E. Rollins Jnr, Brad Dourif, Moses Gunn, Kenneth McMillan, Donald O'Connor

'It's limp . . . it always seems to be aiming about halfway toward the effects that Doctorow achieved in his literary extravaganza.' – *New Yorker*
'The book, despite its defects, was funny, radical and angry. The film, despite its virtues, is solemn, liberal and passive.' – *Sunday Times*

† The film cost 32 million dollars and took eleven.
🎬 screenplay; Miroslav Ondricek; Randy Newman; Elizabeth McGovern (supporting actress); Howard E. Rollins Jnr; art direction; song 'One More Hour'

The Raid ★

US   1954   83m   Technicolor
TCF (Robert L. Jacks)

In 1864 six confederate soldiers escape from a union prison, and from a Canadian refuge carry out a revenge raid on a small Vermont town.

Interesting little action drama, crisply characterized and plotted, and based on a historical incident.

w Sidney Boehm, story *Affair at St Albans* by Herbert Ravenal Sass d Hugo Fregonese ph Lucien Ballard m Roy Webb

☆ Van Heflin, Anne Bancroft, Richard Boone, Lee Marvin, Tommy Rettig, Peter Graves, Douglas Spencer, Will Wright, John Dierkes

Raid on Rommel

US   1971   99m   Technicolor
Universal (Harry Tatelman)

In North Africa during World War II, a British officer releases prisoners of war and leads them in an assault on Tobruk.

Dispirited low-budget actioner apparently first intended for television.

w Richard Bluel d Henry Hathaway ph Earl Rath m Hal Mooney

☆ Richard Burton, John Colicos, Clinton Greyn, Wolfgang Preiss

---

and ignore the insistence on *unpleasantness; still, there are boring bits in between, and the story doesn't make a lot of sense.*

w Lawrence Kasdan d Steven Spielberg
ph Douglas Slocombe m John Williams
pd Norman Reynolds

☆ Harrison Ford, Karen Allen, Ronald Lacey, Paul Freeman, John Rhys-Davies, Denholm Elliott

'Both de trop and not enough.' – *Sight and Sound*
'Children may well enjoy its simple-mindedness, untroubled by the fact that it looks so shoddy and so uninventive.' – *Observer*
'Kinesthetically, the film gets to you, but there's no exhilaration, and no surge of feeling at the end.' – Pauline Kael, *New Yorker*
'An out of body experience, a movie of glorious imagination and breakneck speed that grabs you in the first shot, hurtles you through a series of incredible adventures, and deposits you back in reality two hours later – breathless, dizzy, wrung-out, and with a silly grin on your face.' – *Roger Ebert*

† Tom Selleck was the first choice for the lead, but was tied up with his TV series *Magnum.*
†† It was followed by two sequels: *Indiana Jones and the Temple of Doom* and *Indiana Jones and the Last Crusade* (qqv).
🏆 editing (Michael Kahn); visual effects
🎬 best picture; Steven Spielberg; Douglas Slocombe; John Williams; Norman Reynolds
📺 Norman Reynolds

Railroaded ★

US   1947   72m   bw
Charles F. Reisner/Eagle Lion

A detective is on the trail of a ruthless mobster.

A new post-war toughness was evident in this sharply made second feature.

w John C. Higgins, Gertrude Walker d Anthony Mann ph Guy Roe m Alvin Levin

☆ John Ireland, Sheila Ryan, Hugh Beaumont, Jane Randolph, Ed Kelly, Charles D. Brown

Rails into Laramie

US   1954   81m   Technicolor
Universal-International

Railway construction is hampered in Laramie by a salon keeper who keeps the workers too happy.

Solid co-feature Western, quite enjoyable.

w D. D. Beauchamp, Joseph Hoffman d Jesse Hibbs ph Maury Gertsman md Joseph Gershenson

☆ John Payne, Dan Duryea, Mari Blanchard, Barton MacLane, Harry Shannon, Lee Van Cleef

'A film for adults to take their children, too!'

The Railway Children ★★★

👫 GB   1970   108m   Technicolor
EMI (Robert Lynn)

Review

As you have seen in this chapter, cinema is an important and complex medium. Like other media products, it is a commodity, produced, in the main, by large and influential institutions. As a commodity, it has to be carefully marketed to ensure that it appeals to as wide an audience as possible. Indeed, as an industry, cinema depends for its survival on this ability to manufacture products that audiences want to consume.

7

Media technology

The way in which we consume the media is often affected by changes in technology. The invention of photography, the first recording of sound, the introduction of sound into the cinema, or talkies, and the birth of television have all had a major impact on the media and its audiences. Today technology seems to be moving at a breakneck pace, making more and more media available for us to consume. Some people fear that this will result in a divided society. Not only will there be rich people and poor people in terms of material wealth, but also there will be rich and poor when it comes to getting hold of media technology and the information and entertainment it provides.

For example, people who are able to pay for access to digital channels are able to view sporting events and films not available to those merely with access to the terrestrial channels. Being able to use the Internet, either at home or at work, means people are able to save time and money by buying goods and services 'on line'. Not only can this make it easier and more convenient to do such everyday things as order groceries on line and have them delivered, it also makes it possible to save money for example by booking holidays using a discount site on the Internet rather than through a high-street travel agent. These are benefits in addition to the convenience of having a wealth of information and entertainment at your fingertips.

In this chapter we look at some of the changes taking places in media technology. We consider how these are likely to affect us not only as individual members of an audience, but also as part of the society in which we live.

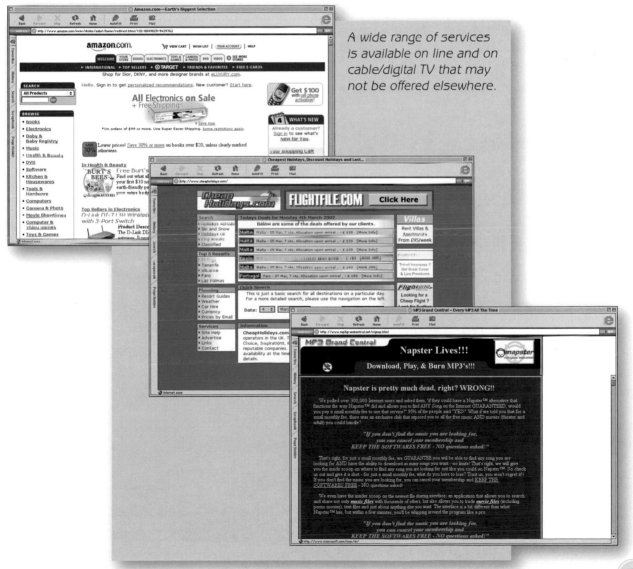

A wide range of services is available on line and on cable/digital TV that may not be offered elsewhere.

Availability and accessibility

One of the key changes is the way in which the media is now able to target individual members of an audience rather than simply broadcasting to a mass market. As individual members of the audience we are likely to be offered a much wider variety of media products to consume, most of them available to us both at home and on the move. These products are much more likely to be designed to meet our individual interests. There is already evidence that the audience for mass media products such as television shows, and mass circulation newspapers and magazines, is in decline. In their place we may end up with a media that is not only targeted at our own specific tastes and needs, but also one that we can call up on demand. No longer will we have to organise our lives around an episode of our favourite soap. Instead we will arrange our consumption of the media around our lives.

Increasingly, services are available which allow viewers more contol over the programmes they watch.

Digital radio

Most people who listen to the radio do so by receiving an analogue signal. This signal, which may be AM or FM, can be received on a variety of different radio tuners. These may form part of a hi-fi system, be a small portable radio, perhaps with earphones, or a radio fitted into the dashboard of the car. Some people use their computer to listen to the radio over the Internet. There are a number of problems with using an analogue signal to receive radio programmes. One of the ones you will have noticed is that the signal is easily distorted by atmospheric conditions, such as a

thunderstorm, or when it bounces off hills or tall buildings. If you listen to a particular station in your car you may find you have to keep retuning. This is because on the FM waveband a radio station needs several frequencies to cover a large area.

Digital radio signals are able to solve both these problems. They use a binary system, like a computer, which makes them less likely to be distorted than an analogue signal. In addition they are able to use a single frequency network which means that all transmitters will use the same frequency for a single programme. If you are driving round the country, therefore, you do not need to retune to keep listening to the same station. Probably the most important advantage of a digital signal is that it allows several programmes to be carried on one block of frequencies, or a multiplex, its technical name. These programmes can be broadcast simultaneously using in effect a single frequency.

Currently there are seven multiplexes designated for use in the United Kingdom.

- One for national BBC stations
- One for national commercial radio
- Five for local radio broadcasting

Digital radio offers a much clearer sound quality, in the same way that you notice a difference between playing music on CD and vinyl formats. It also gives audiences a much wider choice. Most people will be able to listen to on average 16 national stations and 16 regional or local ones. In addition to receiving most of the existing radio stations, new stations starting to broadcast include:

Planet Rock: the rock specialist playing uncompromising, classic rock from the 60s, 70s and 80s.

Core: fresh hits for the UK. The best of the chart and club anthems.

Life: playing contemporary music for individual, confident, aspirational adults.

Oneworld: the world's first national commercial station dedicated to plays, books and comedy.

Primetime Radio: an easy listening radio station, playing melodic hits from the last six decades.

Bloomberg Radio: 24-hour City, business and personal finance information.

ITN: delivering news, money, sport, weather, travel and entertainment.

With a digital signal you can do more than transmit just sound. You can also transmit data. As you can see from the illustration, a typical digital receiver is provided with an LCD to allow information to be displayed. For example, a music station will be able to transmit details of the artist, song and album playing over the audio channel. For people listening to radio on the move, information about traffic conditions will be made available, just as it is now. However, this information, either in the form of voice or text, can be automatically sifted by the receiver, so that only information you need for your particular journey is sent. In effect the information is personalised to the needs of a particular individual rather than being broadcast to a mass audience many of whom would find the information irrelevant.

A digital radio receiver.

Activity

ON YR. OWN

Which stations from this list do you think you might like to tune in to? Write down your reasons for wanting to tune in. Working as a group, consider if there are any stations missing from the list that you think would find an audience? Choose one of these stations and write a brief summary of what you think it should broadcast and what sort of audience might listen.

Print media

Print media, such as newspapers and magazines, have been forced to react to changes in technology in the same way as they had to respond when faced with competition from radio and television. Compared to electronic media, print is much slower at getting its message to the audience. Events that are happening while you sit in class will not be reported in the newspapers until tomorrow morning. Most people will know all about them through television or radio news bulletins before they read about these events in a newspaper. As you can see in the chapter on newspapers, print media have met this challenge in a number of ways.

More recently, however, a new challenge has presented itself in the form of on line news through the Internet. When you connect to the Internet, your ISP's home page usually provides the latest news headlines with a link to the full story behind them. In fact it is possible to customise many home pages so that you can decide precisely what type of news and information you want.

For example you may decide that you only want to read sports and showbiz news rather national and international news. This is another

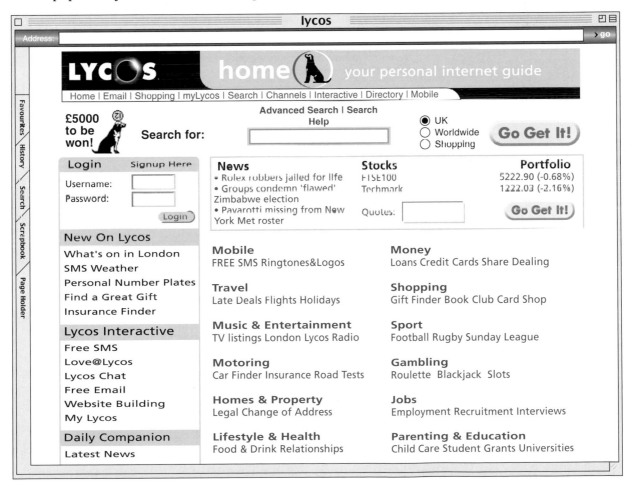

The Lycos homepage.

☐ ═══════════════════ **yahoo** ═══════════════════ ▣▤

Address: [   ] ❯ **go**

MY YAHOO!
UK & IRELAND

Welcome Matthew! – Yahoo! – Update – Account Info – Info – Out

[move to bottom] [   ] [Search] Advanced

Front Page

[Change colors] [Choose Content] [Change layout] [Add/Delete Pages]   [hide buttons]

Album Releases [Edit] [X]

Rock/Pop

Week of 03/12/2002
- Become You – Indigo Girls
- VH1 Presents The Corrs Live In Dublin – The Corrs
- The Fats Domino Jukebox... – Fats Domino
- Souljacker – Eels
- Songs From Take–Off To Landing – Garrison Starr

Week of 03/19/2002
- Rude Awakening – Megadeth
- Land (1975–2002) – Patti Smith
- The Elvis Broadcasts: On Air – Elvis Presley
- Sphinctour – Ministry
- Postcards Of The Hanging: Grateful Dead... – The Grateful

Jazz/Blues

TV Listings				[Edit] [X]	
7:00 pm	7:30 pm	8:00 pm	8:30 pm	9:00 pm	9:30 pm

Horoscopes [Edit] [X]

○ **Pisces**

Horoscope (by astrocenter.com)
You will find that your emotions are calming down a bit to the point where you can deal with them on a more rational level, dear Pisces. It will become easier detaching yourself so that you can make more objective decisions overall. This is a great time to sort out issues of love and romance. It could be that you have acted a bit too hastily in recent weeks. Now you have the opportunity to stand back and make an accurate assessment of these actions. Your intellect and your emotions seem crystal clear.

Front Page Headlines Mar 14 4:18pm [Edit] [X]

Top Stories from Reuters Mar 14 4:18 pm
- Israel Presses Offensive; Italian Journalist Killed
- U.S.–Afghan Troops Proclaim Victory, Pursue Rebels
- Cheney Says U.S. Is a Mideast Force for Peace

The My Yahoo homepage can be customised for the interests of the user.

example of the way in which the audience is able to shape the precise nature of the product that the media is delivering to it. Unlike a newspaper which tries to cater for all its readers, a website can be organised to meet the needs of one individual member of the audience.

Activity

Look at the home pages above and on p99. What sort of people do you think would customise each of the home pages to look like this? Write down a list of features that you would want to see on your own home page.

One way in which print media have risen to this challenge from the Internet is to join it. Most newspapers and magazines now have their own websites. Many of these are very similar to the printed or 'hard copy' edition. They employ the same headlines and include the same news stories and features. Web-based editions also have a number of advantages over the printed version. The main one is that they can archive, or keep on file, back copies of the paper. Many sites offer a search facility so that a reader looking for an article in a previous edition or seeking information on a topic can use a keyword search. This search will result in a list of articles with hypertext links to take the reader straight to them.

The Guardian Unlimited website allows users to search for articles that have been archived.

In a similar way most magazines have set up their own websites that include features from the current print edition. They do not, however, usually allow access to the entire magazine contents. There is a simple reason for this. Access to most websites is free. If people can read a newspaper or magazine for free, then they will not go out and but it. Clearly the argument is not really as simple as that. A high proportion of people still enjoy the convenience of a newspaper or magazine in its print form. Even though some people have laptop computers with Internet access, connecting on a crowded bus or train is a lot more troublesome than simply reading a newspaper. In fact many print media see their website as a way of promoting the print, or hard copy edition. If people see the newspaper or magazine on the web and enjoy reading the articles, they are likely to go out and buy a copy to read the rest.

Many high profile magazines now have their own website.

Activity

Imagine that you can customise your favourite newspaper or magazine to be delivered electronically. Make a list of the features would you most want to see. Are there any you would get rid of. Are there any new ones you would like to be included?

One of the benefits of on line information sources is the increasing use of email to deliver selected news information to the audience. For example, if you want to keep up to date with media stories, *The Guardian* website allows you to subscribe to their daily Media Briefing, which will email you each morning details of all the stories about the media in that day's newspapers.

Television

It is in television that digital technology has had the greatest influence over the way in which we consume the media. Until just over 20 years ago, most people had just four terrestrial television channels from which to choose their viewing. Two of these, BBC2 and Channel 4, were considered 'minority' channels with a limited appeal. BBC1 and ITV competed for the mass audience, especially in the evening prime-time slots.

The launch of satellite broadcasting in 1989, with four channels, and later Channel 5 meant that audiences were offered a wider range of programming and the opportunity to see films much sooner after their release at the cinema. Although choice had increased, the capacity for broadcasting via analogue technology remained limited. The arrival of digital technology in 1998 allowed an immediate growth to 140 in the number of channels broadcast using satellite technology. Look at the channel guide for Sky TV on page 193 and you will see the range of choice available to viewers able to receive this service. Of course, choice comes at a price and many people feel that a subscription charge of nearly four times the annual television licence fee for the all-inclusive package puts this technology beyond their reach. Some people also argue that there is too much choice so that it is impossible to keep up with what is available let alone find time to watch it.

The potential of digital technology is only just beginning to be explored and choice is only one of the so-called benefits it offers the audience. Until now, audiences have had little or no control over the image on their television screens, other than being able to change channels or switch off. Digital technology allows audiences to control what they see on the screen. For example most television programmes are shot using a variety of different cameras, each with it own angle. The image that appears on our screens is chosen by the director. When we watch a football match, for example, it is the director who decides when we get a close-up of a particular player or whether an action sequence is replayed in slow motion. Digital technology can allow the audience itself to make some of these choices. For example, it is possible to look at a particular incident from the viewpoint of one of the players, wearing a tiny camera called 'playercam'.

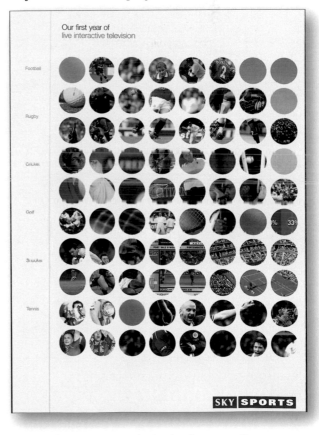

Advert for 'playercam' which allows audiences a choice of viewpoints.

In the same way, we can also select news items that we want to know more about by using the interactive features of Sky News. As you can see, digital technology is capable of handing control of the images on the screen over to the audience to play with it to suit their own needs and pleasures.

Alongside the development of digital satellite broadcasting, broadband technology will have a huge impact on the way the media affects our daily lives. Broadband can come in many forms: down a telephone line, through a fibre-optic cable or via a satellite signal. What it can do is bring into your home huge amounts of information at high-speed. It allows Internet access at around 40 times the fastest speed generally available. It is likely that people will pay a monthly fee for unlimited access to the Internet so that they will be permanently connected without having to dial in each time they want to use it. At these speeds, it will be possible to download and watch films as well as having reliable access to music and games.

What is most likely to change the way we use the media is the idea of convergence, which means bringing all this technology together. At present, most of the electronic equipment in your house tends to be used separately. Some people link their hi-fi to the television and VCR while others may use their television to send and receive e-mail. What new multimedia technology is likely to do is bring together broadband technology, Internet access and the television in the corner of your lounge. This will not only enable you to receive video on demand, rather than visiting your local rental shop, it will also open up the way to e-commerce. This means we will be using our television in a much more interactive way to buy goods and services without leaving our favourite chair. This on line retailing is already beginning to be known as t-commerce.

We will also be able to send and receive video e-mails and have a 'virtual' get together of family and friends. What is more, this technology is likely to be available to us both when we are on the move and when we are at home.

Technology on the move

Mobile phone communication is also likely to be improved by broadband technology. Today's third generation WAP phones offer limited access to Internet and e-mail services as well as text messaging. Broadband will make it possible to use your portable phone in the same way you might use a portable television. News bulletins, films, our favourite television programme, the latest CD and on line shopping are all likely to be available to us as we move around the country. In fact mobile phones of the future may well become an extension of our homes, enabling us to take with us much of the information and entertainment technology we are used to using in our homes.

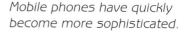

Mobile phones have quickly become more sophisticated.

Interactive technology

Using interactive media means that we have access to a lot of information, much more than any generation previously. The very fact that it is interactive means, however, that the people who provide this information will in turn have a large amount of information about us. If you use a mobile phone, for example, the phone company knows where you are each time you use it. We are used to being watched by surveillance cameras in shopping malls or on motorways. When we use interactive media, information can be gathered about all the things that we consume, from fast food to fast cars. Knowing what people spend their money on and when they spend it is important information to advertisers. The more they know about people's lifestyles the better they than can target their advertisements. So if you use your remote control to order a pizza during the football match every Sunday afternoon, pizza companies will be queuing to send an advertisement to your screen telling you why you will enjoy their product better than the one you usually buy.

You may have already noticed when you use the Internet that advertisements pop up for products that are linked to particular information you are seeking. Some people think that one day we will be constantly targeted in this specific way as vast databases of information about our individual lifestyle are built up. For example, people who like to gamble may be offered odds during a televised football match on whether a player will score from a penalty. Of course many people see a lot of danger here, arguing that our rights to privacy and individual freedoms are being taken away form us. For example, usually when you use the Internet to visit a website, the webserver places a 'cookie' on the hard disk of your computer. These cookies are used, often without your knowledge, to store and transmit information about the sites that you visit. It does not take long for a lot of complex and useful information to be built up about a person's interests and tastes.

On the other side, people also argue that all of this technological change has led to people having more control over the media. A popular pastime for some people on the Internet is to set up a site enabling them to communicate with a potential audience of millions across the globe. These sites often take the form of personal home pages which people use to provide the world with information about themselves, their families and their interests. Some people build sites to celebrate their favourite bands or football teams and share their knowledge and enthusiasm with the world.

Examples of fanzine websites – there are thousands of such sites on the Internet.

One impact of new media technology is the way in which it is changing many people's views of the world. For example, people have usually been suspicious of surveillance cameras set up around public spaces, such as shopping malls, to keep an eye on what they are doing. These cameras have been seen as a way of controlling people by watching their every move, like Big Brother in George Orwell's novel *1984*. Now people actually encourage the use of surveillance cameras in the form of webcams on the Internet. These are set up in people's homes to broadcast intimate details of their lives to anyone who chooses to watch.

The idea has been taken up on television by programmes, a genre known as Reality TV. The best known of these in fact calls itself *Big Brother*. Contestants on reality TV shows enjoy making an exhibition of the most intimate moments of their personal lives in return for the short-lived celebrity status that

Activity

ON YR. OWN

What do you think is the appeal of appearing on a webcam? What do you think makes people want to do it? Would you be happy to have a webcam installed in your house?

There are thousands of webcam sites on the Internet.

such programmes give to them. We, the audience, play our part by watching in our millions and buying newspapers that tell us the secrets of the off-screen lives of these instant celebrities. Surveillance seems no longer to be feared but has become an important source of media pleasure as people invite us to poke our noses into their private affairs.

Big Brother itself was one of the first programmes to exploit the potential of the Internet. Not only was the access to the Big Brother house available 24 hours a day on the Internet, but the audience was able to use e-mail to make their own direct contribution to the programme. This is a good example of the kind

of convergence that is taking place with media technology. Other reality TV shows allow viewers to apply to appear on the show and vote on how issues should be resolved as well.

Activity

ON YR. OWN

What other reality TV programmes have you watched? What do you think makes them so popular? Do you think we should be concerned about programmes of this sort or are they just good fun? Are they a passing phase that will be replaced with another genre?

Many popular TV programmes will have their own official websites.

8

Newspapers, magazines & comics

History

On street corners throughout the world, newspaper-sellers invite people to read the 'latest'. In airports and stations, kiosks and shops offer eye-catching displays of magazines to entice travellers. In doctors' waiting-rooms, dog-eared piles of old magazines help patients take their minds off their troubles. Newspapers, magazines and comics are some of the most familiar objects on earth.

Humans have communicated using writing for thousands of years. However, it was the development of printing in the 15th century that made the written word so powerful. It meant that large numbers of copies of a

document could be made, using printing blocks that were covered in ink and repeatedly pressed onto paper. This was revolutionary, as it meant that, for the first time, written information could be circulated to a large number of people. Previously documents had to be copied by hand, which limited their number and therefore people's access to them.

At first, though, the development of printing meant little to most people, because they could not read. That is why the earliest newspapers and magazines in the UK were produced for and read by the rich and powerful. The first recognised newspaper or pamphlet to contain information about world events was the Oxford Gazette, which was first published in 1665. It was produced to keep the royal court (which had fled to Oxford to escape the plague) informed of events in London. It later became known as the London Gazette and is still published today. The first daily newspaper was the Daily Courant, published for the first time in 1702. The news it contained was hardly hot off the press, as it carried only stories from papers published on the continent. The history of newspapers really began in the UK in 1885, with the first appearance of *The Times*.

The development of newspapers and magazines into items familiar to virtually everyone in the UK was brought about by two main factors: education and distribution. The development of road, and especially rail, transport meant that newspapers and magazines published in London and other big cities could be distributed throughout the country. But it was only in the 20th century, when most people could read as a result of education reforms, that large audiences for printed material were created.

NEWSPAPERS

Thousands of different newspapers are published in the UK each week. They can be separated into groups according to where they are published, and when and how often they are published. Virtually all newspapers fall into the following categories.

Types of newspaper

National daily papers

The national daily papers are the big papers that everyone is familiar with – *The Sun*, *The Mirror*, *The Times*, *The Guardian* and so on. They are published in London each night and are on the news stands every morning, except Sunday. Newspapers can be divided into two groups, depending on their size.

Broadsheet newspapers are printed on sheets of paper 116.83 × 81.28 cm (46 × 32 inches). There are five such broadsheets: *The Daily Telegraph*, *The Times*, the *Financial Times*, *The Guardian* and *The Independent*. The *Daily Telegraph* is the bestselling broadsheet paper, with sales of around one million copies a day.

Tabloid newspapers are half the size of broadsheets, with pages measuring 58.42 × 40.64 cm (23 × 16 inches). There are six national daily tabloids: *The Sun*, the *Star*, *Daily Mail*, *The Mirror*, *Daily Express* and *Daily Sport*. *The Sun* is the tabloid that sells most copies, around 3.5 million a day. This makes it the UK's best-selling daily paper.

National Sunday newspapers

As well as national daily newspapers, the UK has a number of national papers that are published only on a Sunday. There are four national Sunday broadsheets: the *Sunday Times*, the *Sunday Telegraph*, the *Observer*, *Independent on Sunday*. The *Sunday Times'* sales are the largest – over 1.3 million every week.

There are five tabloid papers published nationally every Sunday. They are: *News of the World*, the *Mail On Sunday*, the *People*, *Sunday Express* and *Sunday Mirror*. The *News of the World* sells around 4 million copies each week, making it not only the biggest selling Sunday newspaper, but also the UK's best-selling paper overall.

Regional papers

Dailies In addition to the national newspapers produced in London, the UK has a strong regional press. Nearly 90 daily newspapers are published in cities and towns throughout the country. Regional papers tend to be grouped according to what time of day they are published (either in the morning or in the evening), rather than according to whether they are broadsheet or tabloid in size. There are only a few morning regional newspapers. They include the *Daily Record*, which is published in Glasgow and is the UK's biggest selling regional daily paper, with sales of over 600,000 copies a day. Most regional daily papers are evening papers. The London *Evening Standard*, for example, is the second largest regional daily with around half a million copies bought every day.

Regional morning papers were once popular, but went into decline, largely as a result of competition from national morning papers. In 1999, *Metro*, a free morning newspaper for commuters was launched. It is distributed in London, Manchester, Birmingham, Leeds, Sheffield, Newcastle, Glasgow and Edinburgh. Every weekday morning, some 826,921 copies are distributed across the UK making it the world's largest free newspaper. According to The Newspaper Society, 84% of all adults regularly read a regional or a local newspaper.

Weeklies Most regional papers are published only once a week. These publications can also be separated into two groups, according to whether they are paid

The UK has a very strong regional press.

for by the reader or given away free. The idea of giving papers away free to readers and making money only from the adverts that they contain became popular in the 1970s. However, economic recessions that led businesses to reduce their advertising budgets forced many free newspapers to close.

Sundays There are also a number of regional papers that are published only on a Sunday. These include the *Sunday Life*, which is published in Belfast, and the *Sunday Sun*, published in Newcastle.

Specialist newspapers

As well as national and regional papers, there are newspapers that cover specific areas of interest. The *International Herald Tribune* is a daily paper that covers world news. The *Racing Post* is a national daily paper that covers events in the world of racing. The *Morning Star* is a daily left-wing political paper that is published nationally. The *New Musical Express* publishes the latest news from the music world, along with reviews and features each week. The *Angling Times* is among many weekly newspapers that cater for leisure interests.

On your own

Go into a large local newsagent's and jot down the names of as many papers as you can. Decide which type of paper they are and draw up a chart to show the results of your research.

How are the newspapers in your local newsagent displayed? Is it possible to see all of the front page before you buy a paper? Or can you simply see the masthead and the headline? What factors do you think influence people when they decide to buy a newspaper?

What's in a newspaper?

The process of putting any paper together is basically the same, although there are thousands of newspapers, each one of them different. Most newspapers have several distinct departments:

- Editorial, which is responsible for the words written by reporters and the pictures taken by photographers
- Advertising
- Production
- Sales.

Who does what?

The advertising department

Like all media organisations, newspapers have to make money if they are to survive. They get their money from two sources:

Cover price. The price of the paper, which is paid by the reader when they but it.

Advertising fees. These are paid to the publishers of the paper by the businesses that buy space to promote their products.

The amount of money that a paper makes from its cover price and advertising depends on its circulation, or the number of copies that it sells each day or week. If a lot of papers are sold, as is the case for national dailies, then a large part of the publisher's income comes from the cover price. If fewer papers are sold – for instance – in the case of local weeklies, most of the money comes from advertising. The general rule is that the smaller a paper's sales, the larger the percentage of adverts in it. Free papers that are delivered through every door in a set circulation area make all their money from advertising.

Advertising is crucial to newspapers. The Times used to carry nothing but adverts on its front page.

The advertising sales department, under the control of the advertising manager, has the task of selling advertising space to businesses. The advertising manager has a team of sales representatives, who contact businesses either by visiting them, or phoning them; the latter known as telesales. Advertisers can pay for their adverts to be put in specific places in the paper, such as the front or back, or can simply leave the position of the advert up to the newspaper, which is known as 'run-of-paper' advertising.

The types of adverts found in papers include:

Display adverts, or adverts for products, with photographs and graphics, placed by businesses.

Classified adverts. These are small adverts in columns, usually placed by individuals. They cover such areas as second-hand goods, cars and births, marriages and deaths.

Advertorials. These are advertising features about products, which are written like news stories and are usually accompanied by pictures.

Press advertising is covered in more detail in the chapter on advertising (see pages 160–173). However, at this point it is important to realise the crucial role that advertising plays in newspapers. Without money from adverts, most papers would go out of business. (In fact, for decades, the front page of *The Times* consisted of nothing but advertisements.) because of this, great importance is given to advertising by publishers. Adverts are usually placed on a page first and the stories produced by reporters are arranged around them. This means that the way a newspaper looks depends to a large degree on the adverts that are on it. They make up what is called the 'page scheme', which the editorial department has to work around. Page schemes are plans of news pages that have been drawn up by the advertising department. They show where the adverts that have been sold are placed on the page.

In pairs

IN PAIRS

Contact your local newspaper and get an advertising rate card. Look at a copy of the paper and work out:

● How much of it consists of advertising.

● How much money the newspaper made from the advertisements in that particular issue of the paper.

The editorial department

The editorial department produces the 'news' in newspapers – in other words, the stories and photographs that appear around the adverts. The editorial department is usually made up of:

The editor, who is in charge of the whole department. Editors make sure everything runs to plan and have the final say on what appears in the paper. They work closely with the advertising manager to make sure that the paper makes as much money as possible.

The chief sub-editor is a senior journalist with design and layout skills. Chief sub-editors receive page schemes from the advertising department and decide which stories will go on each page. They distribute the page schemes and stories to sub-editors.

Sub-editors are journalists who place stories and photographs on page schemes. They do this on computer screens. Before placing a story and writing a headline for it, they must first check that it is accurate, does not break the laws of libel and is spelt correctly. They do all this under the guidance of the chief sub-editor.

The news editor is a senior journalist who is in charge of a team of reporters. News editors look at all the stories coming in and decide which ones to follow up. They give the stories that they are interested in to reporters and tell the photographic department what pictures will be needed. They also check stories written by reporters before they are sent to the chief sub-editor.

Reporters are senior and junior journalists who research and write stories. Reporters may cover all kinds of stories, or they may be specialists, concerned with a specific area of the news, such as sport or crime.

Photographers take and develop the pictures needed for each edition of the newspaper. They are usually controlled by a chief photographer and report to the picture editor, who overseas the photographic needs of the newspaper.

Designers are artists who produce graphics for editorial features and advertisements.

On your own

ON YR. OWN

Look at the copy of any newspaper.

- Look for the 'by-lines' (the text that shows who a story or photograph is by).
- Note down the names and titles (for example, Julian Honer, Chief Reporter, or Jane Turner, Crime Reporter, if any are given.
- Next to the names, write the titles of the stories or a description of the photographs for which each person is responsible.

This will give you an idea of the editorial structure of the newspaper.

The production department

The production department is responsible for putting the paper together in its final form, as well as for having it printed. The production editor oversees the printing of the paper, working with a team of plate-makers and printers. Printing is the most expensive area of newspaper production: the cost of printing presses runs into millions of pounds.

Printing presses are the most expensive equipment used in the newspaper production process.

Over the last 30 years, developments in printing technology have revolutionized the production of newspapers.

Hot-metal printing Until the 1960s, papers were printed using movable metal type, which was built up into pages. The ink was placed onto the type and newsprint was then run over the top of the plates. This form of printing was known as 'hot metal', as the metal type could be melted down and remoulded to make different letters, words and symbols.

Photo-typesetting With the invention of photo-typesetting, stories (or 'copy') were typed on computers and then printed onto a special type of photographic paper called bromide paper. This paper was then cut to size and pasted onto page plans, which were photographed. Printing plates were made from the photographs.

Offset litho printing This was the invention that changed the face of UK newspapers. It involves using photographic negatives of bromide pages to make printing plates with raised images. The plates are placed on printing drums and rotated so that they come into contact with ink rollers. The drums then impress an image onto rubber sheets. Newsprint is pressed onto the rubber sheets and the pages are printed.

In groups

AS A GROUP

You are a publisher who is launching a newspaper for schools or colleges in your area.

You have to decide how many copies of the paper you will need to distribute to your readers and how much this will cost. To do this, you will have to:

- Work out your potential readership. How many schools or colleges will you target? How many students does each have?
- Find out how much it would cost to print the number of papers that you would need. You will have to contact printers to do this.

In groups

- Investigate the ways in which newspapers have tried to increase their sales. To do this, you will have to look at advertisements for newspapers on television and in other media, special offers, competitions, free gifts, cheaper prices or coupons for holidays. Most promotional activities have very little to do with 'news'.
- Use your findings as the basis for a class discussion on the subject of what these developments tell us about the role of newspapers in our society.

The sales department

Once a newspaper has been printed, it has to get to the readers. This is the responsibility of the sales department. Under the sales manager, the department tries to maximise sales of the paper through as many outlets as possible. Outlets include:

- Newsagents and other shops
- Paper sellers on the street
- Home deliveries.

Sales representatives try to persuade shops to take more copies of the paper. They also contact individuals at home to encourage them to have the paper delivered. Special offers are often used to tempt readers to order regular copies of a newspaper.

Distribution

Newspapers are distributed using all forms of transport. National newspapers use road, rail and air links to send out their publications. Local paper delivery vans are a familiar sight in most towns, as they take the latest edition to the shops. Paper-sellers go to a distribution point to pick up bundles of papers before setting off for their carefully chosen spots throughout towns and cities. Many students are part of a newspaper distribution network, working to deliver papers for a newsagent.

From story to page

Newspaper stories, like all media products, are the result of a production process that involves a team of workers. To reach the printed page, a story goes through the following stages.

Choosing the story

'News' does not just happen; it is created. Someone has to decide that it is news before it is printed or broadcast. The people who decide this are journalists. In the case of newspapers, it is usually the news editor who judges what the news is. They sift through the stories that come in and decide whether to follow them up or not (for a list of sources of stories, see the chapter on television news, page 199). There is a difference between:

- The stories that are reported to a newspaper, and
- The stories that a newspaper reports.

Not all the information that arrives on a news editor's desk ends up as news in a paper. The news editor decides whether the material that comes to their attention will become news by being turned into a story, or remain unreported information. In this way, news editors influence what the audience thinks of as news. By sorting information and deciding what to follow up, they set a news agenda, which is drawn up on the basis of the news editor's personal decisions, not on the basis of information that they receive. This is why the news is something that is created, rather than simply reported.

NEWS AGENCIES ● ● ● ●

News agencies are private companies that sell stories to the news media. They exist because news organisations' coverage of events is limited by the number of staff and the amount of money that they have. Agencies have their own reporters, photographers, and film and radio crews, who produce ready-made news that newspapers, radio and TV can reproduce. Agencies range in size from small, regional press agencies to multinational, multimedia companies.

The Press Association is one of the UK's biggest news agencies, employing over 400 journalists. It supplies news, sports coverage and photographs to newspapers, radio and television. Reuters is one of the most famous agencies and supplies news to media organisations throughout the world.

News values

Several factors influence whether a story will be selected for coverage. These are often called 'news values' and include:

Where the event occurred. If an event happened within the area covered by the newspaper, it will be more interesting to readers than an event that took place outside it.

When an event occurred. An event that has just happened is more newsworthy than one that happened a week ago. This is simply because people are more likely to know about something, the longer ago it happened.

Who is involved in the story. A story is more likely to be reported if the person involved is famous or well known in the newspaper's circulation area.

News sense. This is a word used by journalists to describe a gut-feeling about what makes a good story that will interest readers. It is often talked about as if it were a kind of magic power. However, it is really a professional way of looking at information, which is built up through the experience of working in a news environment.

In groups

Each group represents a national daily newspaper.

- Look closely at copies of the newspaper your group represents and decide what its news values are.

- Which three stories from the following list does each group think their paper would be most likely to cover? Use the news values you have identified to help you to make your choice.

  - A top pop band splits up
  - A plane carrying diplomats crashes in China
  - The government announces a drop in taxes for the rich
  - The star of a TV soap has a baby
  - A Russian minister is sacked
  - A big fraud case involving city bankers comes to trial
  - A princess wears a daring dress to a film première
  - The space shuttle is launched on another mission

Getting the information

If a news editor thinks that a story is interesting enough, they give it to a reporter. It is the reporter's job to gather all the information they think is necessary to write the story. The news editor briefs the reporter on what the story is about and supplies any information that the newspaper has about it. This may be addresses and telephone numbers, a press release, a report from the emergency services, or copy from a news agency. The reporter then begins to add to this information by interviewing people face-to-face or on the telephone, visiting the site of the event and gathering information from organisations, libraries or other newspapers.

Writing the story

Once a reporter has enough information to write the story, they sit down at a computer and key in the words that make up the copy. This is done using a set of professional codes, or ways of writing that have been learnt from other journalists (see the chapter on language for an explanation of codes, pages 16–17). In writing the story, they select what information will be included and what will be left out, and decide the order in which the information will appear.

Most news stories are written in the following format:

Intro. This is the first paragraph of the story and it is the most important one. Research into how people read newspapers shows that most people read the headlines first and, if they find them interesting, will then read the first paragraph of the story. If the first paragraph is not interesting, most readers will not continue with the story. As a rule, the most exciting or interesting aspect of the story is written about in the first paragraph. After reading the intro, readers should be able to tell what the story is about. The intro paragraph acts as a 'hook' to drag readers into the story.

It is the reporter's job to research and write news stories.

Elaboration The next few paragraphs tell readers more about the story outlined in the intro. They tell readers what happened, when, where and to whom it happened. The elaboration should also say how it happened and, if possible, why. In all news stories, the more important thc information is, the closer it is placed to the beginning of the story.

Quotes Virtually all news stories contain comments from those involved. These are called quotes, and are meant to be word-for-word records of what the person said. They usually come after the story has been elaborated, and are an important element in keeping a balanced view of a story.

Projection Many, though not all, news stories tell the reader what might happen next in relation to the event or people in the report. This may take the form of a police officer saying what they will be doing in an enquiry, or an MP outlining what action they will be taking over a particular issue. This sort of information is generally used to end stories.

An important element a journalist must keep in mind when writing a story is that of balance. Journalists must try to give equal weight to the points of view of all those involved in the story in order to avoid bias. In theory, if a story is critical of a particular person or organisation, that person or organisation should be offered the chance to respond to this criticism. In practice, however, balance is a controversial issue, as many people believe they have been unfairly treated in they way they are portrayed. Journalists may find it difficult always to represent equally the views of all those

involved in stories. Some people, however, accuse journalists of misrepresenting people in order to 'spice up' stories. The issue of balance is important in debates about how different groups in society are represented. As was discussed in the chapter on representation, many groups feel that the media is biased against them (see page 33). Many left-wing councils have complained that stories written about them by journalists who work for right-wing newspapers are biased and without balance. The Press Complaints Commission, discussed in the chapter on institutions (see pages 56–57), was set up to deal with complaints about unfair treatment in news stories, amongst other things.

Air stowaway seeks asylum

Intro — **A MAN** is claiming asylum in Britain after stowing away in the baggage hold of a flight from New Delhi to Heathrow. The man, an Indian national, was treated for hypothermia after his 10-hour ordeal in the freezing hold and is now at Harmondsworth immigration detention centre.

Elaboration — He must have slipped through the tight armed security at New Delhi airport, aviation experts say. The man was found much the worse for his journey wandering around without the necessary identification documents at Heathrow's Terminal 4 by a British Airways dispatcher.

Quotes — One official said: 'He stowed away in the baggage hold of an aircraft where temperatures drop extremely low – he is very lucky to be alive.'

Projection — Airlines face fines of up to £2,000 for bringing into Britain anyone without the necessary travel documents.

The typical structure of a newspaper story.

TYPES OF STORY ● ● ● ●

Journalists separate stories into types, depending on their length or the position they are intended to take on a page. Some of these story types are:

SPLASH – the main story on the front page of a newspaper.

PAGE LEAD – the main story on a newspaper page. It is usually the longest story on the page and has the biggest headline.

SUPPORT – usually the second largest story on a newspaper page, 'supporting' the main story.

SHORTS – stories that are usually between three and eight paragraphs in length.

FILLS – stories of no more than one or two paragraphs, which are used to fill gaps on a page.

NIB – or news in brief. Nibs are one- or two-paragraph stories that give only basic facts. Nibs are often arranged in lists with small headlines on the front page of a paper. They usually refer to stories carried inside the paper and give the page number on which the full story appears, so that readers can find it.

NAG – or news at a glance. These are short news summaries that give the main points of a story.

Class activity

AS A CLASS ▌▌▌▌

Examine stories from a range of newspapers, both broadsheet and tabloid, and local and national. Are the stories 'balanced'? Does everyone mentioned in the story get a fair hearing? Can you spot any bias?

Examine carefully a story that deals with a controversial issue in a broadsheet and a tabloid newspaper.

- Write down in not more than 50 words what you think the story is about.
- Do you think the story is balanced? This means that it shows all sides of the argument and gives everyone mentioned a fair say.
- If not, which side do you think the newspaper supports?
- Do you think that it's right to support this side? Give reasons for your answer.

In pairs

IN PAIRS ▌▌▌

Take a page of any newspaper. Look at each story and decide which type of story it is.

The deadline is the time by which the reporter has to have a story ready. The reporter must make sure that the copy appears on the news editor's screen in time for it to be checked, before being sent to a sub-editor. The news editor reads through the story to make sure that it makes sense and that the reporter has followed up all the possible avenues of information. If they are not satisfied, they will send it back to the reporter with suggestions as to how it could be improved – for example, by interviewing another person.

Getting the picture

Every news story is considered not only in terms of words but also in terms of the photographs or graphics that could accompany it. The news editor looks at each story and decides if there is a photograph that could go with it. If they think that there is, they discuss with the picture editor or chief photographer what sort of picture would be suitable. It may show an event happening, for instance, a demonstration or a meeting, or it may show a person involved in the news. Once it has been decided what sort of a picture is wanted, the task is given to a photographer to go out and take it. The photographer has a deadline for the photograph and has to make sure that it is developed in time to be used in the newspaper.

As well as using photographs, the news editor may decide that a story could be illustrated with graphics in the form of illustrations, tables or decoration. In this case, they talk to the design department and a graphic designer is briefed to come up with the necessary graphics.

Sub-editing the story

When the copy and photographs are ready they are sent to a sub-editor. Sub-editors are given page schemes by the chief sub-editor. They are also given a list of stories and photographs to fit onto the pages scheme. Their job is to display the stories and photographs to the best effect in the space surrounding the adverts. Their job involves:

Making sure stories do not break the law by libelling people Libel is a law that defends people's right not to have things said about them in print that are not true and which damage their reputation. If a newspaper prints a story that libels someone, the victim can take the newspaper to court and demand cash in compensation.

Correct spelling and grammar Even trained reporters make mistakes.

Writing headlines Headlines are 'doors' through which readers get into stories. They have to be interesting and inviting, or the reader may pass the story by. This is especially true on the front page, as it is the main headline that often persuades a reader to buy the paper.

In newspapers, photographs are as important as words.

Placing photographs to best effect

Photographs are 'windows' through which readers see what is going on in a story. If the photograph is used badly, it will be ignored and fail to attract the reader to the story. As with headlines, this is especially true on the front page. The picture that is used on the front page of a newspaper has to be good to encourage readers to buy the paper.

Writing captions for photographs that tell the reader what they show.

Making sure the story fits into the space set aside for it on the page, usually by cutting words from it. Once a sub-editor has laid out the page, it goes to the chief sub-editor on the computer network to be checked. If it is approved, the page is then sent to be printed.

In pairs

Try to come up with headlines for the following stories:

- Angry mothers march on a school to protest about the lunches
- Local dog wins Cruft's dog show
- Martians land in your town.

Sub-editors place stories and write headlines.

Newspaper identities

All newspapers have their own identities, which are expressed through a combination of the following:

- Design and layout
- Content
- Language

price

date

tag

THE Mirror

Tuesday March 12 2002

NEWSPAPER OF THE YEAR   32p

INSIDE: YOUR UNBEATABLE GUIDE TO **Cheltenham 2002**

FREE **£2 BET** CORAL

AS THE U.S. MOURNS ITS DEAD SIX MONTHS ON.. DICK 'LON' CHENEY SEEKS SUPPORT FOR A NEW WAR

An American Warwolf in London

FEARSOME: Dick Cheney as Lon Chaney Jnr's film wolfman

By JAMES HARDY, Political Editor

WARMONGERING US Vice-President Dick Cheney was last night luring Tony Blair into invading Iraq.

Six months after September 11, President Bush's deputy told the Prime Minister at Downing Street that he suspected Saddam Hussein might supply chemical weapons to al-Qaeda.

But more than 70 MPs have signed a motion opposing any military action.

FULL STORY: PAGE 2

by-line

headline

intro

Design and layout

Most papers are either broadsheet or tabloid in format. The size of a newspaper has an effect on how it looks: for example, broadsheet papers have more stories on a page because the pages are bigger. However, the design and layout of broadsheet and tabloid newspapers are very different in other ways, too.

Tabloid newspapers tend to be brasher in their presentation. They use large photographs and big headlines. In fact, the front pages of most tabloid newspapers are dominated by the splash headline and a striking photograph. Stories in tabloids tend to be short. Many of the photographs are used simply because they are visually interesting, rather than because they are newsworthy. Pages are designed to be eye-catching, with lots going on.

Broadsheets are more restrained in their presentation. Headlines are usually informative, rather than startling. Photographs are used to illustrate stories, rather than used as stories in their own right. Stories are laid out in blocks on the page and tend to be longer than those in tabloid papers

Content

Newspapers also develop their own identities through the type of story they print. Tabloid papers, especially the popular ones such as *The Sun*, the *Star*, *The Mirror*, *News of the World* and the *People*, generally carry stories concerned with crime, sex, gossip and scandal. This has led to them being called the 'gutter press'. They have been condemned by some for lowering moral standards by publishing stories regarded as being in bad taste. Tabloid editors, however, argue that they aim to entertain their readers as much as to inform them. They also say that the fact that their papers have the highest

circulations shows that their readers are interested in the subjects they cover. Of course, not all tabloid papers are like this. What are known as the 'quality' tabloids, such as the *Daily Express* and *Daily Mail*, take a less sensational approach and carry a lot more 'serious' news.

Broadsheet newspapers see their job as that of informing their readers about what is going on in the world. Their stories tend to deal with political, economic and international news. It is unusual for a broadsheet to lead on a sex scandal, unless it affects politicians or other people in positions of authority.

In pairs

IN PAIRS

Carry out a content analysis exercise on two broadsheet and two tabloid newspapers (see the chapter on representation, pages 30–41, for tips on how to do this). Which subjects feature more heavily in one type of paper than the other?

Language

A major part of a newspaper's identity is the language that it uses in its stories. The words used play an important role in the way the paper addresses its readers. In the chapters on language and audience, it was shown that different media products use different tones of voice to communicate with their users. Tabloid newspapers use short, simple words. They tend to use slang, as some people do in

On your own

ON YR. OWN

Can you find examples of language used in tabloid newspapers that may be offensive to particular groups of people?

conversation, for example, 'cops' instead of police, and 'squaddies' instead of soldiers. They often refer to famous people by nicknames, like 'Posh' and 'Becks'. They also use puns and word play to make headlines entertaining. Popular tabloids have been attacked for using sexist and racist language to describe minority groups and foreigners.

Broadsheet papers tend to use more formal language. Stories often contain longer words and sentences than are used in tabloids. Headlines are written 'straight', in that they rarely use humour or wordplay. People in stories are usually given their proper titles, such as Mr Blair, Mrs Gupta or Ms Anderson.

PAGE FEATURE PROFILE

The *Star* is Yorkshire's biggest-selling newspaper.

TYPE: Evening Paper.

FORMAT: Tabloid.

PUBLISHED: Six days a week.

CIRCULATION: Around 10,000 copies a day.

EDITIONS: *Sheffield Star, Rotherham Star, Doncaster Star* and *Barnsley Star.*

HEAD OFFICE: Sheffield.

PRINTING PRESSES: Produce 50,000 copies of the paper an hour.

EMPLOYS: Around 600 people.

OWNER: United Newspapers.

In groups

AS A GROUP

Using this as a guide, produce a profile for your local newspaper.

Readership Profile

GENDER

MALE	149,000	50.9%
FEMALE	143,740	49.1%

Readership of The Star is split evenly between men and women.

AGE

15–34 year olds	98, 654	33.7%
35–56 year olds	89,561	30.6%
55+ year olds	104,512	35.7%

The Star is read by all age groups.

SOCIAL CLASS

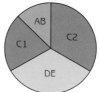

AB	39,914	13.5%
C1	58,843	20.1%
C2	93,387	31.9%
DE	100,706	34.4%

1 in 3 readers of The Star are ABC1's.

MAGAZINES

The word 'magazine' comes from the French 'magasin', which means 'shop' or 'storehouse'. This is an appropriate name, as magazines tend to be storehouses of knowledge and information about a particular subject or area of interest. The first magazine to be published using the word in its title was the *Gentleman's magazine* of London, which was first published in 1731.

Magazines are very different from newspapers. They are generally thicker, printed in colour on glossy paper, and are published less frequently. One major difference between newspapers and magazines is their content. As magazines as published less often, they cannot keep readers informed of day-to-day happenings, as newspapers do. Therefore, magazines tend to focus on feature material, in the form of interviews with 'newsworthy' people, or investigations of particular subjects.

Magazine publishing is one of the most lively areas of media production. There are over 3,000 titles published, generating £1.6 billion from sales to customers. Approximately 350 new titles are launched each year, of which half become established.

There is a magazine for virtually every subject you can think of.

So many magazines

Over 7,500 different magazines are presently published in the UK. They range from the *Radio Times* to *Dog World*. Magazines are generally divided into two groups:

Business and professional titles These are specialist publications aimed at people in specific areas of business and industry. Such magazines make up the majority of those published in the UK: around 5,000 titles fall into this category.

Consumer These are magazines aimed at the general public, or at specific segments of it. They include the publications that most people think of when the word 'magazine' is mentioned, for instance *Just Seventeen*, *Cosmopolitan*, *The Face*, *More*, *FHM*, *TV Times*.

There are so many magazines because they are relatively cheap to produce in comparison with newspapers. This means that there is less risk involved in setting one up. As most magazines do not have their own printing presses, all they need is staff, computer equipment and enough start-up cash to pay a printer. Desk-top publishing (DTP) packages which allow professional-looking pages to be produced on personal computers have revolutionised magazine publishing. Working from a rented office, a small team can have a magazine in the newsagent's within months of the initial idea to set it up.

In groups

AS A GROUP

Do a survey of the different magazines read by members of your class. Present your findings in the form of a chart for display in class. What have you learnt from the survey about how people of your age use the media? Why do you think boys and girls read different magazines?

In the chapter on audience, audience segmentation, or the splitting of audiences with particular interests from wider audiences, was discussed (see pages 64–65). The magazine market has seen a large degree of audience segmentation. The low cost of publishing means that a very small readership with special interests can be catered for at a profit. So a publisher might look at existing fishing magazines, decide that they are too general and that money could be made by launching a magazine solely for those interested in fly-fishing.

However, not all magazines are published to make a profit. Fanzines are magazines with a small circulation that are produced by fans about their particular area of interest, for example, a band or a football team. Fanzines are published on very low budgets, often using nothing more than a typewriter and a photocopier. They tend not to make a profit and are produced out of love for the subject they cover. Increasingly, publishers of fanzines are using the Internet as a cheap and easily accessible alternative to print. (See chapter on new technology).

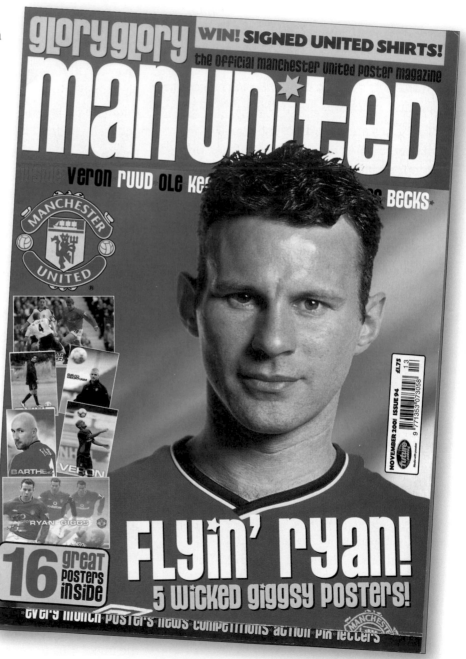

'Glory, Glory Man United' is an example of a fanzine.

Making money

Like newspapers, magazines can make money from their cover price (which the reader pays to buy a copy), from advertising or from a combination of both. Most business magazines are sent free to readers and make all their money from advertising. Consumer magazines generally charge for copies. However, advertising is still their major source of revenue.

Magazine advertising departments work in a similar way to those on newspapers. They sell adverts on the basis of how much space they take up on a page, and which page the advert is on. Most quote a price for a full-page advert in their magazine and, for a smaller advert, work out a percentage based on that price. The more copies a magazine sells, the more it can charge an advertiser, as it can say that more people will see the advert. In 1998, taking out a full-page colour advert in the *Radio Times*, which had a circulation of 1,390,981, cost £18,500. In comparison, a full-page colour advert in *Just Seventeen* magazine, with a circulation of 378,000, cost £7,930.

One way in which magazines create income that they can rely on is through the subscription system. This is where a reader pays for a set number of copies of the magazine in advance, usually at a price lower than they would pay in a shop. The magazine is then sent to the reader by post. The advantage for the magazine is that it receives a lump sum of money that it can invest in its operation.

A major factor affecting how much money magazines make is the cost of paper. A steep rise can force a magazine to increase its cover price or even to close down.

Setting up a magazine

More and more magazines are being launched. Unfortunately for their publishers, many sink. To make sure that a magazine has a chance of success, potential publishers have to take many factors into consideration.

Identifying a market

A publisher must be sure that there are people who will buy their magazine. It is no use producing a magazine for worm racers if there are only three in the country.

Publishers must also be sure that there is enough to write about and photograph on a specific subject to fill a regular magazine. The number of worm racing facts and action shots may be somewhat limited.

Low production costs mean that magazines can be published for very small readerships.

Assessing the competition

Before launching a new magazine, a survey of the market must be done to see what magazines are already published in the same subject area. If there are already a lot of them, it may be difficult to justify launching a new one, as readers have only so much money to spend. The publisher may decide to go ahead with the magazine, however, if they are convinced that it will be better than others already being published and will lure readers away from them. When a particular subject area is seen to be completely covered by magazines, it is known as 'market saturation'. It could be argued that men's lifestyle and computer magazines have reached market saturation point.

Most new magazines are produced because their publishers believe that they have spotted a gap in the market, or an area that is not catered for by existing magazines and that could generate a profitable readership. Look at the number of magazines on the market that cater for the public's appetite for news and gossip about celebrities. Probably the best known is *Hello!* magazine, which specialises in stories about celebrities and features photographs of their homes and families. Launched in 1988, *Hello!* magazine is distributed in 65 countries. It has a UK circulation of 450,000. Its main rival is *OK* magazine with a circulation of 525,000. *Heat* magazine appeals to a younger audience by publishing stories and photographs of celebrities at events such as parties, clubs and events such as film premières. It sells 233,000 copies per month.

Activity

ON YR. OWN

Why do you think people like to read about celebrities and look at photographs of their so-called private lives?

Why do you think celebrities want to be photographed?

Do you think you would like to be a celebrity feature in *Hello!* magazine?
What do you think your friends and family would say?

Attracting advertisers

As most magazines depend on advertising to survive, a publisher has to be certain that some businesses will want to buy space in the new publication. The publisher will have to convince businesses that enough people will read the magazine to make it worth paying for an advert. To do this, they will outline to potential advertisers the readership that they have identified.

Securing finance

The publisher will need cash to set the magazine up. They will have to buy or rent offices and equipment, employ staff and pay for printing. The money may come from a bank loan or from investment by other businesses in the project.

Organising distribution

For a magazine to make money, people have to be able to buy it. Most magazines are sold in newsagent's. The two biggest sellers of magazines in the UK are W.H. Smith and John Menzies. To be successful, a publisher must persuade newsagents and other shops to stock their magazine.

Producing a magazine

Magazines, like newspapers, are all different. However, like newspapers, their individual production processes are essentially the same. A typical production process includes the following stages:

Planning The editor and advertising manager discuss how many pages the magazine will have. This is called pagination and is decided on the basis of how many adverts have been sold for a particular edition.

Writing The content of the magazine is produced. Like newspapers, this comes from two sources, the advertising department and the editorial department. Most magazines carry classified advertisements, and the glossy, full-colour format of the majority of magazines offers a good platform for eye-catching display adverts. Editorial in most magazines is made up of a combination of features, photographic spreads, columns, news items and readers' letters. A lot of feature articles are written by freelance journalists, who are writers who work for themselves and sell articles to many magazines. Journalists who are employed just to work on a particular magazine are called staff writers. Photographs are also often taken by freelance photographers.

Designing Designers and sub-editors lay out the adverts and editorial on pages. They work according to what is called a flat plan, which is a map of the magazine that shows every page and what will appear on it.

On your own

Come up with an idea for a new magazine by answering the following questions:

What would your magazine be about?

Who would read it?

Who would advertise in it? (Make a list of firms and products that would be of interest to the readership.)

What would it be called?

How often would it come out?

What would the competition be?

Could the market support your magazine, or has saturation point been reached?

	title page	imprint page	contents	unit 1	unit 1	unit 1	unit 1	unit 1	unit 1
	1	2	3	4	5	6	7	8	9

unit 1	unit 1	unit 1	unit 1	wordlist 1	unit 2	unit 2	unit 2	unit 2	unit 2
10	11	12	13	14	15	16	17	18	19

unit 2	unit 2	unit 2	unit 2	unit 2	wordlist 2	review 1	review 1	unit 3	unit 3
20	21	22	23	24	25	26	27	28	29

unit 3	unit 3	unit 3	unit 3	unit 3	unit 3	unit 3	unit 3	wordlist 3	unit 4
30	31	32	33	34	35	36	37	38	39

unit 4	unit 4	unit 4	unit 4	unit 4	unit 4	unit 4	unit 4	unit 4	wordlist 4
40	41	42	43	44	45	46	47	48	49

A flat plan is a map of the magazine, which is used to decide where everything will go.

Printing Most magazines are published in full colour. To produce them, special printing plates have to be made of each page using a technique called 'colour separation'. Pages are printed using only four colours: black, yellow, red (or magenta) and blue (or cyan). Every photograph has to be 'separated' into these four basic colours by being photographed four times, using filters that allow only one colour through. This produces four pieces of film, which are laid over one another and exposed onto a printing plate. All the colours needed to produce a full-colour photograph are made by mixing different sized dots of these four basic colours. Colour separating and printing are usually done by printing companies, not by the magazines themselves.

Class activity

AS A CLASS

Have a go at producing your own magazine.

- To do this you will have to appoint an editorial team, with an editor, an advertising manager, writers and designers.

- Set a production schedule with a deadline for each stage.

- You will have to:

Find and write stories

Get and design adverts (these could be made up or produced for local businesses)

Design the magazine and put it together

You could produce one copy of the magazine for the class or, if you have a budget, print copies to distribute around the school or college.

COMICS

Development

You may think comics are something produced simply to keep young children amused. However, comics are an important part of the modern magazine market and they have a long and eventful history. They are also big business, and not just for children. In fact, in Japan, comic books out sell most leading newspapers.

Comics are books of stories that are told in the form of cartoons. They started life as comic strips, which were introduced into newspapers at the end of the 19th century to attract more readers. In the early 20th century, comic strips began to be collected from newspapers and published as magazines in their own right. Comics really became popular in the UK in 1937, when D. C. Thompson published *The Dandy*. A year later, *The Beano* was launched and became the UK's bestselling comic.

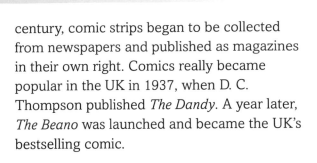

The Beano *and* The Dandy, *the UK's first really popular comics.*

during the 1960s and 1970s that a recognisable comic culture developed, complete with serious collectors and specialist shops. The introduction of 'manga' comics from Japan into the UK and America in the early 1990s led to an explosion of interest in comics. Manga is a style of Japanese animation.

Cartoon animals were an early development in the history of cinema, and there has always been a close relationship between comics and films. Many cartoon characters that first appeared on the cinema screen, such as those of Disney, have their own comic books, as do such television characters as Sooty and Scooby Doo. Other comic characters that were created for the

The introduction of manga comics into the UK led to an explosion of interest in comics.

In America, the 1930s saw the birth of many of the cartoon characters that have become household names throughout the world – Superman, Batman, Spiderman, Wonder Woman, Buck Rogers and Flash Gordon. Most of these characters appeared in comics published by Marvel.

Comics have never been aimed only at children. In the 1960s, the adult comic was born. Some of these comics dealt with serious subjects, using cartoons to make political statements. Others were sexually explicit or depicted extreme violence. It was page have gone onto the screen, many of them being played by real actors, for example, Judge Dredd and Tank Girl. Japanese comics inspired 'anime' (the Japanese word for animation), which is the video animation of popular manga publications. Even toys, such as Care Bears and Barbie, have their own comics.

Genres

In the chapter on language, the concept of genre was examined (see pages 27–29). Genre is the word used to describe types of media text that can be grouped together because of their shared themes and structures. Genres are very important in the field of comics. Comic genres include science fiction and fantasy, war, superhero and educational. Each genre has its own 'rules' that readers expect to be followed, for example, that the superheroes will always win. Genre influences how the cartoons are drawn, the storylines that characters are involved in and the language that they use.

Elements of comics

Comics communicate a narrative to the reader through a combination of images and words. The story is told through a series of scenes in the form of boxes. Each box is like a snapshot, in that it depicts one piece of action. In themselves, the scenes mean little, but arranged in a sequence they build up to form a narrative.

On your own

ON YR. OWN

If you have a specialized comic shop in your town, make a visit and see how many different genres of comic you can spot. What is typical of each genre? Are there genres within genres, for instance, science fiction westerns?

The narratives are usually:

- Simple, dealing with straightforward situations
- Action-based, dealing with adventures
- About a set character or group of characters. New superheroes do not usually appear each week
- Self-contained, with a beginning, middle and end. They tend not to continue over several issues.

The images may be:
- Simple line drawings, as in childrens' comics
- Artwork that is very complex and even beautiful, as in many comics aimed at adults
- Photographs, as in photo love stories.

The characters depicted can be:
- Fantastic, for example, monsters
- Superhuman, or human with special powers, for example, Spiderman or Judge Dredd
- Anthropomorphic, in other words, animals with human characteristics, such as the ability to speak
- Realistic, either because the characters are drawn realistically, or because the stories are made up from photographs.

The words in comics are usually kept to a bare minimum. They are secondary to the images. However, they still have important functions to perform:
- Words anchor the image – they tell the reader how to interpret the pictures
- Words express information that is difficult to communicate visually, for instance, thoughts and feelings
- Words give extra information, such as introductions that set the scene for the comic narrative.

Producing a comic

Comic stories are the result of a production process that involves creative input from two types of people:

Writers, who come up with ideas for stories or scripts. They may invent a character and then write storylines involving that character, or they may be asked to write stories involving existing characters.

Illustrators, who draw the cartoon images. They may come up with the idea for a character, or be asked to draw a character that has been suggested by a writer.

The production process of putting a comic book together is similar to that of a magazine. The comic book is a combination of editorial (in this case the comic strips) and advertising. The editorial and advertising departments work together to produce a flat plan of the comic. The comic strips are designed and placed onto pages along with adverts. The finished pages are then sent to be printed.

On your own

Produce your own comic strip, using computers or art materials. Remember, you must first come up with characters and a script. Your comic could be in the form of a cartoon, or you may want to produce a photo story, using members of the group as models.

Comics, sex and violence

Controversy has dogged comics since they were introduced. They have been attacked for corrupting not only children, but also adults. In America in 1954, the Comic Code was passed to limit what was seen as most comics' love of crime and violence. Comic producers were encouraged to create more wholesome characters and storylines. Despite this, comics have been criticised for being:

Violent Adult comics have been condemned for being too graphic in their depiction of violence. Children's comics have been attacked for treating violence as funny and not showing its tragic effects.

Racist There have been complaints that some comics, especially those dealing with war, portray people of different races in an offensive way. For example, in some British comics with stories about the Second World War, Japanese and German soldiers are shown in this way.

Sexist Children's comics have been criticised for reinforcing sexual stereotypes (see pages 37–40). They do this, it is said, by showing girls to be passive and well behaved and boys to be adventurous and violent. Adult comics have been attacked for sexist depictions of women. Critics say that women in science fiction and horror comics are shown semi-naked and are used only as props for male characters. Some cartoon characters, such as Tank Girl, have gone against this stereotype somewhat by showing a strong female character who is at the centre of the action.

Immoral Comics have also been condemned for promoting bad behaviour. In children's comics, characters who are well behaved and study hard are shown as swots. In adult comics, violence and crime are often shown as the only way to gain power or enjoy life.

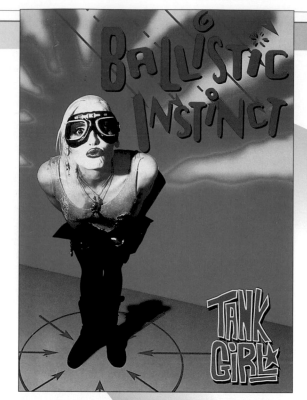

The character of Tank Girl goes to some extent against the sexual stereotyping that is sometimes seen in comics.

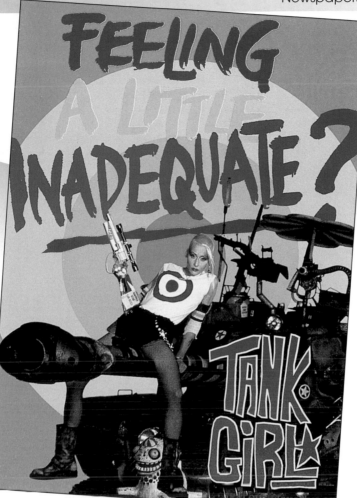

ON YR. OWN

Review

Looking along a newsagent's shelf takes only a few seconds. However, a survey of the print media shows how much work goes into producing just one of the publications that can be seen in the newsagent's. next time you are in a newsagent's, take down a magazine and look at how much information it contains. Imagine how long it would take you to read every newspaper, magazine and comic in the display. Our society is awash with printed words and the companies that produce them play a major role in our lives.

In groups

AS A GROUP

- Collect examples of comics and identify characters, storylines and language that could be defined as racist, sexist or immoral.
- Do you think that the examples you have found could influence the views of those reading the comics?

9

Music industry

Whatever we're doing and wherever we're going, we can now have music there with us. Car stereos, radios as small as coins, portable CD and Mini-Disc players, Walkmans and other technology allows us to listen to our favourite tunes anywhere. Billions of CDs, tapes and records are sold worldwide and the lives of pop stars make headline news. The music industry has ensured that the human race is truly wired for sound.

However, all this is a relatively recent development. Until the early years of the 20th century, there was no such thing as a music 'industry'. This is because before the invention of sound recording there was no way of selling music to a mass market. The only way to hear music was to attend a performance or play it yourself. In order for music to become an industry, a way had to be found of turning it into a product that could be sold. The birth of recording technology was the spur for the development of a business now worth around £27 billion.

Phonographs allowed music to be played at home.

From phonograph to DAT

The music industry owes its beginnings to Thomas Edison, who made the first recording of a human voice in 1877. A year later, he patented the first phonograph for playing back recordings, using cylinders made of tin-foil. Tin-foil cylinders were soon replaced by wax ones, but there was still no way to mass-produce them. It was Emile Berliner who really set the turntables spinning by patenting the gramophone in 1888. The gramophone used flat discs to produce sounds, and it was easy to make copies of them. This opened the way for the mass marketing of sound recordings, and the 1890s saw the first sales of commercial recordings.

Sound reproduction technology took a big step forward in 1896 when Johnson Eldridge fitted a motor to the gramophone, doing away with the need to wind it up with a handle. Johnson set up the Victor Talking Machine Company, and in 1906 it produced the first gramophone with an internal horn, or amplifier, known as the Victrola. Victor went on to become RCA Victor, one of the world's largest record companies.

The birth of KDKA, the first American commercial radio station, in 1919 was a mixed blessing for the early recording industry. Record sales fell initially as people could listen to music on the radio for free. However, record companies soon realised that radio was the perfect advertising vehicle for their products. The invention of the jukebox in the 1930s led to a new demand for records. The 1930s also saw the publication of the first 'hit parade', or chart listing the most popular recordings.

Getting it taped

The next leap forward for the music industry was the development of sound recording using magnetic tape. The German firms BASF and AEG first demonstrated the use of tape recording with their Magnetophone in 1936. The technique was developed in America by 3M, and Ampex produced recorders that could match the quality of recording onto wax.

The 1950s saw the introduction of stereo recording. This involved recording two separate channels of sound onto one tape. It added 'depth' to musical performances on record and led to a demand for improved record players.

Until the 1960s, buying music on tape was not popular, as the tape had to be fed into a recorder by hand. In 1964 Philips launched the first tapes encased in plastic housing, which could simply be slipped into tape machines. Throughout the 1960s, a battle raged between companies that produced eight-track and four-track tapes and those that made cassettes.

Cassettes won, and the introduction of Dolby Noise Reduction, which removed the hiss from tapes, increased their popularity. Cassettes were more portable than records, and sales took off, especially when players began to be fitted in cars. The portable tape player, or Walkman, first marketed by Sony in 1979, created an even bigger demand for tapes.

CD and beyond

The search for better sound quality led the music industry to look at the possibilities offered by computer technology. In 1982 the compact disc, or CD, was launched by Sony and Philips. In the manufacturing process, recordings by musicians are changed into digital information that can be read by a computer. The quality of sound reproduction that this allowed was much better than that offered by cassettes at the time.

As the price of CD players fell, they began to dominate the recorded music market. As well as new recordings, companies began to release recordings they had made in the past, known as their back-catalogues, on CD. This was seen as a brilliant marketing move, as it led many people to replace recordings they had owned on vinyl with ones on CD: in other words they bought the same recording twice.

A new chapter in the story of tapes began in 1987 when Sony introduced the helical scan recording technique, which had been developed for video into sound recording. The result was the digital audio tape, or DAT. Before this development, different sounds were recorded onto different tracks that ran parallel to each other on the tape. The helical scan system records sound onto tracks that cross each other diagonally, which provides better

The jukebox was invented in the 1930s. Since then, technology has developed rapidly.

The Internet is also beginning to have an important effect on the way in which we consume music. Not only is it possible to buy CDs at a discount price via the web, it is also possible to buy music direct by downloading MP3 files onto your computer's hard disk. As the speed of Internet connections increases, this is set to become a fast and effective way of obtaining music.

Napster is an Internet service that angered music companies and artists by allowing people to download music for free. It was forced off line by court action, but is set to re-launch as a subscription service that will guarantee payment to artists.

In pairs

IN PAIRS

List all the forms of musical reproduction hardware you can. Think not only of the types of hardware, but also where they are used. Early gramophones were targeted for home use, but the jukebox opened up a new market. Where are music reproduction systems an accepted if not an essential part of the atmosphere?

reproduction. The sound quality offered by DAT soon led to it being widely used in recording studios, although the price prevented large sales to the general public. Small digital compact cassettes with high-quality sound reproduction were launched in the 1990s.

In 1992 Sony introduced the MiniDisc, a compact disc that can be used to record in the same way as a blank cassette tape. This format combines many of the advantages of the CD in a more portable format.

Music video

Video changed the face of the music industry. Seen initially as a way to advertise records, music videos have become an industry in themselves. Today it is inconceivable for a major, or even new, band to release a recording without a video to accompany it. The complexity of videos has also increased. The first videos usually showed a band performing on stage or in a carefully chosen scene. However, their success led to increased budgets and pop music mini-epics made by film directors.

A major factor in the growth of the pop video was their popularity with television producers. Videos provided TV with ready-made footage that they could simply broadcast for free. They fitted easily into the format of the BBC's *Top of the Pops*, and provided the material for ITV's *Chart Show*, which showed nothing but videos.

It was the birth of the satellite channel MTV, or Music Television, that provided the biggest platform for music videos. Launched in 1981 and broadcast all over the world, much of MTV's output is made up of pop videos, punctuated with music news bulletins.

Now it is possible to tune into a range of different MTV channels, each reflecting the way in which the audience for popular music has become segmented.

The music industry today

To begin with, recording companies were simply recording companies. Their main product was the reproduction of hardware – they produced records so that people who bought their gramophones would have something to play on them. They had no real interest in music as a money-maker in itself.

Recording companies became aware, however, that they could make only so much money from selling record players. Record players have always been an expensive purchase and once people have bought one they tend to keep it for a while before replacing it. Realising that the real money lay in the software – the records – the recording companies began to invest money in producing their own recordings by popular musicians. It was this move into the feild of music production that led to the music business as we

know it today. Big industrial companies now own everything from the factories that make the CD and tape players to the studios where musicians record – and even the musicians themselves. The model for this type of music multinational, RCA Victor, was created in 1929 when RCA (Record Company of America), together with General Motors, took over the Victor Talking Machine Company in a bid to exploit the new phenomenon of car radios.

MTV

5.30am	**Fanatic** Westlife and Foo Fighters meet their biggest fans
6.00am	**The Number One Music Channel** The biggest chart hits of the moment
9.30am	**Diary Of A** day in the life of the Latino superstar Jennifer Lopez
10.00am	**Hitlist UK** The British singles chart, with Cat Deeley and Edith Bowman
12.00pm	**TXT Request Live** show in which viewers request their favourite tunes via text messages
2.00pm	**European Top 20** Countdown of the most popular Euro-hits this week
4.00pm	**MTV Top 5** Top hits of an artist or theme
4.30pm	**FANatic** Fans get the chance to meet Westlife and Foo Fighters and ask them searching questions
5.00pm	**The Story of Westlife** The incredible story of the Irish boy band, revealing how they evolved to become chart titans and smash the Beatles record of consecutive...

MTV Base

6.00am	**Beats, Rhymes and Life** Back-to-back tracks
10.00am	**Base Trebles** Heavy tunes
11.00am	**Flashback Quiz-show**, hosted by Henry Kelly
12.00pm	**Biorhythm** In-depth profile of Jennifer Lopez
12.30pm	**Diary Of Chris Tucker**
1.00pm	**Beats, Rhymes and Life** Back-to-back tracks
3.00pm	**The Lick Chart** Trevor Nelson looks at the current releases, including Jennifer Lopez featuring Ja Rule and Alicia Keys
4.00pm	**Beats, Rhymes and Life** Back-to-back tracks
7.00pm	**Top 10:** Musicians and Actors Rundown of tunes
8.00pm	**Michael Jackson's Ghosts'** Short film combining big budget effects with Michael's music
9.00pm	**Videography** Base checks out film's funkiest tunes
12.00am	**Run Richie** Run Richie's on a mission, but obstacles are placed in his way. Watch him try to keep out of harms way.

MTV Hits

6.00am	**More Hits, More Often!** Back-to-back hits
12.00pm	**More Hits, More Often!** Back-to-back hits
1.00pm	**Fresh Hits on Hits** Latest additions to the playlist
2.00pm	**More Hits, More Often!** Back-to-back hits
6.00pm	**More Hits, More Often!** Back-to-back hits
12.00am	**More Hits, More Often!** Back-to-back hits

MTV Dance

0am	**Close**
0pm	**Your Resident DJ** The very best in dance tunes
pm	**I Got Mashed in 1994** Featuring D:Ream
0pm	**Your Resident DJ** The very best in dance tunes
0am	**Chill-Out Zone** Relaxing early-morning music
am	**All Nighter!** The resident DJ mixes a dance set

MTV broadcasts music programmes 24 hours a day.

The music industry has always been dominated by a small number of large companies. This happened because the recording companies bought up independent record labels in the 1930s. (They were known as labels because of the distinctive stickers bearing the company's name that were attached to every record.)

Today the industry is controlled by six major companies:

- **Philips,** which owns the Polygram, A&M Mercury and Island record labels
- **Sony,** which owns Columbia Records, S2, Epic and Higher Ground
- **Matsushita,** which owns MCA Records and Geffen
- **EMI,** which owns Capital and Virgin
- **Time Warner,** which owns Warner Brothers and subsidiaries
- **Bertelsmann,** which owns RCA Records.

As an example of the sums of money involved in these companies: when it was split from its sister company Thorn in 1996, EMI was believed to be worth around £5.8 billion.

On your own

ON YR. OWN

Take a look at your CD collection. Write down the names of five different labels that CDs are released on. Are some of these labels better known than others? If so, why do you think that is? Is it possible to find out from the information on the inlay if this is a small independent label or part of a bigger media organisation? Why do you think that it is sometimes hard to find out which labels are owned by large multinational organisations such as Sony?

In groups

AS A GROUP

Major record companies often own a number of different record labels, known as divisions. For example, rap band Cypress Hill releases records on the Columbia label, which is owned by Sony. This gives the appearance that there are more record companies than actually exist.

Ask each member of the group to bring in a number of CDs or tapes. Look at the labels and the packaging and make a diagram showing which labels belong to which companies.

Singers and styles

Singing stars

Just as stars, rather than stories, sell films, so singers, rather than songs, sell music. This is something record companies learnt as they developed: their top priority is to find voices and, more importantly, faces that shift records.

The first and biggest recording star was Bing Crosby. He made his first record in 1926 when the music industry was in its infancy. In 1931 he was signed to CBS Records and became the first nationally famous recorded 'star'. During his career, Crosby recorded 1,600 hit songs, including 'White Christmas', which sold 30 million copies, making it the world's biggest-selling record of all time.

What is called the youth market for records effectively began with Elvis Presley. Presley became famous in 1956 for singing a new form of music called rock 'n' roll. Rock 'n' roll was a mixture of blues music and country and western swing. Although the music itself was

Bing Crosby was the first major recording star.

not created by recorded companies, they were not slow to exploit it. Known as 'The King', Presley sold 41 million albums for RCA during his career.

The biggest-selling album of all time is Michael Jackson's 'Thriller', which has sold 40 million copies. Jackson is signed to Sony. Madonna is one of the biggest-selling female stars in recording history. Her single 'Vogue' is one of the bestselling of all time, and her 'Immaculate Collection' album was only the second greatest hits album to achieve a position in the top ten charts. Madonna is signed to Maverick Records, a subsidiary of Warner Brothers. The most successful group ever were The Beatles, who became closely identified with their record label, Apple.

Madonna is one of the biggest-selling female recording artists of all time.

145

Musical styles

The history of popular music has seen the rise and fall of many musical styles. There are types of music that share certain characteristics, such as beat, speed and lyrical style. They have usually been accompanied by fashions in clothing and behaviour. They began with rock 'n' roll, which in Britain was the music associated with the Teddy Boys, who wore Edwardian-style drape suits and slicked their hair back with grease. Since then there have been Mods, Hippies, Punks and many others.

Record companies are always on the lookout for new musical styles in order to exploit them. Many people make a distinction between groups that originate a style and those who copy them. They believe the originators are 'authentic' in their musical ideals, while those that copy them are merely commercially driven.

In marketing terms, musical styles are a form of audience segmentation (see the chapter on audience, pages 64–65). They can be used to identify types of music consumer. For example, there are general music consumers, who buy records of tunes they like. Then there are specific music buyers, who only purchase a particular type of music by certain types of bands. Record companies judge their performers in terms of their appeal to these different groups.

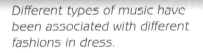
Different types of music have been associated with different fashions in dress.

On your own

ON YR. OWN

- How many different musical styles can you name?
- What makes them different from each other?

Classical music – in other words music written from about the 17th century onwards in such forms as symphonies, sonatas and operas – is seen as serious 'art' music compared with popular and rock music, which is often called commercial music. However, classical music has played a big part in recording history and made record companies a lot of money. Many early recordings were of classical music, and all major record companies have classical divisions. Classical music has become more popular, as indicated by the launch in 1992 of Classic FM, a radio station that plays nothing but classical music.

Getting signed

To be successful financially in the music business, it is essential for a musician or band to sign a recording contract with a major record company. Likewise, record companies are always on the lookout for new performers to sign up.

In order to attract the attention of major record companies, bands and solo artists do any number of the following:

Perform in public Bands invite representatives of record companies to attend what are often called 'showcase' concerts or 'gigs'. In Britain, bands from the regions will often set up a gig in London to make it easier for record companies to see them.

Make a demo This involves making a demonstration recording of their music and sending it to a record company. It is usually in the form of a tape.

Release their own record Many bands pay to have a record released on their own label to promote themselves both to the public and to record companies.

Employ a manager or an agent He or she promotes the band to record companies. The more experienced the manager or agent is in the music industry, the better. Some managers have become nearly as famous as the artists they represent, such as Colonel Tom Parker, who managed Elvis Presley.

Sign a publishing deal Before the birth of recorded music, music publishers published sheet music. Songwriters and musicians give their work to a publisher who, of they like it, will agree to look after it for a fee. This means promoting the music and making sure the artist receives money whenever it is played. All

musicians are supposed to receive a fee every time one of their pieces is sold on record, played live at a concert or broadcast on the radio or television. They also receive money if another artist records one of their songs. These fees are

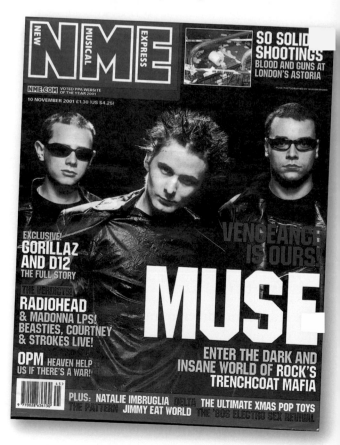

The music press can help new bands by featuring them in their publications.

called royalties. Publishing companies are responsible for collecting royalties and subtract their fee from them before passing them to the musician. Signing a publishing deal can help musicians, as it is in the interest of publishing companies for their artists to sign recording deals. Publishing companies actively represent artists to major record companies.

Attract attention Unsigned bands may try anything to achieve a high profile. They will play as many concerts as possible in as many different places, produce publicity material such as posters and fliers, and badger journalists to write about them. The music press plays an important role in 'breaking' new bands by featuring them is their publications, which are read by record company representatives.

Record companies do not simply sit back and wait for musicians to come to them. They go out and look for new performers and try to sign them before anyone else does. This is done by the company's A&R department. A&R stands for 'artists and repertoire' and the A&R section is responsible for discovering new acts and looking after the musicians once they are signed to the label. Members of the A&R department attend concerts and listen to demos in order to spot up-and-coming talent.

If a record company is interested in a band, it may offer them a recording contract. The individual terms of the contract will differ from band to band, but essentially they give the company the right to release all the band's recordings. This may be forever, but is usually for a set number of recordings, also called releases. So a band may be offered a 'three-album deal', in which they would record three albums for the company and a set number of singles. The contract will also say how much money the band will receive from the sales of their recordings.

On signing a contract, a band usually receives what is called an advance. This is a sum of money given in advance of any record sales and is taken out of the band's royalties once they start to sell records. Advances range in size from thousands of pounds in the case of unknown bands, to millions in the case of established stars changing labels.

Making a recording

Whether making a demo to promote themselves or producing their fortieth album, all musicians need to record their music before it can be sold. This means going into a recording studio, though this may be simply a computer and a keyboard.

A traditional recording studio is made up of two rooms. One, in which the musicians perform, is soundproofed so no other noise can be heard from outside. The other is the control room, which contains the recording equipment. The recording process is supervised by a sound engineer, a technician who ensures that the best possible recording is made. Sound engineers grow famous for the quality and style of the recordings they supervise and may become producers, who are much sought after by bands. A producer is someone brought in to oversee a recording and give it a particular 'feel'. The producer's role often merges with that of the sound engineer, as a producer has to know how a studio works in order to get the sound he or she wants.

The recording process usually involves the following steps:

Mic-up Every instrument and singer must have their own microphone so that they can be recorded.

Digital recording does not require a traditional recording studio.

Sound engineers and producers mix tracks recorded in the studio.

Setting the levels The level at which each microphone records has to be set by the sound engineer.

Laying down the track Recording studios are classified in terms of how many 'tracks' they can record onto one tape, and can be four, eight, twenty-four, thirty-two track or even more. The more tracks a studio has, the more

instruments or vocal tracks can be recorded. For a band consisting of drums, bass guitar, lead guitar and vocals, the tracks would normally be recorded in the following order:

● Drums and bass: this track forms the base for the rest of the instruments and vocals
● Guitars: usually laid down while listening to the drum and bass track

- Vocals: usually recorded last. Most recording sessions begin in the morning, when a singer's voice is not at its best. So recording the vocal track is left until later in the day, when the vocal cords have warmed up.

Today a lot of music is produced using electronic instruments and computers. The sounds generated are stored in the computer's memory, which does away with the need for a traditional two-room studio. It also means that one person can carry out all the functions, from playing to mixing. Recording using computers is called digital recording.

Mixing Once all the instruments and vocal tracks have been recorded they are mixed to produce the version of the track that will be released. This involves combining the sounds using a recording desk. It is at this stage that 'effects' that alter the sound of the instruments, such as echo and distortion, are added. It is during mixing that the producer or sound engineer has a major creative input. They are skilled at getting a certain sound and 'feel' to a recording, and, mix every track to ensure it is right. A development of the 1980s was the phenomenon of remixing. This involved the separate tracks of a recording being combined in a different way to produce a different sound. Many producers are famous for this, and bands approach them to do remixes of their recordings.

A technique known as sampling, in which sounds from existing recordings are used to make new ones, was also developed in the 1980s. Combined with computer-generated sounds, sampling removed the need to be able to play a musical instrument.

Formatting Once a final mix has been decided, it is sent off to be turned into a format, such as cassettes and compact discs, that can be sold to consumers.

The work of a sound engineer
Sound engineers are the invisible people who play a major role in shaping the music that tops the charts. They supervise recordings, making sure that everything runs smoothly. Pete Darnborough, who trains sound engineers, has years of experience in helping recording artists achieve the sound they want.

The sound engineer's job is to manipulate all the equipment in a studio to get the best representation of a band possible. To do this, they have to know the studio inside-out. They have to know how the mixing desk works, the best way to set up a microphone, how to balance sound levels and many other things.

For example, every piece of a drum kit has a separate microphone. The sound engineer has to make sure that every mic is working and recording at the right level. They also have to ensure that the sounds don't 'leak' into one another by using devices called sound gates and compressors.

However, it is not just machinery. A recording studio is a very unnatural environment – it is two enclosed rooms with no natural light and no fresh air. If you have five or six people in a studio for a long time under pressure to produce a good recording, things can get a bit intense. Arguments can break out between members of a band, and it is the engineer's job to keep the peace and make sure the recording gets made. You have to very diplomatic to be a sound engineer.

Most important, however, is the sound engineer's feel for the music. You may be highly skilled in using equipment, but if you don't care about the music, you will never be able to help a musician record to the best of their ability.

Making money

The purpose of most recordings is to make money for those people and institutions involved in their production and sale. These include:

- The record company
- The band or performer
- Compact-disc and cassette manufacturers
- Record shops.

To make money, the price of a CD or cassette has to be higher than it costs to produce. The difference between what a CD costs to produce and what it costs to buy is the profit margin. The profit margin is split between all those involved in the production and marketing process. The biggest percentage goes to the record company. Bands and record companies also make money from broadcasts and performances of their material. In 1999, TV and radio stations paid almost £80 million for the rights.

The charts

The measure of success in the music industry are the charts that show which recordings sell the most copies each week. The first music charts were published by *Billboard* magazine in America in the 1890s. They consisted of lists of the most popular sheet music. However, the charts as we recognise them today began when *Billboard* started to publish its Best Sellers in Stores listing, based on information from record shops throughout America. In 1958 the magazine launched its Hot 100 chart, which remains the main chart in the US.

In Britain it was the *New Musical Express's* Hit Parade, published for the first time in 1952, that pioneered music charts. It listed the 12 top-selling records in the country. Today the

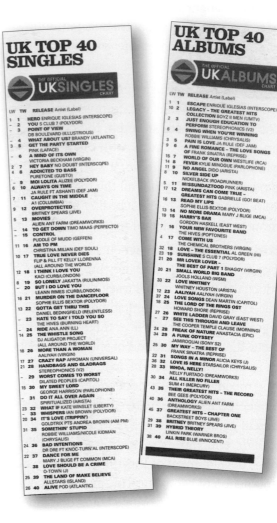

official UK charts are compiled by the Chart Information Network (CIN). The company CIN Ltd is jointly owned by Miller Freeman plc – a UK information company that publishes *Music Week* magazine – and the British Phonographic Industry (BPI), the trade body for UK record companies. CIN makes the charts available to the music business and to broadcasters and publishers worldwide.

CIN employs Millward Brown International, a market research company, to compile the charts on its behalf from sales information supplied by members of the British Association of Record Dealers and other music retailers. Around 3,000 shops in the UK have equipment that allows them to contribute sales information to the charts.

When a record or video is bought, the retailer runs a scanner over the barcode on the product. This information is stored in a file, which grows during the course of the day. After the shop closes every night, the charts' computers automatically telephone each shop and transfer the barcode files into a central processor. Once retrieved, the barcode information is run through a central product file. This contains details of every audio or video product sold through the stores. The barcodes are matched up to the product details from this file. Then the information is scanned by a security programme, which isolates any shop whose sales information does not conform to its usual pattern. The data is multiplied up to represent the full market of the 3,000 stores whose sales information is eligible for the charts. Finally, the sales figures are ranked in descending order and the charts are produced. This procedure is carried out daily and the sales totals grow through the week.

On Sunday morning, the charts are generated from sales mode during the previous Sunday to Saturday. After checking, the official UK singles and albums charts are sent to the BBC and *Music Week* at 12.30 pm – less than 18 hours after the last sale was made. The BBC makes the first broadcast of the charts on Sunday at 4.00 pm. *Music Week* prints it to appear the following day.

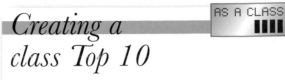

Creating a class Top 10

AS A CLASS

Get a copy of the Top 10 singles from a newspaper or by listening to the radio or watching TV. List the titles of the singles on a form and give one to each member of the group. Each person can make three 'purchases' from the Top 10 list. Once they have made their choices collect in the forms and add up the 'sales'.

- Is your chart different from the official one?
- What does it tell you about the musical tastes of your classmates?

Selling performers

Marketing a performer and their recordings is the major function of record companies. Their aim is to make as much money as possible out of the acts they sign to their labels.

Crucial to the marketing of a performer is their image. This is the way they present themselves to, and the way they are seen by, their audience. It includes the style of their music, the way they dress and the things they do and say. Record companies recognise that image is especially important for performers with a mostly young audience. One image that is particularly attractive to young audiences is that of rebellion against society and the older generation. Throughout the history of pop and rock music, bad behaviour by bands has been a way of creating publicity and selling records. From the earliest days of rock 'n' roll, wearing leather, taking drugs and smashing up hotel rooms have always been good for business.

During the late 1990s much publicity was given to a feud between Liam Gallagher from Oasis and Robbie Williams.

Although some performers have been marketed with the opposite image – that of being safe and wholesome – these performers have always seemed to be more popular with parents than with young people.

Another technique used to market performers has been to set them in competition with rival bands and singers. This leads to fans dedicating themselves to one performer in opposition to another. Image can also harm a performer's success. Many acts are criticised by fans for changing their image, or 'selling out', when they sign to a major record company. A record company may insist that performers tone down or emphasise a particular element of their image in order to attract a wider audience for their music. What's more, musical styles and fashion in clothes

change quickly, and a band that is associated with a sound or a 'look' that has gone out of fashion can find their record sales falling.

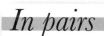

In pairs

How many performers can you think of who have been marketed in competition to one another?

Performers and their management have also manipulated image to good effect to make successful recordings. Malcolm McClaren generated millions of pounds out of his skilful management of the Sex Pistols, who were at the head of the punk explosion of the 1970s. in the 1980s the KLF foundation wrote a book on how to make a hit record and proceeded to do so with 'Doctor in the Tardis', which went to number one in the charts. It is rumoured that the K Foundation later burned much of the money they had earned – £1 million in cash.

Promotion

In order for performers and record companies to be successful they have to make as many people aware of their recordings as possible. They do this using a well-established system of promotional techniques.

Radio

Having your recording broadcast on radio is an excellent way of promoting it. Radio broadcasters and record companies have a close relationship, as they depend on each other. Record companies want people to hear their recordings and radio stations need something to play. A major achievement for a record company is to have its performers 'playlisted' by a big station such as Radio 1. A playlist is a list of records to which a radio station decides to give a lot of air-time by playing them a set number of times during a day's programming. Records that are playlisted tend to be successful simply because large numbers of people hear them. In the 1950s in America there was controversy when it was revealed that some record companies were paying radio stations to playlist their records.

DJs

Disc jockeys, the people who host radio programmes, have a lot of power to promote recordings. If a disc jockey is respected for their knowledge of a particular field of music, such as rock or reggae, their approval and promotion of a record on their show can help sell a lot of copies. The explosion of club culture in Britain has led to the DJs who work in them becoming stars in their own right. They 'perform' at different clubs for big fees and can promote records by playing them as part of their show. Therefore record companies, especially those that produce dance music, are keen to have their recordings backed by club DJs.

DJs play an important part in promoting records.

There are numerous music titles available on the market.

Music press

The music press also plays an important part in promoting performers. There are many publications for those interested in music, each serving a particular type of consumer.

The *New Musical Express*, published weekly, keeps readers up to date with what is going on in the music world. It is aimed largely at young people aged between 16 and 30, and concentrates on 'alternative' bands. These are bands that are seen to be serious about music and non-commercial in their outlook. This does not necessarily prevent them from selling large numbers of records.

Smash Hits is aimed at a younger teenage readership, with features on the latest chart 'sensation' and glossy colour posters.

Q magazine is a 'heavy' music magazine for an older audience. It concentrates on famous performers and covers not only the latest releases, but also back-catalogues of older recordings.

Mojo specifically targets those interested in artists from the past and in re-releases of their material.

Classic FM caters for those interested in high-quality recordings of classical music.

There are many other specialist music magazines and newspapers. Newspapers and general consumer magazines also have music sections, and of course record companies supply them with free copies of recordings so they can review them for their readers.

Advertising

As with any other consumer product, advertising plays a crucial role in music promotion. Record companies place adverts in the press, magazines and on TV. Posters are one of the most common methods of advertising. A controversial practice – because it is often illegal – is that of fly posting. This involves sticking posters advertising record releases on walls, fences and buildings. Sponsorship is another way of bringing in money and advertising at the same time. Record producers often manufacture bands in order to cash in on a set musical trend. The Spice Girls – a band created by carefully auditioning individual members until a marketable product was manufactured. Below are some examples of products that the band have been used to promote:

- *Elida Faberge's Impulse Spice* perfume was the most successful variant launch in the brand's history.
- *Walkers Crisps* introduced five different Spice packs and sold 50% more than the equivalent promotion 12 months earlier.
- *Polaroid* launched a new SpiceCamera and re-built their distribution base across Europe.

- *Sony PlayStation* used the Girls to launch a new low-price format aimed at core non-users (young girls).
- *Pepsi* used the band in advertising, staged their first ever concert and offered an exclusive track with purchase. On the back of this activity, the brand's UK share grew by four percentage points.

The television programme Popstars took the process a stage further. It turned the process of creating Hear'Say into a docusoap as hundreds of hopefuls were narrowed down to the final line-up.

Merchandise

Merchandise is products that carry the name of a performer, for instance T-shirts and jackets. These are a clever marketing device. Firstly, they make money for the record company and the performer.

Secondly, they also advertise the performer, as other people see the product and may go on to buy their recordings as a result.

Fan clubs are a useful way of selling merchandise, as are stalls at concerts. Many bands also have mailing lists of addresses built up through pre-paid postcards included in CDs and tapes, to which they send information on new releases.

On your own

How many types of music merchandise have you seen?

Can you think of a new form of merchandise for a band?

Concerts

In its early days, sound recording was seen as a way of capturing live performances by musicians – so those who could not attend could hear them. However, the playback quality of music produced in studios soon surpassed that of music recorded 'live'. Performers were then faced with the task of trying to produce studio-quality music on stage. Today, concerts are seen largely as a way to promote recorded music. A band will tour 'on the back of' an album. That is, they make a record and use a tour to sell it. Live albums sell significantly fewer copies than studio-recorded ones.

In the shops

How many people buy their products is of great concern to record companies. Early gramophone records were sold in music shops, along with musical instruments and sheet music. Before long, however, stores began to open that sold only recorded music. Department stores also began to incorporate record sections in their layouts. As well as general record shops, specialist shops sprang up selling recordings of particular types of music, such as jazz or classical.

Record companies, however, needed to ensure that there were enough outlets for their products and decided not to rely solely on independent retailers. They began to buy up existing chains or opened their own. In doing this, the multinational music companies took control of every part of the process, from recording performers to producing the records and selling them. Today, EMI owns the HMV chain of shops, while Virgin has its own successful retail outlets.

In the 1990s, music megastores were opened. Pioneered by the Virgin group, these shops brought the selling of recorded music full circle. CDs, tapes and vinyl records are only a part of the range of products sold in these shops, which also stock videos, computer games, clothing, books and sheet music. This move from record shops to what Virgin calls 'home entertainment stores' has been followed by other music retailers.

Review

The main aim of the recording industry is not to make music but to make money. Music is simply the product that the industry sells. To be successful, a record company has to present the consumer with a popular product, such as a band, in an attractive package, such as an album, recorded on an accessible format, such as a CD or tape. The music you play on your CD may have been written by the performer in their bedroom, but, on its route to you, it has gone through a complex industrial and marketing process as part of a multi-million pound business.

Advertising is the promotion of goods or services in such a way as to encourage people to buy or use them. Each section of the media uses its technology to make advertising presentations. Money paid to media institutions by advertisers funds much of their activity, and without it many television programmes would not get made, newspapers and magazines published, or records played. Most media, therefore, depend on advertising revenue for their survival. In fact, some people say that the main function of the media is not to inform or entertain audiences, but to deliver audiences to advertisers.

In the UK there is a publicly funded television organisation, the BBC. It does not rely on advertising as it gets its money from the sale of TV licences, which viewers must have if they are to watch its programmes without breaking the law. However, it is worth noting that even the BBC carries adverts for its own products, such as videos, tapes and books associated with its programmes.

On your own

List the occasions on which you come into contact with advertising. You will be surprised how often this happens.

Forms of advertising

Television commercials

Advertising on television usually takes the form of short films broadcast between and during programmes in what are called commercial breaks (although it could be argued that the programmes are merely made to be shown between the adverts). These commercial breaks are called slots and TV companies sell them to advertisers. The cost of a particular spot depends on the popularity of the programme broadcast around it. Typically, a 30 second peak times slot on Carlton would cost £23,000

Advertising costs have grown and grown. On its first night of broadcasting in May 1956, Granada TV charged £14,215 in total for commercial break air-time. On Granada in 1996 it cost around £600,000 for a 40-second commercial during Coronation Street. Television advertisements in the 1990s cost an average of £400,000 to make.

Advertising slots on TV tend to be sold to advertisers in packages. This means that they buy a set number of slots in commercial breaks, throughout the day, some at peak time, during the evening, others at less popular times in the morning and afternoon and late at night. Most television commercials are made by commercial production companies on behalf of advertisers.

Radio adverts

Adverts are played during most programmes on commercial radio stations. Radio commercials are less expensive to produce than those for television, and the cost of air-time is also significantly lower. This means that more companies can afford to advertise on radio, especially small local ones.

Radio commercials usually take the form of a short presentation using music and speech. Many use a catchy piece of music with simple lyrics, called a jingle, to get listeners to remember the advert. The majority of radio adverts are made by local radio stations that have their own production units. Others, especially those that are broadcast nationally, are made by commercial companies.

'TINGLING-FRESH'
-and you're toughening your gums too

The first advert broadcast on TV in Britain was for Gibbs SR toothpaste 1955.

In groups

AS A GROUP

Using a tape recorder, produce a radio advert for a new product of your choice. To do this, you will have to write a script and choose appropriate music. Remember that most radio adverts use a catchy jingle. It may be helpful to tape some examples from the radio and study them before you begin.

Press advertising

A large proportion of newspapers and magazines is taken up by advertising. In fact, some papers are made up of nothing more than adverts. Publishers design their products around what are called 'advertising ratios'. This means how much of a magazine or newspaper will be made up of adverts and how much will be taken up by stories and pictures (editorial). The percentage of adverts in newspapers depends to a large extent on their circulation figures. National daily newspapers tend to have the smallest amount of space devoted to adverts, while small local papers usually have the largest percentage of adverts.

In pairs

Using a calculator, work out the advertising ratios for the following:

- A national Sunday paper
- A national daily paper
- Your local evening paper.

This will give you an idea of how much space in newspapers is sold to advertisers.

Advertising in newspapers and magazines falls into three types:

Display adverts: these use visual images in the form of photographs or graphics to attract the attention of the reader, and are generally placed by commercial advertisers. They can range from adverts for small local firms, containing a simple company logo in black and white, to full-page, full-colour adverts for internationally famous products.

Display advertising.

RELAX

AT HOME ON

SPAIN'S GOLDEN

COAST

An endless sandy coastline and picturesque landscape form a perfect setting for your private beachside home in this wonderful year-round climate.

Oliva Nova is truly a complete leisure resort with every facility you could imagine - including a beautiful 18-hole golf course designed by the master himself - Seve Ballesteros.

"I really enjoyed designing the Golf course at Oliva Nova. I am sure you will enjoy playing it!"

Seve Ballesteros

From its perfect location near Denia, Oliva Nova is without doubt one of the finest addresses on this stunning golden coastline.

For a detailed brochure call now on **020 8940 9406**

Prices include 7% VAT and may fluctuate in accordance with the exchange rate

OLIVA NOVA
BEACH & GOLF RESOR
★★★★★

TOWN HOUSES
from £98,000
VILLAS
from £190,000

Please fill in the coupon & return to the address below for more information

Name

Premier Resorts Ltd., 9 Duke Str
Richmond, Surrey TW9 1HP

On your own

Design a display advert for a new product of your choice. Think who would buy the product and what sort of advertising image would appeal to them.

Advertorials: these are pieces of writing about companies, describing and promoting their products. They can be accompanied by photographs. By law, such pieces of writing must have the words 'advertising feature' printed next to them so that people do not confuse them with news stories.

An advertorial.

Classified Ads.

Classified adverts: these as a rule do not use visual images and consist almost entirely of words. They are generally arranged in columns towards the back of the publications and are often known as the 'small ads'. They include things such as births, marriages and deaths, job adverts and adverts placed by members of the general public.

ADVERTISING RATES

best

Positions	Pages	Spreads
A	£25,065	£50,130
B	£23,395	£46,790
C	£20,055	£40,110
D	£18,380	£36,760
E	£16,710	£33,420
Promotions	£16,250	£29,250

Esquire

Positions	Pages	Spreads
A	£10,245	£20,490
B	£9,560	£19,120
C	£8,195	£16,390
D	£7,515	£15,030
E	£6,830	£13,660
Promotions	£6,695	£12,050

COMPANY

Positions	Pages	Spreads
A	£12,710	£25,420
B	£11,865	£23,370
C	£10,170	£20,340
D	£9,320	£18,640
E	£8,475	£16,950
Promotions	£7,955	£14,315

FOCUS

Positions	Pages	Spreads
A	£6,000	£12,000
B	£5,600	£11,200
C	£4,800	£9,600
D	£4,400	£8,800
E	£4,000	£8,000
Promotions	£6,145	£11,060

COSMOPOLITAN

Positions	Pages	Spreads
A	£24,005	£48,010
B	£22,405	£44,810
C	£19,205	£38,410
D	£17,605	£35,210
E	£16,005	£32,010
Promotions	£15,840	£28,510

Good Housekeeping

Positions	Pages	Spreads
A	£22,610	£45,220
B	£21,105	£42,210
C	£18,090	£36,180
D	£16,580	£33,160
E	£15,075	£30,150
Promotions	£15,230	£27,415

Rates effective from 1st November 2000

A newspaper advertising rate card.

Prices for advertising in print publications depend on how much space the adverts take up on a page, and are charged by the column centimetre. Publishers provide potential advertisers with a rate card that tells them how much an ad of a particular size will cost (see above).

Where the advertisement appears in the paper or magazine also affects how much it will cost. An advert at the top of a page close to the front of the publication will cost more than one at the bottom of the page towards the back.

Sponsorship

Another popular form of advertising that uses the power of the media is sponsorship. This involves an advertiser paying for the right to have their name associated with a media event. This is common with sporting events, when the advertiser's name forms part of the event's title, such as the Barclaycard Premiership for football or the Embassy World Snooker Championships. Advertisers also sponsor teams and have their names and logos printed on players' shirts, or have posters put on hoardings around sports grounds. The idea behind this is that large numbers of viewers will see the names when matches or tournaments are broadcast on television. This is one way firms can actually get advertising courtesy of the BBC, even though it does not carry paid-for advertisements.

The sponsorship of actual programmes on commercial TV stations is increasingly popular. Advertisers pay to have their name shown or read out at the beginning and end of the programme and either side of the commercial breaks. So a police drama series may be seen produced in association with an insurance company, or a high profile film with a soft drinks manufacturer.

Product placement is a form of advertising that is gaining in popularity.

A film advert displaying product placement.

try to persuade them to place advertisements with their publication, radio or TV station.

If a business wants to advertise, the next step is to produce the advert. For television commercials, advertisers approach a production company to make the advert for them. This involves a team of scriptwriters coming up with an idea for the commercial. Once an idea is agreed upon, a storyboard is drawn up. This is a series of drawings showing how the action in the advert will develop. A production team, including camera operators, sound recordists, actors and a director then goes into a studio or out on location and films the advert. The finished product is delivered to the TV company ready to be broadcast in the agreed advertising slots.

It involves advertisers paying the producers of films to have characters use their products. For example, the main character in a film may wear a certain brand of jeans or drive a certain make of car. The jeans or car will be provided by the company that makes them and they will pay for them to be used.

These are examples of what is known as covert or hidden advertising where a product is promoted indirectly to the public.

How are adverts produced?

All commercial television, radio and publishing companies have departments dedicated to selling advertising space. Companies that wish to place advertisements contact people working in these departments, known as advertising sales representatives. Representatives also approach businesses and

In the case of radio, newspapers and magazines, the sales representatives usually contact their own in-house production department. For radio, a script is written for the advert by a copywriter and then recorded in a studio by engineers and presenters. In newspapers and magazines, copywriters work with artists, known as graphic designers who come up with the images to be used. Once the designs have been approved by the advertiser, they are positioned in the page design of the publication.

Advertising agencies

Instead of looking after their own advertising, many big firms use professional advertising agencies to ensure they get the best from the opportunities offered by the media. Advertising agencies specialise in handling all aspects of advertising, from designing the commercials to buying the air-time or page space. They are particularly good at conducting advertising campaigns that use all forms of the media. A typical campaign would involve the following steps:

- The Client contacts an agency to develop a publicity campaign for its product. The client gives the agency an idea of how much it wishes to spend. The contract to carry out advertising for a company is known as an account.
- The agency carries out research to discover who would be interested in buying the product.
- Adverts are designed to appeal to the people whom the agency thinks will be attracted to the product.
- All options for advertising are considered, such as, TV, radio and press. A decision is made about which type of advertising is best for the product: this may include just one or all three of the different media.
- If a television commercial is needed, the agency contracts a production company to make it. Press and magazine adverts and scripts for radio commercials are developed by creative teams at the agency.
- Agency buyers purchase at the lowest price possible the best spots for the adverts on TV and radio and in the press.
- Research is carried out following the campaign to see how successful it was in generating sales of the product.

In groups

Design your own advertising campaign. Each group acts as an advertising agency for an imaginary product chosen by the class leader. Each group should work out how to advertise the product.

- Think of all the different forms of advertising available and decide which would be best for your product.
- If possible, work out the cost of your campaign by checking advertising price rates with media producers.
- Remember that advertising agencies have to work to tight budgets given to them by their clients.

The class can vote on which agency they think would be the most successful.

Controversial Adverts

One company that has gone out of its way to produce provocative advertising is the clothing manufacturer, Benetton. For nearly 20 years, their campaigns were controlled by fashion photographer Oliviero Toscani. He used such images as car bomb explosions, a dying Aids victim, child labour, an electric chair and a black woman breastfeeding a white baby. One of his most controversial campaigns was a series of posters that featured 26 inmates of Death Row, awaiting execution in an American prison.

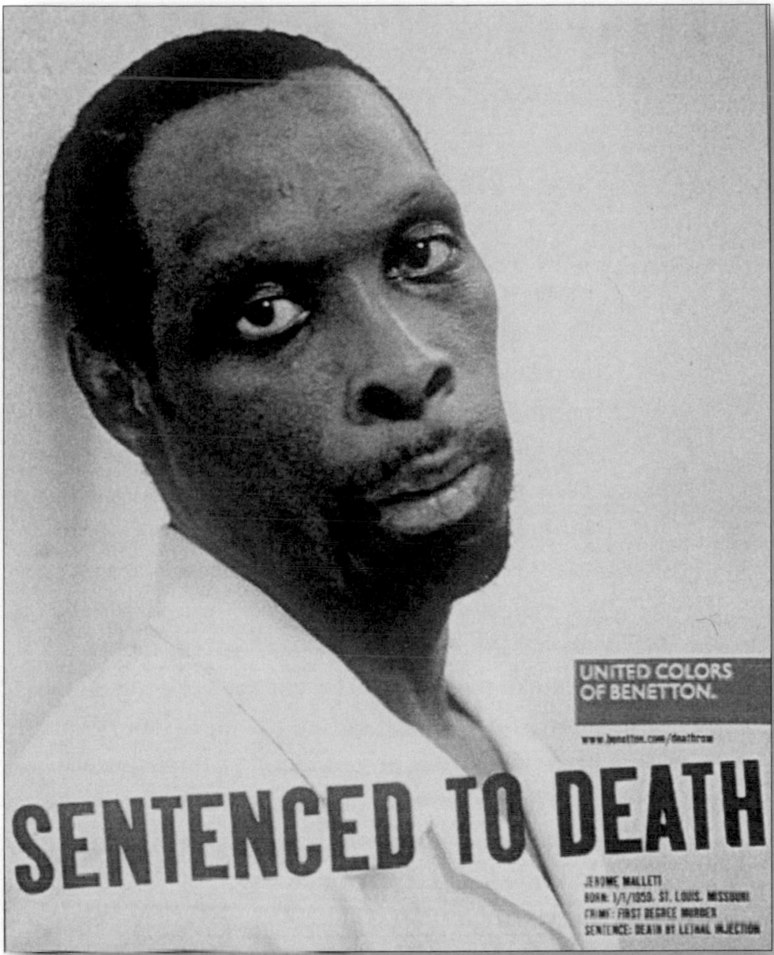

UNITED COLORS
OF BENETTON.

www.benetton.com/deathrow

SENTENCED TO DEATH

JEROME MALLETT
BORN: 1/1/1959. ST. LOUIS, MISSOURI
CRIME: FIRST DEGREE MURDER
SENTENCE: DEATH BY LETHAL INJECTION

The power of advertising

Money talks

The relationship of advertising to the content of media products has been the subject of much debate. Critics say that because of the amount of money advertisers pay to the media, they can, if they wish, influence what is shown or printed. They also argue that TV programmes, newspapers and magazines will not broadcast or publish material that is harmful to their advertisers. So, they say, a story about defects in a particular product may not be published by a newspaper if the company that makes that product advertises with it. They also say that the line between news and advertising may become blurred when the subject of the story is linked with a major advertiser. For example, a new product may become the subject of an editorial feature if there is a promise of a lucrative advertising contract with the magazine.

Although rare, there have been incidences of advertisers putting direct pressure on media producers. However, these have largely been in the form of advertisers using their financial muscle to protest against particular stories or features in the media, rather than blatant attempts to avoid bad or achieve favourable publicity. In 1993 *The Mirror* printed pictures of Princess Diana working out in a gym and many

In groups

AS A GROUP

Look at the image used by Benetton.

What do you think is going on in the image?

Does the advertisement tell you anything about Benetton clothes?

Another company that produces advertising designed to upset people is French Connection UK which uses its initial letters provocatively to promote its fashion wear.

Advertisers threatened to stop advertising with some magazines in protest at the use of extremely thin models, which they said could encourage eating disorders.

large companies withdrew adverts from the paper in protest. In 1996, the watch manufacturers Omega stopped advertising with *Vogue* to protest against what is saw as the promotion of the skinny 'waif' look through the magazine's use of very thin models.

However, the real power advertisers have over the media works in a more subtle fashion. The majority of the media in Britain exist to make a profit. To do this, they must attract as many advertisers as they can and charge them as much as possible. Advertisers are interested in media products because they reach large numbers of potential customers. To charge high advertising rates, a programme or newspaper must prove that it reaches a big audience through viewing figures or sales. This leads to the media producing products not on the basis of their ability to inform or entertain, but, to attract large audiences. So if a commercial television station has a choice between showing a documentary about an issue of importance that will attract an audience of hundreds of thousands, or showing a game show that will attract an audience of millions, the game show is likely to be chosen.

A similar process can be seen to operate in the planning and marketing of new media products. The decision to launch a new magazine usually boils down to whether there is an audience ready to buy it. If the publishers can sell a magazine to a lot of new readers, they can convince advertisers it is worth paying to promote their products in its pages. The birth of 'lifestyle' magazines for men grew out of recognition that men would buy publications dedicated to male interests in the same way that female readers had been buying 'women's' magazines for years. In turn, advertisers used the pages of these new magazines to promote products for men, such as skin care products and high fashion, traditionally aimed at women.

Advertisements from male lifestyle magazines offer advertisers a platform to sell men products they hadn't considered buying before.

On your own

ON YR. OWN

List the types of manufacturers who would be likely to advertise in a new magazine for middle-aged people. Do you think such a magazine could be successful, judging by your list of potential advertisers?

Around 30 million adverts are published in the UK every year.

How seriously do we take adverts?

How justified are fears about the supposed grip that advertising has on the media? Advertisers may try to use the media in as many ways as possible to promote their products, but how do audiences use advertising? As we saw in the chapter on audience, many people believe that viewers, listeners and readers are not brainwashed by the media (page 62). In fact, the reverse is true: audiences use the media for

their own ends and have a healthy scepticism of what it produces. Points that should be taken into account when looking at the power of advertising include:

● Just because an advert looks good does not necessarily mean that it is effective in selling more products. Viewers may enjoy it purely because it is funny or entertaining and never have any intention to go out and buy the product.

- People tend to be highly suspicious of claims made in adverts and take most with a pinch of salt.
- Adverts may be 'invisible'. That is, people may switch channels in commercial breaks or go and make a cup of tea in order to avoid watching advertisements. They may also skip past adverts in newspaper and magazines, concentrating only on stories they are interested in.

Class discussion

AS A CLASS

- What are your favourite adverts?
- Why do you like them?
- Are they for products you would buy?
- If so, do the adverts have an effect on you? Do you go out and buy because you have seen the ad?

The Advertising Standards Authority

The Advertising Standards Authority (ASA) was set up in 1962 as an organisation independent of both the advertising industry and the government, to make sure that all advertisements that appear in the UK are legal, decent, honest and truthful. (It does not regulate advertisements that appear on TV and radio: these are regulated by the Independent Television Commission and the Radio Authority respectively. For radio advertising, see pages 189–190).

The ASA is funded from the money spent on display advertising (advertising in newspapers, magazines and on posters) and on direct mail advertising (advertising material sent through the post). Advertisers pay a levy of £1 for every £1000 they spend on display or direct mail advertising. The money is collected by the Advertising Standards Board of Finance, a body that is independent of the ASA.

The British Codes of Advertising and Sales Promotion

These codes say what is and what is not acceptable in advertisements. They were drawn up by the advertising industry itself and have two main aims:

- to make advertisers take responsibility for backing up the claims they make for their products in their advertisements;
- to avoid causing offence.

The codes are monitored by the Committee of Advertising Practice, which works alongside the ASA. The codes are in addition to the 120 laws passed by successive governments that apply directly or indirectly to advertising.

The codes include a set of general rules that apply to all published adverts. These rules are based on the following principles:

- all advertisements should be legal, decent, honest and truthful;
- all advertisements should be prepared with a sense of responsibility to consumers and to society;
- all advertisements should respect the principle of fair competition generally accepted in business;
- no advertisement should bring advertising into disrepute;
- advertisements must conform with the advertising codes. Primary responsibility for observing the codes falls on the advertisers. Others involved in preparing and publishing advertisements, such as agencies, publishers and other service suppliers, also have to abide by the codes.

The codes should be applied in the spirit as well as the letter of the law.

Issues such as decency, truthfulness, safety, the depiction of violence, privacy, guarantees and political bias are all covered in the general rules. The codes also contain a number of rules relating to specific categories of advertisements. These include adverts for alcoholic drinks, cars, medicines and slimming products. They also cover advertising relating to children and adverts making environmental claims. A separate code applies to adverts for cigarettes.

Monitoring advertisements

Only cigarette adverts have to be cleared before they can be published. However, thousands of advertisers, agencies and publishers seek advice and guidance from the ASA on the content of their adverts.

The ASA dealt with 12,262 complaints relating to 8,457 adverts in 2000. Nearly one in seven of these complaints was upheld, or supported, and action was taken against the advertiser (see below). The ASA carries out its own regular surveys of adverts in the press, on posters and on adverts sent through the post. In addition, the ASA's research department keeps a watch on adverts in areas of particular concern such as medicines and slimming products.

The government and the European Union consult the ASA whenever they are drawing up policies referring to advertising.

If the ASA decides an advertisement is unacceptable because it is misleading or likely to cause offence, the advertisers are told to remove it. Failure to do this can lead to the following:

- bad publicity generated by the report that the ASA sends round of its judgements;
- suspension or withdrawal of trading privileges or financial incentives, or the refusal of publishers to sell space to the advertisers;
- a court appearance, if the advertisers are referred to the Office of Fair Trading by the ASA for refusing to abide by the codes.

Nearly a thousand of complaints were about an advertisement for Opium perfume which used a naked photograph of the model Sophie Dahl. Many complaints said that the advert was offensive to women and unsuitable for display in a public place. The ASA ordered that the advertisement be removed from billboards but ruled that it was acceptable in magazines and newspapers.

Review

Advertising is the foundation on which most of the media is built, and so deserves close investigation. We have seen in this chapter that media producers get money from two main sources:

- audiences who pay for their products;
- businesses who pay to advertise in their products.

The money paid by audiences is usually not enough both to support the production of films, programmes and publications, and to allow them to make a profit as well. Because of this, advertising plays a major role in financing media production. In fact, without funds from advertising, most media products would not get made. This has led to serious concerns about the influence advertisers have had over what the media produces and what we see, hear and read.

Radio

Guglielmo Marconi sent the first wireless telegraphic message across the Channel in 1899. Two years later, he repeated the feat, but this time the message was sent across the Atlantic, from Cornwall to Newfoundland. On Christmas Eve 1906, in the United States of America, Reginald Aubrey Fessenden broadcast the first radio programme, which featured music, poetry and a talk.

It was not until 1919 that radio was successfully transmitted in the UK. In that year, a transmitter in Chelmsford, Essex, began broadcasting programmes that contained both speech and music on a daily basis. Three years later, as interest in radio grew, the BBC was born. At first it was organised around the interests of manufacturers and broadcasters, but soon the government stepped in and set up the BBC as a public corporation with its own board of governors, and made it accountable to Parliament. Finance was generated through a licence fee. In this way, the concept of public service broadcasting was born.

Radio is a medium that audiences can consume while they are doing other things. Unlike television or newspapers, it doesn't demand your whole attention: radio is an ideal medium to use while you are busy with your everyday life. Because of this, radio has some interesting functions. For many people, it provides an important source of companionship and acts as a friend who chats to them and keeps them company. It also helps people to concentrate on the tasks they have to do by shutting out the outside world. When you see someone wearing headphones listening to the radio, it is as though they are saying to other people, 'Don't try to talk to me. I can't hear you.'

Every week, nine out of ten people listen to the radio for around 21 hours. They listen to it as soon as they wake up in the morning, on their way to work, in the car or on the bus or train. They tune in while they are working, on their way home at night, while they eat their tea or do their homework. Some even fall asleep listening to the radio last thing at night.

On your own

- Make a list of the radios that you can use.
- Where they are?
  What kind of radios they are?
  Who uses them most?
- If you travel in a car, who decides what station you are tuned to?
- If you travel abroad in a car, do you still listen to the radio?
- Write a short report on your family's listening habits.

Radio or some kind of background music is often played in shops and factories. It can help make people feel comfortable and soothe them while they work or shop. Radio is like wallpaper, in that it is in the background, making people feel at ease with their surroundings.

Although radio is a popular medium with audiences, especially the younger age groups,

WAVE BANDS

Most radios have both FM (Frequency Modulation) and AM (Amplitude Modulation) wavebands for receiving programmes. In general, people prefer to listen on the FM band whenever possible, because it offers better quality sound and is also capable of stereo and surround-sound reproduction. (Surround-sound amplifies sound through four or five speakers to create the effect that the sound is all around the listener. For example, an aircraft can be made to sound as though it has flown over the listener's shoulder. This technology also allows the listener to reproduce the acoustics characteristics of specific venues, for example a concert hall.)

surprisingly little attention has been paid to it in Media Studies. Perhaps because it seems less glamorous than television, film and the print media, far fewer books have been written about the medium of radio.

A good way of starting to investigate the medium is to listen to it. Begin by tuning to the FM band of your radio. The frequency is measured in megahertz (a unit that measures wavelengths in cycles per second). Move slowly from the bottom of the waveband (usually 87.5MHz) to the top (108MHz). You may do this by turning a dial and watching a pointer, or you may have a digital tuner, where you press a button and the display changes. As you move from the bottom of the frequency to the top, listen carefully to each station for a short time. Depending on where you live, the number of stations you hear will vary, as will the quality of the sound. If the signal (the electronically coded message sent out from the transmitter) is not strong enough, the reception is often in mono. (Mono sound is amplified through a single channel and is usually heard through just one speaker. Stereo production, on the other hand, splits sound into two channels and amplifies it through two speakers.)

Of course, you need to remember that the brief sample of the stations' output that you have heard may not be typical. It is a good idea to listen again at a different time of day to see if the style and content have changed,

Each radio station aims to establish its won identity so that the audience will recognize it and want to make it the station that they tune to automatically. Different stations have different approaches to broadcasting, in terms of their style of presentation and the content of their programmes.

Some digital tuners have RDS (Radio Data System), which allows them to identify the station that is playing by showing its name on the display. Analogue tuners use a pointer on a scale to show the frequency.

In pairs

IN PAIRS

Write a brief description of each station you hear, together with its frequency. Your description should cover such information as:

● Was the station playing music? If so, what sort of music was it?

● Was anyone speaking on the station? What were they talking about? What did their voice sound like – did it have a regional accent, or use slang?

● What was the presentation of the station like? Was it lively and informal, or was the tone more serious?

● Did you like the station and want to listen to more?

● What sort of audience do you think the station is addressing?

Group discussion

AS A GROUP

One way in which stations establish their identity is by using jingles. These are short pieces of music which a presenter plays in order to let listeners know they are tuned into a particular station. What other methods are used to establish a station's identity? You might want to think about:

● How often the presenter mentions the station's name and frequency

● Slogans

● How the station is identified with the local area

● Style of presentation

● Logos

● Sponsorship of events.

Types of radio station

Radio stations can be placed in broad categories in terms of both their identity and the audience they attract.

Funding

The first division is between commercial radio and what is known as public service broadcasting (PSB).

Commercial radio stations are financed by money from advertisers. They sell advertising time between and during programmes, just like commercial TV stations.

Public service broadcasting refers to radio stations operated by the BBC, including the national stations Radio 1, 2, 3, 4 and 5 Live, as well as many local radio stations, such as BBC Radio Cleveland and BBC Nottingham. Just like BBC television channels, these stations are financed with revenue from the BBC licence fee, although you don't need a licence for a radio now.

> ### RADIO LICENCES
> At the outbreak of war in 1939, nine million households had a radio licence. The radio licence was abolished in 1971.

Transmission area

Radio stations can be categorised according to their transmission area, which is the part of the country to which they broadcast.

National radio stations broadcast right across the country, although some regions may listen to them on slightly different frequencies.

Regional radio stations transmit over areas that already have local services. Scot FM, for example, broadcasts to central Scotland, which also has a number of local radio stations.

Local radio stations broadcast to smaller areas. Their transmission areas are often focused on a large city or county. For example, BBC Radio Sheffield and Hallam FM both cover the city of Sheffield and the surrounding area, including such towns as Doncaster and Rotherham. In addition, in some areas there are community radio stations that cover much smaller areas.

There are many local radio stations around the UK.

Material

Radio stations can also be categorised according to the type of material that they broadcast.

Music-based stations Many stations are, in essence, music stations. Their main output is music, with some news and related programmes. People listen to these stations chiefly for the music content. Of course, music does not necessarily mean popular or chart music. For example, the main output of Classic FM is classical music.

Speech-based stations Other stations are speech-based. Their output consists largely of people talking. For example, BBC Radio 5 Live provides a news, sport and current affairs service.

Of course, most stations will have some combination of music and speech. To describe them as music- or speech-based is to focus on their main output.

Class discussion

AS A CLASS

- What is the music policy of your local commercial station?
- Is any air-time given to new bands?
- Do any local bands get a chance to have their music played?
- Are specialist music interests catered for?

RADIO STATION PROFILE

1 Draw up a profile of your favourite radio station, using the categories described left. Look at the schedules for the station, which are usually printed in a TV and radio listing magazine, or a local newspaper. Listen to the station at a variety of times.

- Does the station broadcast to different audiences at different times?
- What is the station's main audience (think about their age, sex, social class and educational background)?

2 Now try listening for a few days to a radio station you would not normally tune in to, for example, Radio 5 or Classic FM.

- How is it different from the radio station that you usually listen to?
- What is the main audience for this station?
- Write a few paragraphs comparing the two radio stations that you profiled. Mention the strengths and weaknesses of each.

NEW TALENT

Some local commercial radio stations are accused of playing only music by established bands who are already known to the audience. Critics say that this policy of 'playing safe' means that many talented new bands do not get the chance to reach a wider audience. Radio 1 says that it has a policy of trying to give such opportunities to up-and-coming bands. It also uses presenters with a specific interest in one particular type of music such as dance rap, indie or jungle. In this way it tries to cater for specialist tastes, rather than simply offering middle-of-the-road music that is already familiar to most listeners.

SATELLITE RADIO

A wide variety of radio programmes is available by satellite. The dish and receiver that are used to receive television programmes also pick up British and foreign radio stations. These stations transmit using the same channels as the TV programmes, but with a different sound channel. They can be received either on a normal television channel or wired through a hi-fi system direct from the satellite receiver.

STATION	SATELLITE	FREQUENCY	LANGUAGE	TYPE
BBC RADIO 1	ASTRA 2A epg 911	11.798 H (27.5)	ENGLISH	POP
BBC RADIO 2	ASTRA 2A epg 912	11.798 H (27.5)	ENGLISH	OLD POP
CLASSIC GOLD	ASTRA 2A epg 919	12.402 V (27.5)	ENGLISH	60s-80s
VIRGIN R	ASTRA 2A epg 917	12.324 V(27.5)	ENGLISH	OLD/NEW POP
THE MIX	ASTRA 2A epg 920	12.402 V (27.5)	ENGLISH	VAR POP
CORE	ASTRA2A epg 922	12.402 V (27.5)	ENGLISH	NEW POP
PLANET ROCK	ASTRA2A epg 921	12.402 V (27.5)	ENGLISH	ROCK
CAPITAL GOLD	ASTRA2A epg 923	12.324 V(27.5)	ENGLISH	60s-80s
HEART FM	ASTRA2A epg 939	12.324 V(27.5)	ENGLISH	VAR POP
XFM LONDON	ASTRA2A epg 924	12.324 V(27.5)	ENGLISH	ROCK
YOUTH FM	ASTRA2A epg 935	12.324 V(27.5)	ENGLISH	NEW POP
STORM-LIVE	ASTRA2A epg 946	12.324 V(27.5)	ENGLISH	VAR POP
TOTAL ROCK. R.	ASTRA2A epg 950	12.402 V(27.5)	ENGLISH	VAR POP
LBH RADIO	ASTRA2A	12.109 H(27.5)	ENGLISH	VAR POP
COSTCUTTER	ASTRA2A	12.324 V(27.5)	ENGLISH	IN-STORE
FIDELITY	ASTRA2A	12.188 H(27.5)	ENGLISH	NO-DJ
SYNERGY	ASTRA2A	12.188 H(27.5)	ENGLISH	NO-DJ
STYLE	ASTRA2A	12.188 H(27.5)	ENGLISH	NO-DJ
VIRGIN R	ASTRA 1	11.372 V	ENGLISH	OLD/NEW POP
R. CAROLINE	ASTRA 1	10.994 H	ENGLISH	ROCK (SAT/SUN)
SKY RADIO	ASTRA 1	11318 V	DUTCH	POP
BBC R1	ASTRA 1	10.979 V	ENGLISH	POP/DANCE
OLDIESENDER	ASTRA 1	12.012 V (27.5)	DUTCH	60s-80s
VERONICA	ASTRA 1	12.574 H (22)	DUTCH	POP
KINK FM	ASTRA 1	12.574 H (22)	DUTCH	POP/ROCK
SKY RADIO	ASTRA 1	12.574 H (22)	DUTCH	POP
RADIO 538	ASTRA 1	12.574 H (22)	DUTCH	POP/ROCK

Some of the stations from all over Europe that can be received via satellite

The radio studio

Before an audience can receive a radio station, someone has to put together the words and music they are going to listen to. This is usually done in a radio studio. Most radio studios are similar in their layout and organisation, regardless of whether the station is speech- or music-based.

The nerve centre of any radio operation is the desk, or main control panel, at which the presenter sits. This consists of a series of channels, each with its own fader. Each channel controls one particular source of sound, such as a microphone, CD player or tape machine. Faders control the volume of a particular sound source. They can be opened or closed by sliding them up and down. The presenter can select each of the sources by opening and closing the fader to bring up or shut down the sound. At the end of a record, for example, the presenter can fade down the music and fade up their microphone to talk to the audience. One of the most valuable tools a presenter has available is the cart machine, which uses a continuous loop of audio tape so that, once it has been played, it can be cued again very quickly. Using this, pre-recorded trails (which tell the audience about programmes that are to be broadcast in the near future) and jingles can be cued, so that they are ready to play immediately. Listen out for examples used by presenters on your favourite station.

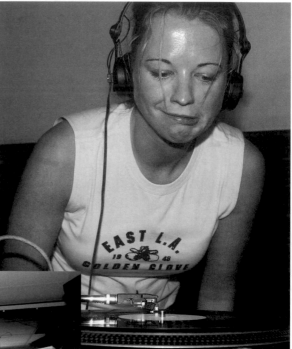

A presenter has to be skilled at cueing records and tapes and fading them up or down to make the show seem professional. While one record is playing, the presenter needs to cue (or find the beginning of) the next piece of music to go on air, so that the music will be ready to play as soon as the presenter has introduced it.

Programme content

Imagine you have been asked to work as a presenter on a local commercial radio station. What would you have to do to produce a show that would keep your audience listening? The first factor you would need to think about is the time of day the show went out. If your show were a drive-time show, which generally attracts a large audience, you would be broadcasting for people getting ready for, or on their way to, work or school, or who were coming home in the evening. Many would be listening in their cars, so it would be important to include information about road conditions, for example.

During the day, the audience is likely to be made up of people who are at home all day, possibly looking after children or doing housework. Evening radio shows compete with television, so this might be a good time to put out a specialist programme for a minority group.

Presenters try to keep a balance between the different elements that make up a show. Talk must be balanced with music. The music itself must be a blend of different types and different moods. Some of it should be familiar to the audience, some of it less familiar. Slow, sad ballads should be balanced with lively, upbeat, happy sounds.

Although presenters can choose much of their own music, they have a playlist of tracks that the stations want to be played most often, which have to be built into the shows. Any music used in a show has to be paid for. Such 'needle-time' is paid for via organisations that represent the interests of record companies and performers, such as Phonographic Performance Limited. A presenter, therefore, needs to find other ways of filling up air-time if a show is to stay within its budget.

On a commercial station, advertising slots have already been allocated, so a presenter has to structure the programme around them. Such regular items as news, weather and travel updates are also built in. Additionally, the presenter may include recorded material from a reporter, who has been out collecting information to be broadcast as part of the show. This is called a 'package' and is likely to consist of interview material and actuality (sound-recorded or broadcast, of real events or activities that are actually taking place), with the reporter's voice providing links to guide the listener through the material. The reporter gives the presenter a cue sheet, which is read out to introduce the package.

Having guests in the studio is another possible feature that a presenter might include. Most studios have three microphones (one that is used by the presenter and two extra ones), so that studio guests can contribute to the show in the form of a discussion or interview. This approach is sometimes called a 'zoo format', which means that other voices besides that of the presenter contribute to the programme. The other voices may be identified as studio guests, or they may be anonymous voices of other people working in the studio, who chip into the discussion or bounce their

In pairs

Imagine that you were presenting a show that went out from midnight until 4 o'clock in the morning.

- What type of audience would be listening then?
- What sort of music would you play?

comments off the presenter. This can produce lively listening, especially if the contributors are able to think up witty, off-the-cuff remarks. For the programme to keep a sense of order and shape, the presenter must be able to control the proceedings.

Group discussion

AS A GROUP

- Have you ever called into a radio station or had a request played?
- What do you think makes people want to hear themselves or their name on air?

Phone-ins have become increasingly popular. Not only are they cheap to produce, but they also involve the audience in the show and help to keep their interest. Of course, on live radio a phone-in could cause embarrassment if a caller started to swear, for example. Generally, callers are not allowed straight on air, but are screened by a production assistant, who tries to get some idea of what the caller wishes to contribute to the show. In some circumstances, the presenter has a delay button. This means that transmission of the 'live' show is, in fact, delayed by several seconds, so that any obscene or embarrassing remark can be covered up, with a bleep for example, before the audience can hear it. On-air competitions, where listeners try to answer questions asked by the presenter, are also a useful way of keeping listener's interest in a programme, as is the playing of their requests and dedications.

Although a radio show may seem quite natural, with studio banter and guests dropping in, a good deal of time and effort go into its preparation. Like many other media products, it takes a lot of work to make the show seem natural and unrehearsed.

A roadshow is an effective way of raising a station's profile and providing lively programmes for its audience.

Radio Sheffield studio.

Local radio

Today we take local radio for granted. It was not, however, until the mid 1960s that local radio stations were launched. The BBC led the way with Radio Leicester which started broadcasting on 8th November 1967. BBC local radio stations now cover most of the country.

In many regions BBC radio is in direct competition with commercial stations and in areas were there are a lot of people, it is possible to find several stations targeted at a local audience. In London, for example, listeners can choose from such stations as LBC, London Live and Capital.

Whether BBC-funded or commercial, a local radio station is designed to appeal to the interests and tastes of local audiences. Commercial stations tend to play rather more music and carry advertisements for local businesses and organisations. Both BBC and commercial stations carry local news bulletins and provide information and commentaries on local sporting events. The BBC boasts that one fifth of the population listened at some point to BBC local radio in the last three months of the year 2000.

Radio Sheffield is typical of many BBC local radio stations up and down the country. It broadcasts from a newly built studio in the trendy Cultural Industries quarter of Sheffield City Centre. Despite its location and its name, Radio Sheffield is at pains to remind listeners that its catchment area includes the surrounding towns of Barnsley, Rotherham, Chesterfield, Doncaster and Worksop – most of South Yorkshire and North Nottinghamshire, in fact. The station has studios in each of these places to ensure that local news and events are covered.

Radio Sheffield organises its daily output to try to meet the demands of its audience. For example, the Breakfast Show has a focus on news and information and keeps listeners posted with regular updates on travel throughout the area, which includes a busy stretch of the M1 Motorway. After the 9am news bulletin, the programme takes on the role of a phone-in. Listeners are invited to call the studio and debate a topic that has been previously announced by the presenters – currently Everard and Trish. These topics range from the serious to the more light-hearted.

Late in the afternoon a similar news and information programme is broadcast, aimed at people on their way home from work. Since people listen to these programmes in their cars, this type of programming is often called drive-time. A typical drive-time programme is likely to consist of a mixture of news, travel information, music and chat.

Radio Sheffield tends to appeal to an older audience than its rival, Hallam FM. A typical programme is that presented by Tony Capstick each weekday afternoon. This is a 'magazine' format programme, with a combination of music, reports, studio guests, competitions, news and chat. Tony, who speaks with a pronounced local accent, has spent many years in the entertainment business and brings his love of the showbiz world into the programme. For example, one feature of the show is Tony's Turns' Mike in which local entertainers such as bands and singers are given the chance to perform in the studio. Besides performing, they take time chance to chat to him on air about their careers.

Nostalgia is an important feature of the programme. A regular slot has a local historian talking about the past, often inspired by some local landmark or building. Such an item will clearly appeal to an audience of retired people who are likely to be tuned in at this time of day.

One of Tony's trademarks as a presenter is his interest in and curiosity about the lives of ordinary people. For example he often includes a report that features him visiting a local firm or organisation and chatting to one of the employees. He also places a lot of emphasis on his own local roots, frequently referring to places where he has lived and pubs he has visited. This strong sense of pride about the local area, its people and its culture are an important part of Radio Sheffield's identity.

Tony Capstick

It seems a far cry from the days when the BBC was dominated by stuffy upper-class, home counties accents, or 'posh people', as Tony would no doubt call them.

Activity
ON YR. OWN

When you hear a presenter's voice on the radio, what mental picture do you have of what they look like? Try looking at the website of your local radio station to find photographs of the presenters. How well does their face match what you imagined they would look like?

After 7pm most evenings, Radio Sheffield along with most BBC local stations takes on a rather different style. The media wave transmitter carries The Asian Network programme while on FM Nightsport offers coverage of local sporting events such as commentary on the two Sheffield football clubs or nearby teams such as Barnsley or Rotherham. At 10pm The Late Show features Andy Peebles. This programme is a multi station broadcast carried by all BBC Local stations in the north until 1am when Radio Sheffield switches to output from Radio 5 Live until next morning.

Activity
ON YR. OWN

Are there any local radio stations broadcasting in your area? What are they like? Try listening at a time of day when you would not normally tune in. What sort of programme is on? What sort of audience do you think it will appeal to?

Controlling radio

Of course, there are limits to what can be broadcast, for example, material that some people would think was obscene or offensive would not be considered suitable. Also, stations cannot simply broadcast on any frequency that they choose, although there are pirate, or free radio stations, which transmit on empty frequencies.

PIRATE RADIO

- Are there any pirate stations in your area?
- If so, what type of station are they?
- Are they aimed at a specific audience?
- Do they exist because this audience is not well served by mainstream radio?

The Radio Authority

The Radio Authority was set up at the beginning of 1991 to license commercial radio stations and to regulate the material they broadcast, including the advertising they carry. The authority was created under the 1990 Broadcasting Act and was given three main tasks:

- To plan frequencies
- To grant licences to organisations who want to broadcast
- To regulate programming and advertising.

RADIO
AUTHORITY

Planning frequencies

The job of planning frequencies is obviously an important one, with over 170 local commercial stations each transmitting a signal. The airwaves are constantly overcrowded, as stations compete with one another for both space and audiences. Part of the authority's job is to give out frequencies to stations in a way that avoids interference with other broadcasters' stations. The FM waveband, for example, is divided into sub-bands, of which three are allocated for use by independent stations, both local and national.

The FM band

In the UK this extends in frequency from 87.5 MHz to 108 MHz. FM is divided into sub-bands, used, with some exceptions, as follows:

87.6 to 88 MHz	Restricted services
88 to 94.6 MHz	BBC National and regional radio
94.6 TO 96.1 MHz	BBC local radio (and Radio 4 in places)
96.1 to 97.6 MHz	Independent local radio
97.6 to 99.8 MHz	BBC Radio 1
99.8 to 102 MHz	Independent national radio (Classic FM) and local radio
102 to 103.5 MHz	Independent local radio
103.5 to 105 MHz	BBC local radio (and Radio 4 in places)
105 to 108 MHz	Independent local radio

How the FM band is divided into different types of station.

Granting licences

When the Radio Authority grants licences to organisations that wish to broadcast, it must take account of what is in the best interests of the people who live in the transmission area. Choice is the key word here. There are many stations that already broadcast a fairly predictable diet of music and news. A new station might be expected to come up with a proposal that would offer listeners something different in the way of programme content and style.

The Radio Authority has awarded three licences to national commercial stations. They are:

Classic FM which began broadcasting classical music in September 1992.

Virgin 1215 (AM nationwide and 105.8FM in London and south-east England), which went on air in April 1993, with a rock music-based playlist.

Talk Radio which was launched in 1995 as a listener-led interactive debate service. It relaunched as **TalkSPORT** in 2000.

In addition to all the local commercial stations throughout the country, the Radio Authority also grants licences to restricted services, which broadcast over a limited area. So far it has granted 2,585 of these for temporary services than can be received by such audiences as a university or college campus, or a hospital.

Regulating content

The Radio Authority's job of regulating programming and advertising makes it an important watchdog. Stations that have been granted a licence must make broadcasts that are fair and decent. An important part of the Radio Authority's job is to make sure that this happens. Radio stations are required to keep a

The Radio Authority also grants licences to restricted services, which broadcast over a limited area.

Class discussion

Imagine that you had the opportunity to make a bid to put a new radio station in your area.

- What sort of programme would you broadcast?

- What types of presenters would you employ?

- Are there any sections of the community that are left out by the stations that are on air at the moment?

- If so, how would you meet their needs?

tape of all the material they broadcast for 42 days. If a listener wishes to make a complaint, they can write to the Radio Authority giving details of their complaint, including the station on which the item was broadcast, and the time and date it went out. Provided that the complaint is received within the 42-day period, the Radio Authority can ask for a copy of the broadcast to help it to investigate the complaint. Important guidelines are laid down by the Authority in the form of codes, which broadcasters are expected to follow. The codes set out what broadcasters may and may not do in relation to:

- Programming
- Advertising and sponsorship
- News and current affairs.

In the Radio Authority's advertising and sponsorship code, there are, for example, important rules about advertisements aimed at children (who are defined as being aged 15 and below).

On your own

ON YR. OWN

Look carefully at the radio advert opposite. How does it break the Radio Authority's advertising and sponsorship code covering advertising and children (see opposite page). Write a letter complaining about the advert to the Radio Authority, explaining why you think it breaks the code. Don't forget to mention the time and date that you heard the advert, and the name of the radio station on which it was broadcast.

The new Zogatron computer game can solve all your problems! Don't let the other kids at school laugh at you because you don't know how to play it. Order one now and a free cuddly Zogatron could be yours. Don't leave the Zogatron to be destroyed by the evil Vortix starfighters. Tell your Mum and Dad – at just £32.99, it's a snip!

Advertising and children

Rule 1 Misleadingness

Advertisements addressed to the child listener must not exaggerate or mislead about the size, qualities or capabilities of products or about the sounds they might produce.

Rule 2 Prices

Prices of products advertised to children must not be minimised by words such as 'only' or 'just'.

Rule 3 Immaturity and credulity

Advertisements must not take advantage of the immaturity or natural credulity of children.

Rule 4 Appeals to loyalty

Advertisements must not take advantage of the sense of loyalty of children or suggest that unless children buy or encourage others to buy a product or service they will be failing in some duty or lacking in loyalty.

Rule 5 Inferiority

Advertisements must not lead children to believe that unless they have or use the product advertised they will be inferior in some way to other children or liable to be held in contempt or ridicule.

Rule 6 Direct exhortation

Advertisements must not directly urge children to buy products or to ask adults to buy products for them. For example, children must not be directly invited to 'ask Mum' or 'ask Dad' to buy them an advertiser's product.

Rule 7 Direct response

Advertisements must not invite children to purchase products by mail or telephone.

Rule 8 Competitions

(a) References to competitions for children are acceptable provided that any skill required is appropriate to the age of likely participants and the values of the prizes and the chances of winning are not exaggerated.

(b) The published rules must be submitted in advance to the licensee and the principal conditions of the competition must be included in the advertisement.

Rule 9 Free gifts

References to 'free' gifts for children in advertisements must include all qualifying conditions, e.g. any time limit, how many products need to be bought, how many wrappers need to be collected, etc.

Rule 10 Health and hygiene

(a) Advertisements must not encourage children to eat frequently throughout the day.

(b) Advertisements must not encourage children to consume food or drink near bedtime.

(c) Advertisements for confectionery and snack foods must not suggest that such products may be substituted for balanced meals.

Rule 11 Children as presenters

(a) The participation of children in radio commercials is acceptable, subject to all relevant legal requirements.

(b) If children are employed in commercials, they must not be used to present products or services which they could not be expected to buy themselves. They must not make significant comments on characteristics of products and services about which they could not be expected to have direct knowledge.

Rule 12 Testimonials

Children must not personally testify about products and services. They may, however, give spontaneous comments on matters in which they would have an obvious natural interest.

These are the rules that advertisers must observe when they target radio adverts at young people.

TASTE AND DECENCY AND THE PORTRAYAL OF VIOLENCE

LANGUAGE

The gratuitous use of offensive language including blasphemy must not be used in programmes specially designed for children or broadcast in circumstances such that children might be expected to be listening.

There is no absolute ban on the use of bad language, but its use must be defensible in terms of context and authenticity. It is one thing, for example, when such language occurs in a documentary programme, and quite another when introduced for its own sake in, for example, a music-based entertainment programme. Many people who would not be unduly shocked by swearing are offended when it is used to excess and without justification.

SEX

The portrayal of, or allusion to, sexual behaviour must be defensible in context and presented with tact and discretion. Smut, titillation, crudity and sexual stereotyping must be avoided.

No portrayal or description or sexual activity between humans and animals or between adults and children may be transmitted and it can be referred to in programmes only after consultation at senior radio management level.

The same considerations apply here as to bad language. Popular entertainment and comedy have often relied to some extent on sexual innuendo: but this does not justify smut, titillation, mere crudity, the portrayal of perversion, sexism, or the degradation of either sex. Much of the world's great drama, music and fiction has been concerned with love and passion, and it would be quite wrong (if not impossible) to require writers or lyricists to renounce all intention to shock or disturb: but the aim should be to move, not offend.

BAD TASTE IN HUMOUR

(a) Licensees must avoid humour which offends good taste or decency. There is a danger of offence in the use of humour based on particular characteristics like race, gender or disability.

Even where no malice is present, jokes can all too easily, and plausibly, exploit or humiliate for the purpose of entertainment. This not only hurts those most directly concerned but can repel many listeners.

(b) Recorded Items:

Items not used immediately must be checked before transmission to ensure that jokes or scenarios are not rendered tasteless by intervening events, such as death, injury or other misfortune.

CHILDREN AND YOUNG PERSONS

The Radio Authority believes that adult radio listeners have the right to enjoy material which would not be thought suitable for children. However, Licence Holders must be aware of circumstances such that large numbers of children and young persons might be expected to be listening. Adult material must not be broadcast at times when a Licence Holder regularly directs his programmes at children and young persons by the inclusion of music, stories, or speech items acknowledged to be specifically attractive to children and young people below the age of 18.

Adult programmes include drama where strong language or violent scenarios might occur, discussion or 'phone-in' programmes that cover explicit violent or sexual topics in a frank manner and musical items with violent or sexually explicit lyrics, unless the programmes have educational aims.

this extract from the Radio Authority's programme code shows how hard it is to say exactly what bad taste is.

Class discussion

What are your views on the Radio Authority's programme code? Do you think that it is right to control what can be broadcast in this way? Or do you think the audience is less easily shocked and upset than the Radio Authority thinks?

The programme code covers a range of issues, such as religion, good taste and decency and the portrayal of violence. The news and current affairs code concerns itself very much with impartiality, bias and the reporting of politics. It insists, for example, that all news broadcasts should be accurate and impartial. When dealing with controversial subjects, the station should broadcast a range of views from people within its bulletins. Equally, the host of a discussion or phone-in programme should make sure that everyone has a chance to express their views.

As well as sticking to these codes, broadcasters are expected to broadcast the type of material that they outlined when they applied for their licence. A description of this material is contained in each station's licence, under the heading 'A promise of performance'.

In considering a listener's complaint, the Radio Authority must decide if any of its codes or the promise of performance have been broken. If it decides that they have, the Radio Authority has a number of options open to it:

● It can tell off the station
● It can ask it for an apology or correction to be broadcast
● In serious cases, it can fine the station, and shorten or even take away its licence.

The Authority publishes a list of all the complaints it has followed up. It also gives a response, details of whether the complaint was upheld or not and what actions, if any, it decided was necessary.

Review

Radio is often given a low priority by Media Studies students, just because it is easy to take it for granted. Radio is a medium that is often on in the background. People can listen to it without concentrating totally on it. They often listen while they are doing something else, such as homework or cooking dinner.

In this chapter, you have learned that radio is, in fact, a complex medium, which is just as interesting and worthwhile to study as television or film. So next time you find yourself listening to the radio, think about what you have learned about the medium and ask yourself some important questions about what you are listening to:

● What station am I tuned in to?
● What is the station's identity, and how is this established?
● How is it financed?
● What sort of audience does it cater for?
● To what sort of geographical area does it broadcast?
● What rules must it stick to in order to carry on broadcasting?
● What do I like about the station?
● How could it be improved?

Television news

As human beings, we need to know what is happening in our environment. We need to know, for example, where we can find food and water, where there is shelter, what poses a danger to us, and much more. We need this essential information to survive. However, most of us also have a desire to know things about our surroundings that are not essential. We want to know about other people's triumphs and tragedies, their good and bad deeds, and their loves and hates; about accidents, wars, disasters and famines. In fact, we want to know just about anything and everything. We are very nosy animals.

If you were asked to find out what is going on in the world, who is doing what, and what issues people should be concerned about, where would you look? It is a safe bet that you would turn to the news. News is central to our way of life today. It exists to satisfy our desire for vital information, as well as for all kinds of facts, figures, views and gossip.

In Media Studies, the term 'news' does not mean simply telling someone about something. News is a product presented to an audience by the media. Most people in our society get their news from television. The main evening news programmes can regularly attract some of the largest TV audiences, especially when an important national or international event has just occured. Television news is popular because of its ability to let the viewer be there when the action is happening.

People used to be able to get news only through newspapers, which was like receiving a letter about an event. The invention of radio allowed a more direct experience of happenings, but it was only as good as receiving a telephone call about them. The TV camera allows viewers to look at events as if they were with the camera operator. This sense of immediate reality has been increased by the development of satellite television stations, offering live news from around the world as it happens.

News is a product presented to an audience by the media.

People find it hard to live without news. This hunger for news, together with the increase in numbers of channels available to us through satellite and digital technology has led to what are known as rolling news stations. There are three British-based channels: Sky News, which started broadcasting in 1989, BBC News 24 and the ITN News Channel, which arrived on the scene much more recently. There is also the US-based CNN.

As the chapter on representation showed (pages 30–41), the impression that television news simply records exactly what is going on in the world is a false one. Most news is carefully packaged for us through the use of editing and the techniques of presentation. Even live 'as-it-happens' news cannot hope to reflect everything that is happening. It is limited by what the camera lens can pick up and by the direction in which the camera operator points the camera.

This chapter will take a close look at how one TV station produces the news for its viewers. You will see that a lot of work goes into making the news: it is a commodity put together by professionals, according to well-established methods.

Viewers tend to watch a rolling news channel like Sky News by dipping in and out of the service and watching for a short period of time rather than remaining glued to the screen for hours. By establishing a regular pattern of bulletins on the hour, every hour and headlines every 15 minutes, the audience knows when best to tune in for the latest information. The channel also has two special programmes – the Nine o'Clock News and Sky News at Ten. They summarise the big stories of the day and compete with those put out in the evening by the terrestrial channels.

	Morning from 5:30 am	Afternoon from Noon	Evening from 5:30	
BBC1	6 Breakfast Intl and financial latest		6–6:30 BBC News Intl	
ITV	5:30–6 ITV Morning News	12:30–1:30 ITV Lunchtime News Intl	6:30–7 ITV Evening News Intl	10–10:30 ITV News at Ten Intl
Channel 4			7–7:55 Channel 4 News Intl	
Channel 5	6–6:30 Sunrise Round-up of intl news		5:30–6 5 News Intl headline update	7:30 5 News Intl headline update
Sky News	6 am–10 Sunrise Round-up of national/intl news	12–2:30 Sky News Today Indepth headline review	10–10:30 Sky News at 10 Round-up of day's stories	

A chart showing the main television news bulletins of the day.

Sky News

SKY NEWS

Sky News has bulletins on the hour, every hour, headlines every 15 minutes and extended bulletins at 9pm and 10pm. During the rest of the day when some of the terrestrials have their morning/lunchtime/early evening news programmes, Sky News has rolling news bulletins: Sunrise 6am – 9am, Sky News Today 9am-5pm and Live at 5 which runs from 5pm to 8pm.

One advantage that rolling news offers an audience is the way that it can organise its coverage of major news events or breaking stories. Such stories as a major political row, a disaster or the sudden death of a major public figure will all be fitted into the rolling news format. Sky News likes to think that when a major story breaks, audiences turn to it to find out what is happening. General entertainment channels such as ITV, however, would be forced to reschedule programmes to extend their coverage of a major story, such as a rail crash or the death of a major public figure. The rolling news format also allows live coverage of such events as Prime Minister's Question Time from the House of Commons every Wednesday afternoon, when Parliament is sitting.

The newsroom is the heart of any newsgathering operation, and Sky Centre in west London is no exception. When the studio presenters read the news, the audience is seeing the end of a news-gathering process that has involved a large number of people and

Sky's newsroom.

a lot of technology along the way. Every morning, a meeting involving all the senior members of the news team is held to decide what are likely to be the main news stories of the day. Many news stories are known about well in advance, although they are often presented to us as though they had happened without any planning. Reporters call these 'diary jobs'. They would include a government minister or member of the Royal family visiting a disaster scene or opening a hospital. Court cases involving serious crimes such as murder or a celebrity caught drunk-driving or taking drugs all make good news stories and will be in the news editor's diary. The newsroom will make sure that reporters and camera crews are sent out to cover these events.

Of course, some stories will happen unexpectedly. That is what we tend to think of as news. Major accidents, such as plane or train crashes, floods, riots or serious crimes all come into this category, and there are always members of the news team on call in the studio ready to go out and cover these events.

The morning meeting will discuss the main stories taking place that day and decide what stories the news bulletins for that day will contain. They also try to decide which is likely to be the most interesting, or 'lead' story as this will go first in the bulletins. Of course, as unexpected stories occur, the contents of the bulletins will have to change.

In a news bulletin, stories have to be organised into what is called a running order. This means that the lead story goes first in the bulletin and then is followed by a less interesting story and so on. It is rather like the front page of a broadsheet newspaper where the lead story has the biggest headline and the most prominent position. What makes a story more interesting than another is decided according to what journalists call news values.

The morning meeting.

Television news

This is quite a difficult term to define but you will notice that stories that happen unexpectedly in this country to people who are famous tend to be reported more prominently than, say, an earthquake in a remote part of Asia, even though the latter might have much far serious consequences for the lives of the people involved.

Once the morning team has decided what its priorities for the day will be, news crews are sent out to go and get the stories. A news crew usually consists of a camera operator, a sound recordist and a reporter. The news crew will be looking to make their story as interesting and dramatic as possible. This way they will make sure that the producer of the bulletin will want to use it. This means they will be looking for:

- Interviews with people involved in the story
- Actions shots of the event, or at least its aftermath
- A shot of the reporter talking directly to the audience, known as a 'piece to camera'.

In addition they will need to get some general shots or 'cut-aways'. These are shots that will help add atmosphere to the report. For example, a report about a factory closure might show workers leaving the premises on their way home. Often the reporter will use these to accompany a voice-over which is when the reporter gives an off-screen commentary to explain the story while these images are shown on the screen. The camera crew will always make sure that they have shot more footage than they are likely to need so that they have plenty of material to choose from when they compile the report.

A running order

The report is usually put together back at the newsroom using one of the editing suites. It is sometimes necessary to edit a report at the scene, and portable edit suites are available for this purpose. The reporter usually works with an editor in the editing suite to turn the raw footage into a completed news report. The reporter will discuss with the producer how the news report will be put together – the points the report will make; the interviewees; and the pictures to be used.

The reporter will select the shots and the editor will join them together. Sound, such as a voice-over, can be recorded over any of the sequences of pictures where it is needed. It is likely that the reporter will have been told exactly how long the report should last in order to fit into the news bulletin. For example the report may have to be just two minutes long. If it is any longer it will not fit and the producer may decide to chop the ending or not use it at all.

Putting a report together

The reporter edits the raw film footage into a running order. This means deciding the order of the shots. The reporter selects the shots that they think tell the story best and places them in an order that leads the viewer through the report in a logical way.

Scripts are the commentary that go with the film footage. This involves writing the words that explain to the viewer what the story is about. The voice of the reporter usually delivers the commentary over general shots, where no one is being interviewed. It is the commentary that holds the report together, as it gives it a storyline with a beginning, a middle and an end.

Once the report is complete, the reporter 'files' it by adding it to the news list. The producer then knows there is a completed news report that can be placed in the running order of the bulletin.

As each news bulletin comes round, the producer has to decide what it will contain. Before the bulletin can be broadcast the news team has to come up with a plan, which involves:

The running order with each item timed precisely so that every minute is filled. While this is going on, they also need to keep an eye out for breaking stories. If an important news event occurs it may be necessary to re-arrange the running order to make room for it. It may even mean that a less important item is left out. As well as the news stories that the presenters will read out and the film reports, there may well be a studio guest such as a politician to be interviewed. There is also a slot put aside for sports news which is usually introduced by a journalist who specialises in sports coverage.

The reporter is responsible for editing the report. This happens in the edit suite.

A **script** will also have to be prepared. This needs to include: Headlines, stories to be read by the presenters, introductions to film reports and links between items.

LVO

A safer NHS - the
Government's resp
the Bristol babie
scandal.

LVO

Powell's pledge t
Afghanistan - we'
you rebuild for a
time to come.

LVO

Protect the pris
the UN's call on
detainees in Cub

LVO

Soul ofthe party
Smith spells out
Tories' new agen

LVO

Four match ban
fails to overtu
Cup red card.

UPSOT

Headlines

A The Government's preparing
to deliver its resp
the report on the
heart babies scanda

As many as 35 chil
and four were left
damaged during ope
the city's Royal
between 1988 and 1

Today, the Health
Secretary, Alan M
will announce pla
the NHS safer and
accountable in th

Among expected me
will be a new wat
monitor the perf
doctos, and prot
so-called "whist

VTR

TAKE VTR

*cgl super SKY
CORRESPONDENT
THOMAS MOORE

*cgl super CHILDREN'S
HOSPITAL BRISTOL

0'21

Stories to be read by the presenters

CANCER: WHITE
2 consultant radiologist, found guilty of
string of blunders at breast cancer unit,
expected to be struck off today - GMC @ 1600

IDS: PERCIVAL
Tories can cut taxes and improve public
services, so says IDS.

DISSENT
* Tory front bencher says in letter Tories are
racist, sexist etc…

SCHOOL: MCCARTHY 1700
Yorkshire school has 13 teachers in 14 weeks…

KENNEDY: PIX
Announces his engagement…

BLAIR: ITN Pool
PM attends international seminar of Christian
and Muslim scholars to be hosted b the
Archbishop of Canterbury - Lambeth Palace @
0915

BLAIR (3)
Appearing on BBCR5 - at 1700… Peter Allen
interview

BLAIR (2) SKY POOL
The P   rime Minister is holding an Inter
Faith Reception for the nine main religions in
UK - 1830

EXPLOSIVES: APPLEYARD
Jury due out in the trial of former agistrate
charged in connection with the

*Introductions to film reports
links between items*

The presenters need to have the script in good time so that they can become familiar with it and, if necessary, re-write bits of it so that it sounds better when they read it out. The presenters sometimes have the script typed onto pieces of paper which you often seen them shuffling at the end of a bulletin. Most of the time, however, they are reading the script from an autocue. This is a device that projects the script in large letters just beneath the lens of the camera. A presenter can read the autocue while looking straight into the camera lens so that it appears as though they are simply talking directly to the audience. In the Sky News studio, the cameras are all operated automatically by remote control, so it is possible for just one person, the floor manager, to look after the studio. The studio manager's job is to ensure that the presenters have their scripts ready, to let them know when the cameras go live and to look after any guests coming into the studio.

On your own

Write the script for a news report on your breakfast or lunch. Think of how you would describe what you ate, how it was prepared, how you ate it, what it tasted like and so on. Draw up a list of camera shots you would need for your report and then put them in the order in which you think they should appear. If you have access to video and editing equipment, you could have a go at producing the report.

On your own

Write a news story and read it out to a group as if you were a newsreader.(If you have access to a video camera, you might like to film it.) Discuss the story with the group.

- Does the way you have written the story make it come alive for the viewer?

- Is it difficult to read?

- How could it be improved?

Discussion

Why do you think news programmes often have two presenters? Why do you think they often feature a male and female presenter together? How do these presenters behave towards one another?

Sources of Stories

Without stories, news programmes would have nothing to broadcast. How do they get their stories? Sources for news stories include:

- **Emergency services** Reporters keep in close touch with police, fire and ambulance services, so that they will hear of any major incident as soon as possible.

- **Press releases** Thousands of organisations send out press releases to draw the media's attention to their news and events.

- **Contacts** These are people who are a good source of stories. They usually have jobs dealing with the public and so are able to pass on snippets of information.

- **Local councils** News organisations receive agendas and minutes from local council meetings, which provide a great deal of information that might be of interest to their viewers.

- **Tip-offs** Members of the public phone in with stories or subjects that they think should be investigated.

- **Other news organisations** These may in the form of 'wire services', which are computer systems that transmit updates of news to news organisations for a fee. They are provided by such companies as the Press Association (see the section of news agencies, page 118). The news media use wire services to get stories and information that they may not have the staff or money to cover themselves. Alternatively, news programmes may buy stories from freelance journalists, who work for themselves. Or they may simply follow up stories reported in newspapers or other news programmes.

Poll Reveals Public Want Ban on Illegally Logged Ancient Forest Timber Coming Into the UK.

Issued: February 19th, 2002.

Greenpeace today delivered a MORI poll to Environment Minister Michael Meacher showing that 87% of the British public want the government to ban illegal imports of wood from the world's ancient forests. Furthermore 80% want the British Government to pledge funding to a proposed international fund to protect the world's remaining ancient forests.

The UK is currently the top importer within the EU of illegal wood from tropical forests (1). We import plywood from Indonesian and Amazon rainforests, some of which is used as hoardings around building sites then trashed. Many doors and window frames come from the destruction of the forest home of Africa's great apes in the Congo Basin.

The poll is being released as Greenpeace launch **Save or Delete** a new campaign to protect the world's remaining ancient forests. To kick off the campaign gorillas and other 'Ancient Forest Messengers' will be roaming London —delivering the results of the poll to politicians, the timber trade and Harrods – who sell furniture made from illegally logged mahogany.

The messengers will also be unveiling billboard posters around London based on a powerful illustration of Jungle Book characters in a devastated jungle. The poster image has been produced for Greenpeace by maverick street artist Banksy - popular in the hip-hop scene for his stencils and graffiti images that portray striking political messages. The posters promote the campaign website saveordelete.com – where the public can take part in an online ref... download DIY campaign kits.

Ancient forests are home to two-thirds of all species of land-dwell... animals including the great apes. 80% of the world's original anci... already disappeared forever and today we are still losing an area ... the size of a football pitch every two seconds. If this destruction ... predict that tropical rainforests in Indonesia and West Africa coul... within decades – leading to the extinction of the great apes in ou...

Ten years ago at the Rio Earth Summit the world's governments ... to protect the world's remaining ancient forests. Yet since the S... ancient forests bigger than France and Spain has disappeared.

This year world governments have the chance to take real actio... remaining ancient forests. In April they will meet in The Hague... Forests Summit (the Convention on Biological Diversity).

Greenpeace is calling on governments to:

Clean up the international timber trade by stopping the impor... destructively logged timber.

Create a global ancient forest fund to pay for forest protection...

ENDS

PHOTOCALL DETAILS: A photocall with the launch poster and Ancient Forests Messengers outside the Houses of Parliament is being held at 10.30am on Tuesday 19th February on Parliament Green, opposite the House of Commons.

FOR MORE INFORMATION: contact Louise Edge in The Greenpeace UK Press Office on 0207 865 8255/07801 212993 or visit the website www.saveordelete.com

(1) The MORI poll was commissioned by Greenpeace. **MORI interviewed a representative quota sample of 1,001 adults aged 16+ across Britain.** Interviews were conducted by telephone between 15 – 17 February, 2002. **Summary of results** (the full poll results are available on www.saveordelete.com

Question One – How strongly do you agree or disagree with the following statement:

the Government should ban the import of illegally logged wood from the world's ancient forests?

87% strongly agreed or tended to agree

3% neither agreed nor disagreed

8% tended to disagree or strongly disagreed

2% didn't know.

Question Two – There have been calls for governments to set up an international fund to the tune of $15 billion each year to protect the world's ancient forests. How strongly do you agree or disagree that the British Government should pledge funding to the proposed international fund to protect the world's ancient forests?

80% strongly agreed or tended to agree.

3% neither agreed nor disagreed.

16% tended to disagree or strongly disagreed.

1% didn't know.

In groups

ON YR. OWN

Write and design a press release to publicise an event, and make a list of all the people you would send it to. The press release might be about a real or imaginary event, for example a protest about a new road, or a school play that is based on local history.

Opening the bulletin

News bulletins at Sky have a lot in common with those of other television channels, but there are also important differences. One big difference is the amount of live news or breaking news broadcast by Sky News.

Smartly dressed presenters sit behind a large desk in a studio. At Sky the presenters aim to present the news in a friendly manner.

Activity

ON YR. OWN

When Channel 5 started broadcasting, its newsreaders were the first to sit on the desk rather than behind it. Why do you think they decided to do this?

Behind the scenes.

Before the bulletin begins, the audience is made to feel that something important is about to happen. A caption announces the headlines of stories 'coming up' and at the bottom of the screen a clock counts down the seconds to the start of the bulletin. As the bulletin starts we read that Sky News reaches an audiences of 80 million people, in 40 countries, 24 hours a day. Music that reinforces a sense of drama is played until the bulletin begins with the presenter's voice reading the headlines as film is played of the day's events. There are usually three or four headlines before an imposing caption announcing SKY NEWS comes on our screens. The camera then slowly zooms into a mid shot, or talking head, of one of the presenters who introduces the lead story, before a report giving details of the story is played. The presenters usually alternate in introducing stories throughout the bulletin.

Throughout the bulletin the director, producer and their team are working in the gallery overlooking the studio. They are in contact with the presenters through earpieces which they wear. This is called talkback and it means that if there is any late change to running order, perhaps because of a technical problem with a film report, the presenter can be told what item to go to next. Presenters need to be good at reacting quickly to changing situation, for example, if a new story breaks while they are on air or a studio guest has to be substituted at the last minute. In this case they will call up information on "the wires" – news provided via a news agency, such as the Press Association or Reuters – which will provide them the latest news and background on a breaking story. The presenters will also use the Internet to find out information. The presenters ad lib too, combining information from the correspondent on the story, from the wires, from the producer speaking through the earpiece and from their own news knowledge.

Profile of Anna Botting/Presenter

A. HOW DID YOU GET INTO TELEVISION?

I started as a researcher for a production company in Manchester – working for free at first! I thought I needed some proper training – so I did a postgraduate course in broadcast journalism. A job as a reporter at numerous BBC local radio stations followed, then regional television, before heading to London and joining Sky News.

B. WHAT HOURS DO YOU WORK?

I get in about 7am, then it's a quick run to make-up, before I madly research the top stories of the day as if I'm about to sit an exam! I go on air at 9am to 1pm – 4 hours.

C. WHAT DOES YOUR WORK INVOLVE?

Sadly it's not just about reading the autocue (though there are some days I wish it was!) We need to do live interviews at very short notice – so we have to brief ourselves on what we KNOW will happen, while also trying to second guess what COULD happen. It means for a lot of the 4 hours you're on air, you find yourself constantly reading for the next interview. If a big story breaks, the scripts and running order go in the bin. The newsroom cranks up a gear to find anyone who can talk about it and their names get shouted in our ear by the gallery producer. We ad lib everything and totally busk it from then on – exhausting!

D. WHAT MAKES A GOOD TV STORY?

Pictures. A story can have all the drama and action in the world, but if you can't SHOW people what's happening, then it might as well be on radio.

E. WHAT DO YOU ENJOY MOST ABOUT YOUR JOB?

Every day is like dipping into an encyclopaedia – with each different news story you learn something new. And you can't help getting a buzz when a big story breaks when you're on air – you're witnessing history being made. That makes me feel very privileged.

F. WHAT ADVICE WOULD YOU GIVE TO SOMEONE WHO WANTS TO GET INTO THE MEDIA?

Have hope and be persistent. Expect a few rejection letters – we've all had them! Don't mind starting at the bottom – you can always show initiative and move on. If you like news and want to be a journalist, I recommend a course (I couldn't have managed without it). And then you have to work out if you want to go into broadcasting or newspapers. I couldn't decide, until someone said – where do you get most of your news from? For for me it was radio and TV – so the answer became obvious.

Regional news

As well as national news bulletins, both ITV and the BBC broadcast regional news programmes. These usually have names that reflect the area that they cover, such as Look North, North East Tonight or London Today. They are usually scheduled next to the national news bulletins or sometimes even form part of it. The format and content of regional news bulletins is very similar to the national news except that they focus on stories that have occurred in the local area. Many of these stories would not be important enough to be included in the national news although some of them might be.

Although these programmes contain quite a lot of serious news, the tone of them is often much lighter than the national bulletin. They have a more 'magazine' feel, which might include studio guests, such as a performer who is to appear at a local venue. Like local radio stations, regional news programmes often feature presenters with pronounced local accents. It is common to have male and female presenters who seem to enjoy poking fun at each other, rather like some couples do. They might, for example, chat about a particular news story and emphasis the ways in which men and women might react differently to it. They are likely to involve the weather forecaster or sports reporter in their banter. By doing so, they establish a relationship with the viewer, talking as though to an old friend using warm and familiar modes of address.

On your own

Draw up a list of qualities that a good TV news reporter should have if they are to be successful.

In groups

Pick members of your group to play the roles of producer, news editors and production assistants. From the list below, choose the items that you think should be included in your 30-minute evening broadcast. The broadcast is split into two parts, so you will have to decide which news goes into which half, in which order and how long each item should last.

Football results

Fashion feature

Road safety campaign

Interview with local author

Weather

Motorway pile-up

Dance group's new show

Pensioner mugged

Dog learns how to skateboard

Brother and sister reunited after 40 years

Local marathon runner wins

On you own

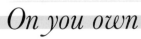

Watch your local evening news bulletin. What sort of stories does it feature? Are they all serious? What other items are included as well as news stories?

What is the news?

As the study of Sky News shows, the news on TV is the result of a long production process. It is constructed by a group of professional journalists and technical staff, who make the decisions about what the audience will see and how they will see it. Certain factors influence the form that television news takes:

Visual impact News stories that are visually exciting will often be chosen instead of those that are not. Big stories that do not lend themselves to TV may not be covered, while more frivolous stories that have a strong visual element may be included.

Journalistic decisions Producers and news editors decide which stories will be covered. Some serious stories may be dropped and replaced with light-hearted ones to add variety to a news programme. Producers and news editors also decide how a story will be told and from whose point of view.

Production decisions Camera footage that may shed a different light on a story may not be included in a report because it does not 'fit', or is of poor quality. Commentaries may be cut or rewritten to fit in with time constraints.

Review

Television is the most popular of the news media, with millions of people tuning in to find out the latest. On the surface, TV news seems to be a 'window' through which the viewer sees events happening in the world. However, television news is actually the product of a long manufacturing process, which involves journalists selecting, ordering and editing information and film reports. What the audience sees on the screen is not 'reality', but a representation of events that has been put together by professional news-makers.

The coursework component of the exam (AQA paper 1) is worth 50% of the total marks. It consists of one major piece of practical production and three assignments.

The practical production

'Candidates are required to undertake a practical production, from conception to realisation, together with a supporting account of 700–800 words.'

This is Section B of the AQA coursework paper, which is worth 25% of the total marks available for the exam. Many Media Studies courses include some similar coursework.

Production work is an important part of your GCSE. Many students find that it is what they enjoy most about their course. However, for others it can be a source of great frustration. You must, therefore, be prepared to put some thought into the early stages if you are to avoid the pitfalls that may lie ahead.

Remember, too, that all the work you put into planning, sometimes called pre-production, can gain you marks. If you want to do well, you must do this thoroughly and be sure you include it as part of the work you want to have marked.

Getting started

Before you can start work on your production, it makes sense to think about a number of issues.

Resources

The first and most obvious thing to consider is what equipment there is for you to use. It is quite natural at thus stage to want to get your hands on sophisticated technical equipment, such as a video-editing facility or recording studio. Not only is it fun to play with, but potentially it can give a better quality finish and hence make your production look good.

Remember, though, that you have to be able to operate such equipment properly if you are to get the results that you hope for. Simply using the equipment is in itself no guarantee of success. On the contrary, you may end up with something worse that if you had settled for more basic equipment that you were more familiar with.

Make a list of equipment that it might be possible to use. Remember that if your teacher agrees, you may be able to use equipment from sources other than your school or college. For example, you may be able to get hold of a video camera for a weekend. You must, however, make it clear if you are given help by people outside.

Now make a list of your current skills that you think might prove useful in working on your production. Then make another list of skills that you might need to learn to help you complete your work. For example, maybe you already know how to use a word processor, but you might feel that it would be useful to learn a software program such as Publisher, Pagemaker or Quark Xpress to help you do layouts for a magazine.

An appropriate medium

Once you have established what is available, the next step is to decide on the most appropriate medium for your idea. Suppose, for example, you decide to base your idea on providing a news service for your school or college. Obviously there are several media you might choose for this:

- Video – recording your own locally based lunchtime news programme
- Radio – a similar approach using recording or broadcast equipment
- Print – a newspaper or magazine for distribution to your fellow students and staff.

Each of these approaches will have its own advantages and disadvantages, so you obviously need to think hard about which is going to be best for what you want to do.

Important tip

Start making a note of all your ideas and the decisions you have reached at this point. It is important information which you need to put in your supporting account (see pages 219–225).

The audience

What is the audience for your production? There is no point in producing a magazine no one wants to read or a video no one wants to watch. Don't assume that if a topic interests you, then everyone else will want to know about it. Remember, getting the attention of the audience is hard, and keeping it is even harder.

Before you launch into your production, it helps to know who your audience will be and how they would like to see the information presented. The best way to do this is by undertaking some audience research, which means asking people the right questions. You can do this in a number of ways. Perhaps you will decide to design a detailed questionnaire for people to complete. Alternatively you may find it as effective to do a survey of your potential audience by simply asking for their views informally. Either way you need to undertake some form of market research to find out about your audience and their interests and needs.

Viz started as a magazine produced by a few friends; it now has a national circulation.

Discussion point

AS A CLASS

- What makes some media texts more interesting than others?
- What is special about your idea? Why will people want to see, read or hear it?

For example, you might want to produce a new football magazine. Start off by finding out what your potential audience reads now and what they like about it. What improvements would they like to see? Many successful publishing ventures have begun with people finding a gap in the market and producing a magazine to fill it.

You may be tempted to choose to produce material for an audience similar to yourself (in other words, your peers). This has the advantage that you will know quite a lot about the needs of this group. There is, though, a disadvantage in that you can easily confuse your own personal interests, tastes and attitudes with those of your proposed audience.

Often it helps to target a group of people with whom you are less familiar. This way you will be forced to pay close attention to their likes and dislikes. Groups of people you might not have considered as a possible audience can include:

- Retired people
- Members of a minority (to which you do not belong).

Ask yourself what distinctive needs these groups are likely to have. How will your product satisfy these needs?

Should I work in a group?

Media production is often a team effort. Look at the list of credits at the end of any film or TV programme to see how many people helped to make it. You may decide to work as part of a team to make your product. However, there are a number of points you need to bear in mind before embarking on a group project:

- Don't try to form a team with too many people in it. Four is an absolute maximum.
- Remember, each group member must produce an individual supporting account.
- Agree before you start how decisions will be made.
- Establish individual roles.
- Agree a timetable
- Make sure you stick to what you have agreed!

A key factor in how well your group works is how you make decisions. You might decide to ask one person to act as the leader, in the same way that a director or editor takes responsibility for a film or newspaper. All members of the group will then have to accept his or her decisions. Another approach is to be democratic. This way all members of the group have an equal say and vote on key decisions. Some 'alternative' and community magazines are run like this. Whichever approach you choose, it is important that you all keep to this way of working. Otherwise your production may suffer because of squabbling within the group.

So, who does what?

If you decide that a group production is what you want to do, there is another important issue to consider. When your work is assessed, it needs to be clear who did what, so that marks can be awarded according to each person's contribution to the piece.

Roles and responsibilities need to be sorted out from the start and written down, so that everyone is clear what they are expected to do. You probably already know that a big problem in group work is caused by people not doing their job. Bear in mind that this can be for a number of reasons: lack of confidence, for example. Be prepared to make allowances, and always be sure you have a plan to cover for people who may let you down. At a simple level, this may mean sharing out the extra work. At worst, it could mean rearranging a whole day's work.

You may find it useful to make a list of different roles that people play in some aspect of media production: all the jobs that appear at the end of a TV programme, for example, or the list of people in the front of a magazine. Now decide what the important jobs on your production will be.

Recap

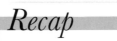

- Find out what resources are available.
- Choose an appropriate medium.
- Find out about your audience.
- Decide whether to work in a group or by yourself.
- If you are in a group, make sure you are clear about roles and responsibilities.

Remember: you need to do all this for your supporting account.

All you need now is an idea to work on! Obviously, you will have thought about this already. It is likely, though, that you may have changed your original idea in response to some of the issues raised above.

Don't be too ambitious. It is important that you are realistic about what you can achieve. A half-hour soap opera or a 100-page magazine is a daunting task, even with several people working on it. Don't be afraid to scale it down: you could maybe produce the opening five minutes of your soap, or the front cover and some key pages of the magazine. This way you will do a much better job and show what you would be capable of, given more time and resources.

The inside cover of a magazine may show you all the different jobs that make up the team that produces it.

Working on your idea

One useful way to begin your production is to research how your topic is treated by existing mass media. This will give you the chance to look at the forms and conventions used to address the audience by media institutions.

For example, the market is full of magazines that publishers want young girls to buy. If you are thinking of producing a magazine aimed at a similar market, look closely at some of the material already on sale. You might like to think about:

- **Content:** what themes do you find most often?
- **Layout:** how is the magazine organized? Is the front cover similar each week? Are some items more important than others?
- **Illustration:** what sort of photographs and graphics are used? How do these relate to the text?
- **Style:** how does the magazine talk to its readers? Does it tell them how to live their lives? Does it suggest role models who they might look up to? Does it feature minority groups, such as young girls with disabilities?

The next important bit of research will be about the subject matter itself. Whether you want to make a video, write an article or produce a radio package, you need to find out about your topic. To do this may involve you in a number of activities:

- You may need to telephone people to ask if you can interview them or get permission to film.
- You may need to prepare to interview someone.
- You may need to find information from existing sources such as libraries or local archives.

Don't forget that the best media production is about people. Even if you are dealing with quite a technical subject, such as a local archaeological dig, tell the story from the viewpoint of the people involved.

Important reminder

Make sure you keep all this research – you need to incorporate it into your supporting account.

Writing a script

A lot of what the media produces tries to look spontaneous, as though it has happened with very little planning or scripting. If you try to work like this, you'll soon discover how much careful preparation goes into quite a straightforward production. Documentaries, which often seem simply to record what is happening, need a good deal of careful planning and organisation.

You need to do some writing before you can even begin to think about using equipment. For video or radio work, this involves producing a script. For a magazine, you need a rough draft of your articles and features before you plan the layout. Remember the work you did on narrative in the chapter on media language. Think about how you will make your narrative work.

1

Julie (to herself): *Why do I have to go home on my birthday?*
Music: *Grange Hill music in background, played very softly but heard*

2

Danny: *Awright Julie, hear it's your birthday!*
Julie: *Yep, and I've got to go home.*

3

Danny: *Well, maybe next year you can go out and have some fun?*
Julie: *Yeh, maybe.*

4

Neighbour: *'Appy birthday luv', have a nice time now!*
Music: *'One foot in the Grave' theme tune, played softly but to be heard [or alternatively, 'Last of the Summer Wine']*

5

Family and friends: *HAPPY BIRTHDAY!!!*
Music: *'Happy Birthday' being sung*
Effects: *cheers and party poppers in background*

6

Julia: *Danny!!! I thought you said I'd be having a party next year?*
Danny: *Yes, another one!*
Music: *'Take my Breath away' from 'Top Gun' film*
Effects: *party noises in background*

An example of a basic storyboard. More information can be added if necessary – for example, the duration of each shot and details of any special effects. You could also get actors to pose for photographs, and use these instead of drawings.

Suppose you want to produce a short piece of TV drama – an extract from a new soap, for example. There are a number of ways to produce a script. One method is to use a storyboard. This is particularly effective for short sequences where you need to focus on the visual elements, such as camera movement.

Notice in the example on page 209 how the sound is linked closely to the visuals. Look at how the visuals vary between types of shot (for example CU, LS) and different camera angles to produce a visual narrative. Being skilled at drawing is less important than having ideas about how to make a video or film sequence visually interesting. A good storyboard is an opportunity to try out ideas to help you save time when you start using the equipment.

Another approach to scripting for film or TV is shown below.

The storyboard and the script show how you can get your basic idea down quickly. Before shooting the sequence, you may want to develop your idea by adding some further detail to give a sense of how the finished sequence might look. You should consider adding information about:

- *Shot size (LS, CU – see pages 18–19)*
- *Camera movement – (pan, zoom – see page 20)*
- *Transition or edit (cut, dissolve – see page 20)*
- *Length of time shot will be on the screen.*

AFRAID OF THE DARK
Script for the opening sequence of a short television film.

Visuals

Establishing shot of a small town viewed from a distance in day light.

Montage of shots of people shopping, going into and out of offices, catching buses, driving cars. Parents collecting small children from school.

Streets at dusk. Streetlamps coming on.

People hurrying to catch a bus or hail a taxi.

Empty street – night time.

Shot of family at home watching TV.

Old man walking through dark and empty streets.

Sound/dialogue

Narrator By day, Weatherfield was just an ordinary town, somewhere in the north of England. People went about their daily business, in the office, at the shops, on their way home from school.

But then, darkness must fall… Suddenly the streets are empty. (*Eerie music played softly in background.*)

Nothing stirs. (*Music fades.*)

Everyone is safe at home, huddled round the television.

Except for one unfortunate soul, who has ventured into the night.

Here the convention is to write the dialogue on the right and to explain the visuals on the left. This format can work well for programmes where words are important, such as the voice-over for a documentary or the dialogue spoken by actors. You can develop this kind of script to include information about camera movement, sound effects and music. If you are using actors, they can have a copy to learn their lines.

Useful tip

If you want to write a dialogue for a piece of fiction, listen to people talking – on buses, in shops or at school. Try to make your own writing natural, as though it were spoken by people you have listened to.

Discussion point AS A CLASS

Does the dialogue on TV soaps sound natural? Or does it sound as though it has been written for actors to deliver?

Now you have made a start on the pre-production work, it is time to look at how to go about the production itself.

NOTE TO TEACHERS

It is a good idea at this stage to get students to fill in a production registration sheet. This has the benefit of focusing students on precisely what they intend to do for the production and how they intend to work. In addition, it provides an opportunity to raise some of the broader issues that will need to be dealt with in the supporting account.

Production skills

It would be impossible in this section to explain to you how to use every piece of equipment available. Not only is there a wide variety of equipment around, but technology changes so rapidly that the information would soon be out-of-date. Instead, here are some general rules and advice on the different bits of technology you might want to use.

Video

Most video cameras have similar features and controls, even though tape formats may be different. One way to learn how to use the equipment is to take out a camera and see what it can do.

Don't expect too much from your first attempts, though. You will need some practice before you get the hang of using a camera.

First, make sure you are familiar with the basic controls. You will need to know how to:

● Switch the camera on
● Load a tape
● Set the camera to record
● Use the pause button

It's also a good idea to know how to check that the batteries are OK and that there is enough light for you to film in. Check in the manual or ask someone who has used the equipment before.

Recording

Be sure you can tell when the camera is recording. It is very frustrating to set up and film a scene only to discover the camera wasn't running.

If you want to make your efforts look professional, you need to try to avoid some of the common pitfalls students often fall into when they first try to make films. A very common mistake is to move the camera too much. This may take the form of using the zoom (moving in and out on the subject), panning (moving horizontally to follow the action) and/or moving vertically. Another temptation is to hold the camera by hand and move around after the action.

All of these techniques have their place. Hand-held camera can be very effective in chase sequences, for example. But often the best shot is achieved by holding the camera steady on a tripod and letting the action take place within the frame. Watch how professionals use a film or movie camera. You will notice how little movement there actually is.

It is also important to try to get variety into the way you frame your images. In the chapter on language (pages 18–20), we saw how visual narratives are composed of different shots. Here is your chance to look at how you can use different angles and sizes of shot to make your film interesting.

How can you include sound on your film? Video cameras have an integral microphone that will record sound synchronized with the pictures. Sound quality is radically improved, however, if an external microphone is used, especially a directional one. This will allow you to get in close when someone is speaking, cutting out any unnecessary background noise. Don't forget, though:

● Keep the microphone out of shot.
● No unnecessary talking when recording is taking place.

If you are intending to edit your video (see pages 214–215), you should also take care to ensure plenty of run-in time before each shot. This means letting your camera run for, say 10 seconds before any action takes place. This way, when you come to edit, vital action should not be lost. For example, if you want to film someone entering a room, keep the camera running and focused on the door for 10 seconds before your character walks through it. If you intend to use a professional edit suite, it is essential to provide enough run-in time.

If you are going to be able to edit your work, you don't have to shoot the film in the sequence in which it will finally appear. Your shooting script, which sets out the order in which scenes are recorded, must be based on the locations you are going to use and the availability of actors and props.

It's always a good idea for one member of the crew to log the scenes you shoot so that you know in what order sequences appear on the tape. If one of you has a video recorder that shows timings in minutes and seconds, this can be done when the tape is replayed at home.

The single camera interview. The interviewer must ask their questions twice so that the interview can be edited to look 'natural'.

(a) The 'establishing two shot', which shows the interviewer and interviewee together in a single frame.

(b) Close-up of an interviewee answering a question. Camera looking over interviewer's shoulder.

(c) The interviewer asks a question or nods in agreement. Camera is now looking over the shoulder of the interviewee.

In pairs

IN PAIRS

Imagine you want to conduct a short interview on location, for example, outside your school or college. Devise a storyboard showing how you would go about this, bearing in mind that you can only use one camera. How will you get any shots other than those of the two people involved in the interview?

Editing

The editing equipment available to you may vary between professional equipment and nothing at all. If the latter is the case, you will need to plan your film very carefully and to edit 'in camera'.

EDITING IN CAMERA

Editing in camera needs a lot of careful preparation and planning. You need to storyboard your film precisely and shoot all your scenes in the exact order in which they will appear in the finished film. After that, it is a question of using the pause control on the camera to get a clean cut between each section of the film. Remember, it is possible to tape over bits you got wrong, but you need to take great care not to erase the bits you got right. The camera's own playback facility is very useful here to show you exactly what you have recorded on to the tape. A pair of headphones will let you hear the sound, too.

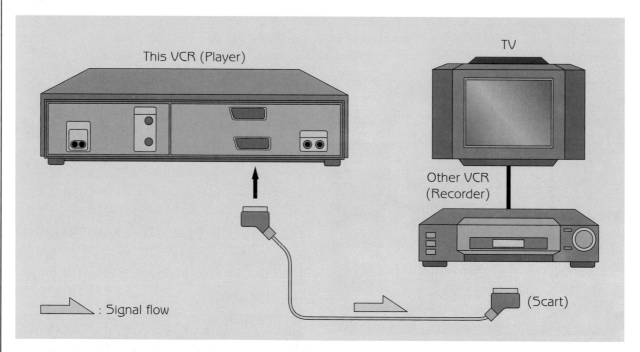

Editing film by linking two domestic video machines with a scart connector. The signal from the left-hand machine is fed to the second machine, which is used to record, via a scart connector. When putting in an edit, both machines should have the video tape laced up and ready over the heads. This way there will be no tear in the picture as the edit 'crashes in' when the pause button on the recording machine is released at the right moment. The instruction manuals of most recorders explain in detail how this arrangement can be set up for their particular model. They also give useful information about audio dubbing and linking up a video camera.

Even if you can't get you hands on proper editing equipment, it is always possible to link together two standard VHS machines, such as you may have at home, and use the pause facilities to 'crash edit' your footage together (see diagram). This is a basic form of 'linear' editing. This means that images and sounds from one tape are recorded onto a second tape in a sequence determined by the editor. Some machines also have an audio dub facility that allows you to replace the existing soundtrack with a voice-over or music. ('Dubbing' is copying from one tape to another.) Some cameras also link to a domestic video recorder to allow editing of tapes.

More common today however is non linear editing. Widely used in the television industry, this technology is becoming increasingly available in homes and educational establishments. A video recorder or digital camera can be interfaced with a personal computer that is loaded with a special software programme. This allows a tape to be edited on the computer.

Titles and end credits can help make your video look professional. Some video cameras have a capacity for generating basic titles. It is also possible to link a computer to your editing suite to create titles. If no such technology is available, then you can always make your own captions, either using copy printed from a computer or simply by writing on a whiteboard and using a camera to record them. If your camera has a switch to create negative images, this can be particularly effective.

While you will want to get the best finish you can for your video, always remember it's the ideas that are important. You will be judged more on your ability to work within the limitations imposed on you by the technology available than on the professional quality of the end product.

Don't forget that once you have finished editing your video, you should remove the plastic safety tab to prevent your work from being accidentally wiped. It's also a good idea to have your tape cued at the start of your film, ready to show it.

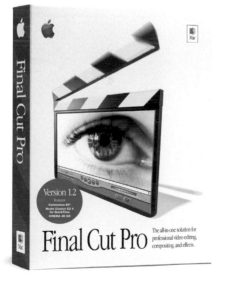

Software available for editing digitally.

Radio/sound

You can easily forget radio as a possible medium for a production. It doesn't have the glamour of video. Yet it is a very popular medium, especially with young people, and you don't necessarily need a lot of equipment to make a high quality programme. If you are lucky enough to have a recording or broadcasting studio, then you will be able to produce high quality work – either as a package, where you record and edit information, or perhaps a live show, using a combination of music and talk to create an interesting piece of radio. Even if you can't get

access to a sophisticated studio, it is still possible to create imaginative and lively radio work.

Obviously, you need some means of recording. A basic tape/Minidisc recorder with either an in-built microphone or, better, an external mike, will get you started.

The technology of radio is changing. Traditionally radio journalists used to record on open reel tape on portable machines and then spliced the tape – literally by cutting out the bits they didn't want with a razor blade and sticking the tape together with adhesive tape. Now most radio programmes are edited and recorded

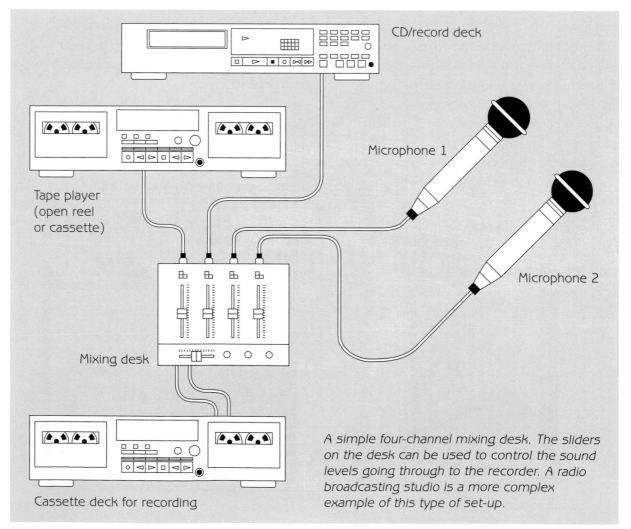

CD/record deck

Microphone 1

Microphone 2

Tape player
(open reel
or cassette)

Mixing desk

Cassette deck for recording

A simple four-channel mixing desk. The sliders on the desk can be used to control the sound levels going through to the recorder. A radio broadcasting studio is a more complex example of this type of set-up.

digitally, using computer based sound editing programmes, similar to non-linear video-editing software. Even if you do not have access to this sophisticated technology, you can achieve a reasonable effect by simply using a twin cassette deck or wiring two decks together.

By using the pause control on each deck you can transfer the bits you want from one tape to another. If the tape deck is a good one, there will be little loss of quality in the process of dubbing sound from one deck to another.

One problem with sound recording is getting the levels right. This means making sure that the bits you record and join together are all about the same volume. It may be possible on your equipment to monitor the volume through a meter and adjust it accordingly, but you will have to be well organised.

If you can get hold of a mixing desk, this can be really useful. Recording studios use this equipment for making records. What it allows you to do is to put together several different sound sources and to fade up and down the level of each. If you want to put together your own radio show, a mixer can be used to fade in and out music and speech to give a professional effect.

However you decide to make your radio product, don't forget your audience. Think about what music they might want to hear or what sort of studio guest they might want to listen to. Equally, consider what news and information is important to them. A good radio programme is more than just playing your favourite music.

Newspapers and magazines

Producing a magazine or newspaper allows you to work independently outside class time without having to use technical equipment. Of course, many of you will want to use computer technology to make your finished product, but in the early stages a lot of work can be done without a computer.

Some students get poor marks for this type of work because they simply copy, or even cut and paste, articles and features from existing sources. Inevitably, some of your ideas may link in with items previously published, but if you are to do well you must generate your own ideas to capture the interest of your audience.

The best magazines are likely to challenge some of the assumptions most frequently made in popular publications. Think, for example, of some of the issues raised in the chapter on representation (pages 30–41) and see how you might look for new ways of representing ideas and addressing your audience.

If you are able to use a computer for your work, then it is worth trying to do your layout and design work using software for on-screen page make-up. If you can't do all of the layout on screen, it may be possible to produce some of the work using a computer and to complete your page design by more traditional methods.

One way in which you can add originality to your work is to take your own photographs. A digital camera will allow you to take photographs and download them straight onto a computer where you can adapt the image to fit in with the page you are designing. Alternatively you can scan photographs and images you have taken or found, and manipulate these. For example, you may find you need to crop and scale them if they are to work effectively. You might decide to organise a fashion shoot, using friends as models, or perhaps take photographs to illustrate a story or feature article.

Cropping means selecting the area of the print you want to use; scaling means deciding the size that will fit best into your layout.

A photo cropped and scaled up.

Remember, too, the importance of a caption to anchor the meaning you want to give to your image. Look at the way captions are used in publications aimed at a similar market to yours.

There are a few simple tips worth keeping in mind if you want to produce a newspaper or magazine that will be attractive to your audience:

- Remember that your front page is like a shop window. Be sure your best stories are on it. You have less than 20 seconds to persuade the average browser to buy it.
- Try to get a mixture of stories – some long, some short, some happy, some sad.
- Create variety with your pictures too. Look for variety of topics, and vary the size of the images.
- Don't put too much detail in photographs – make sure they are clear. Be sure to have the people in them doing things, not just standing in a line.
- Use features such as crosswords, puzzles and comic strips to break up the blocks of text.
- Organise your publication so that people can easily find their way around. Use headlines and pictures as 'signposts' to help them.
- Most important of all: know who your audience is and what they are interested in. Never take them for granted!

Other technologies

We have looked at three popular ways of doing the practical production. The syllabus says that you can use any media format. Such areas as computer games, comics, animation or interactive computer technology are all open to exploration, if you have the relevant skills and interest. Do remember, though, that you are looking at mass media and the codes and conventions under which it operates. That has important implications for the type of production you undertake, particularly in relation to how you define the audience for your product. If you are uncertain, then be sure to check with your teacher that your idea is acceptable and falls within the syllabus. It would be a shame to do a lot of work and then discover that you wouldn't get any marks for it.

Website design is becoming increasingly popular with students, especially as access to computer technology is more readily available. If you do decide to design a website, it's a good idea to take a look at similar sites to the one you want to create. Remember too that you should try to ensure your site has a connection with some aspect of the mass media. A personal home page with details of yourself, your family and the cat is not going to offer the same opportunities to engage with media concepts as a site dedicated to film reviews or news about the music scene.

The supporting account

You must submit a supporting account along with your practical production. Even if you have worked as part of a team the account has to be your own individual effort.

Many students think that once they have completed work on their production, it is time to have a rest. Sadly, this is not true. What you write about your production is just as important as the production itself – and in some cases more important.

Writing the account

A supporting account is a written commentary, linked to the work you did on your practical production. It should show some of the thinking behind your practical production. Therefore, it should help explain how you arrived at your decisions and why the finished product looks or sounds like it does.

I CHOSE MEDIA STUDIES BECAUSE I THOUGHT I WOULDN'T HAVE TO WRITE MUCH

The syllabus recommends a length of about 700–800 words and says that in your account you should relate the work on your practical production to the key concepts. To put this another way, you are being asked to show what you have learned about the media from doing your own practical work. This can best be achieved by making connections between your production and the work on the key concepts that you have done in other parts of the course. This is an important skill you need to develop at any level of media education. You need specifically to look at the context, audience and purpose of your product.

The specification talks about 'writing an evaluation of the production'. You will often hear the word 'evaluation' used in the context of the supporting account. One thing it means is that you should take the opportunity to stand back and look at what your finished product has achieved. Your job is to decide how far your work is effective for the purpose you intended it. In fact, you are being asked to judge your own work in the way that you have learned to evaluate other mass media products.

You should also consider whether the medium you chose – for instance – radio, was right for what you decided to do, or whether it would have been better to have chosen a different medium.

By placing the camera in front of Jason and zooming in, I made it look as though the stranger was much closer to him than he actually was.

Remember that when we were looking at your particular production work, you were asked to make notes on any important research you undertook and decisions you made. You may like to approach this by keeping a diary or log. In this, you would record what you have done at each stage of the process, and, in some cases, evaluate these activities as you do them. This approach is fine as the basis for your supporting account, especially if you are going to use it as a reminder of what you did. It is probably not a good idea, though, to make this the actual account you submit. The danger of this approach is that it simply becomes a description of what you did – or, in many cases, didn't do.

Before starting filming we looked at some documentaries that had been shown on television earlier in the month. We were particularly interested to see how they captured the viewers' attention in the opening sequence.

Don't buy this magazine: it's a waste of money. They have the same articles every week and the reviews of the new albums are dreadful. They think we're all interested in one type of music.

We evaluate media products all the time.

Today we planned to film the sequences where the students get into trouble with the teacher. Unfortunately Rachel and Mike were off sick so we couldn't do it.

Today we had hoped to do the layout work for the article on boys' fashion but John forgot to bring the computer disk.

We did a really good interview with a local shopkeeper about her attitude to the parking ban but unfortunately the tape broke when we took it out of the recorder.

We had some important decisions to make about how we were going to approach the topic of the shortage of decent recreational facilities in our local town. We considered making an item for the regional news programme, which is shown after the national news each evening. We decided, though, that it wasn't really sufficiently newsworthy for a programme covering such a large area. The local newspaper seemed a better idea.

The best way to produce a good supporting account may be to organise it under a series of headings, like those used from here to page 224.

Context

Where do you think your product belongs? If it is a TV programme, what channel would it go on, and what time of night would it be shown? If you have produced a magazine, who might want to publish it? Is it something you would find on the shelves of your newsagent's, or is it likely to be sold in a different way – by subscription or on the streets, like *The Big Issue*?

Some media products have a fairly narrow or local market. A fanzine about up-and-coming bands in your area is a good example. It is still important that you look at the context of the product. How will it be distributed? How will you ensure your audience gets to see it?

You also need to talk about context even if you have chosen to create just a sequence from or a part of a larger product. For example, trails for films at the cinema or radio advertisements are consumed by audiences within specific contexts.

The work you did in the chapter on media language and its codes and conventions (pages 16–17) is important here. Look at your own production and compare it to professional productions that occupy a similar context. How does it compare? Have you adopted the same conventions or have you chosen a different approach?

Audience

You have learned about audiences and why they are important in an earlier chapter (pages 58–75). In your supporting account, audiences are also a key element, especially from the viewpoint of identifying who they are. In this section write about what you found when you did some market research (see pages 66–69).

> I needed to find out if there would be people interested in a fanzine about local bands. A good place to start was the local record shop where I asked the manager if any of the local customers ever asked for a local gig guide or something similar.

What is your audience? Remember that there are often several audiences for a media product. A women's magazine may well have an important secondary audience of male readers. Remember also to think about your audience in terms of gender, age, and social and educational background. What assumptions did you make about their expectations?

How will you reach your audience? Obviously you will need to relate this section to what you have written about the context. Should your audience be offered any additional follow-up materials, such as a telephone helpline or an information pack? You can mention this, even though you may not have prepared one as part of your product.

Purpose

What is your product for? What is its function? You may argue that it has more than one function. If so, explain what these are. Is it there to entertain, to inform, to provoke debate?

Very often the success of your production will depend on you having a clear sense of its purpose. It may be, however, that the purpose has changed during the production process. What started out as a light-hearted piece, the purpose of which was to entertain, may have turned into something controversial and thought-provoking. You need to explain how this came about. What factors and decisions along the way caused it to change?

> I was worried that the purpose of the radio programme was not clear. I wanted to get a message across to people about the dangers of drinking and driving, but at the same time I wanted to produce an entertaining show with plenty of music.

A women's magazine may well have an important secondary audience of male readers.

Evaluation In this section you need to look at your production and decide how successful you have been in fulfilling your original intention – how effective your product has been.

It may be that you have market-tested your product. This would have involved showing or playing it to a sample of your audience and getting their reactions. Don't just write, 'Our audience thought it was really good' (even if they did), but try to get some constructive criticism from them by way of specific responses. Was it interesting? Were there bits that went on for too long? All this information should then be included in your supporting account.

> All in all, I think our production was successful. People who saw it, including parents and teachers, found it entertaining and informative. I still feel it is too long, though perhaps that is because I have become bored after seeing it so many times.

You might also like to think about how you would improve it. Imagine you have the chance to start again. How would you try to make the end product different or better?

Self-assessment Another important area you need to look at is yourself. You probably learned a lot about yourself while working on your production. For some of you, it may have sparked off ideas about your career, getting a job or choosing what course you will do next. As part of your account, you may find it useful to answer the following questions:

- Am I good at managing my time? Do I meet the deadlines that I set myself or those set by other people?

- Do I work well unsupervised, or do I need someone to tell me what to do and to urge me on?
- Am I a good member of a team? Do I contribute well, or do I have to be forced to work? Am I good at sharing ideas with other people? Do I get on with other people?
- Do I have to get my own way all the time, or am I prepared to compromise?

You might also like to write about the roles you played within the group. For example, if you worked with video, did you like to be in front of the camera? Did you enjoy the technical aspects of the production, such as editing or graphics?

> Our group worked well together. Rebecca wrote down everything we agreed and the names of the people who would do things and the date when they should have it finished. This way, if someone didn't pull their weight, everybody knew.

What skills have you learned? These need not just be technical skills, such as using a word processor, but more general skills such as making appointments over the telephone. Do you feel more confident as a result of doing the production?

However you decide to organise your personal account – and there is no right way or wrong way to do it – remember that it is your opportunity to show what you have learned in the process of your production work. Even if you are not very pleased with the end product and feel your production has been a failure, a good supporting account, looking at what went wrong and how it might be improved next time, can gain you valuable marks in this part of the exam. This is especially true if you have some good planning materials, such as scripts and bits of research, that you can include with the practical production.

Presenting the account

There is no set format for presenting your supporting account, so you have some freedom to choose a style that is best for you. What is important is that you present it in such a way that it is both attractive and easy to read. If you can use a word processor, then that will help, but writing the account by hand is also acceptable.

To make it easier to read, consider using a series of headings. These will help the reader navigate through the text. You may like to consider some of the headings used above (pages 222–224) as a means of organising your account.

You can also included diagrams and tables, or even photographs and drawings where these are appropriate, to illustrate a point. For example, you may have made some rough sketches or photographs to show the camera positions for a scene you filmed. These could be included as a part of the explanation of the thinking behind the shot.

Some design work that includes a front cover will also enhance the appearance of the account and provide those among you with a flair for design with the chance to show off your skills.

Remember also that you are set a word limit of 700-800 words for producing this supporting account. It is important that you do not exceed this limit. It is also important that you do not fall a long way short of it. Be prepared, therefore, to edit your first draft, if it is under or over the required length. If you are a long way over, you need to decide which information should have priority and be prepared to leave some out if necessary. If you are just a few words over, you may be able to go through the account cutting words and phrases that are not essential to the meaning. These skills of editing and prioritising information will be important to you one day if you decide to work in the media.

GCSE Media Studies

Name	Alan Trewartha
Centre	Ryton Comprehensive School
Date	15th May 2001
Title	A Fanzine for local bands The supporting account

THE ASSIGNMENTS

'Candidates are required to submit *three* coursework assignments each of 700–800 words or the equivalent in design and production work'

This is Section A of the coursework paper (Paper 1), which is worth 25% of the total marks available for the exam.

This means that you teacher will choose the best three assignments you have produced in the course of your Media Studies programme. Your teacher will make sure that the three assignments chosen cover all three assessment objectives (knowledge, analysis and production skills), show an understanding of the four key concepts of language, representation, institutions and audience, and cover at least two different media. The assignments must avoid the topic of the controlled test (see pages 230–240).

The specification says 'the equivalent in design and production work, because many of the assignments include visual work, such as storyboards, or even practical work such as video recordings. Although these may not include words, the amount of time you have spent producing them will be taken into account and given an equivalent value in terms of word length.

The type of assignment you are given to do will obviously depend on your teacher. Most probably, you will be provided with a sheet of your instructions with a list of tasks to be completed, very like the sample assignment shown here. On some occasions, however, it may be more appropriate for your teacher to give you instructions verbally. Either way, it is important that you make certain that you understand exactly what you are being asked to do. If you are not sure, it is better to ask now rather than find out when you have already done a lot of work that may be irrelevant.

You will find that much of the work you do for an assignment will allow you to respond in your own individual way. Although you will have to show some knowledge and offer some information, most of the time it is your ability to show your understanding and to think critically that is being tested. In many assignments, you will also need to show that you can be creative and come up with ideas. Your coursework may well provide you with several opportunities to develop your own responses and ideas.

ASSIGNMENT:
Looking at newspapers

You have been given the front pages of a broadsheet and a tabloid newspaper published on the same day. Look at them and attempt the following tasks:

Task 1

Identify which is the main story on each front page. If both lead with the same story, write a comparison of the two versions, in terms of the content and style of each. If each title has a different lead story, look at each story individually and analyse the difference in content and style between the presentation of the two.

Task 2

Look in detail at the remainder of each page and answer the following questions:

1 What other information is given on these pages?

2 How is it presented in terms of layout?

3 What information is given about the institution that produced the title?

4 What assumptions about the audience does each newspaper make?

Task 3

Write your own story. Possible sources for this might be:

● TV or radio news

● A story in a local newspaper

● An event within the community, school or college

● Teletext news.

Your story must be written in the style of a new tabloid paper aimed at an audience that normally reads a broadsheet.

Now produce a mock-up of the front page of the paper, including a title and other appropriate details, with your story as the lead.

Working on your assignments

Exactly how you work on an assignment will depend on your teacher. It may be that you will have to complete all of the work in class, perhaps with a time limit for doing it. On other occasions, it may be possible to have a go at some of the tasks in the assignment as homework.

Whatever the circumstances for completing the assignment, you should bear in mind some important principles. First, before you do anything, be sure you have all the essential information you need to undertake the assignment:

- What have you been asked to do?
- How and where are you to do it?
- When must it be finished and handed in?

Secondly, try to get an overview of the tasks to be completed. Decide in what order it is best to do them. Make a note of any information you need to collect or material you need to find for the work. Make arrangements to get access to any special equipment you need – for example, a camera or tape recorder.

Thirdly, take care in presenting your assignment. Try to organise your material so that you are showing off what you know and what you can do. If you are asked to write down information, that does not mean that you have to write it as an essay. This may not be the best format to adopt if you want to get information across clearly and concisely. Think about how using headings to prioritize the information might help. Try bullet points (as in the list above) or numbers to separate out points you wish to make.

Where appropriate, you should use coloured pens or pencils and drawing instruments for sketches, diagrams and layouts. Don't forget some of the important skills you have learned in doing your production work. Marks can be gained for using these in many of the assignments you will be doing. Make sure you lay out scripts and storyboards properly, and do design work such as posters and layouts on plain paper.

Remember, though, that the ideas you are putting forward are the most important things. Drawing skills are less crucial than getting across the idea you want to communicate. If possible, use a format that allows you to display the skills you feel most confident about. If you like writing, then a script might be more manageable for you than a storyboard, for example.

On your own

ON YR. OWN

Have a look at the assignment on page 227 in which you are asked to work in the medium of newspapers. Think how some of the points mentioned would apply to this assignment if you were asked to do it. For example, how might you use headings in Tasks 1 and 2 to present the information you want to get across? What is the best way to approach Task 3? What resources would you need for this task? It may be helpful to look at the section on the practical production to help you with this (pages 211–218).

Imagine for a moment that it is your job to mark all the assignments...

Making the grade

Once all your coursework has been marked by your teacher, you will have some idea of how well you have done on Paper 1. However, you need to bear in mind that the mark awarded by your teacher may not be the final mark you will receive from the exam board.

Each centre (in other words, school or college) has to send off a sample of the work marked by its teachers, to ensure that all centres are marking to exactly the same standard throughout the country. Marks for any candidate may go up or down, therefore, if the exam board feels that an adjustment is necessary.

Your final grade will be a combination of your coursework mark, with any adjustments made by the board, and your mark for the controlled test, which is marked by examiners employed by the board. You will get to know your final grade towards the end of August, along with all your other GCSE results.

If your work is clean, neat and presented in such a way that it is easy to follow, you are likely to get a much better mark than if you hand in messy scraps of paper that make little sense. Once you have completed the work, make sure you look after it properly. Don't get it creased and dirty and above all don't lose it.

Bear in mind that your spelling, punctuaction and grammar are an important part of the presentation of your assignment.

Finally, before you hand in your work, check it thoroughly. Imagine for a moment that it is your job to mark it (along with a pile of others). Ask yourself if it is easy to read and understand. Are the tasks you have completed clearly separated from one another and labelled? Does it give a good impression of your attitude to your work and the care you

have taken? If you can answer 'yes' to all these questions then your work should at least do justice to the effort you have put into it.

When you have completed all your assignment coursework, your teacher will give a total mark out of 75 for the three pieces that are to be submitted for your exam. Remember, this represents a quarter of the marks that are available for the whole exam.

The Controlled Test

'The Controlled Test will take a case study approach, which is likely to include stimulus material intended to encourage individual research into specific aspects of the topic area'

The Controlled Test (AQA paper 2) is worth 50% of the total marks available for the exam. Preparing for it properly and trying your best at the test are obviously important if you want to do well. Your teacher will tell you what the topic area for the test is. It will be some aspect of Media Studies that allows you to do some research. For example, TV News, comedy films or local radio.

What will the test be like? Well, it won't be like a traditional exam where you have to memorise information and sit writing essays or solving mathematical problems for two hours. Instead, the test takes place over a period of time, decided by your teacher, and you will work on it probably over two sessions until you have completed a total of three hours on the test. Many of you will work on the test during normal lessons. You will, however, be working under exam conditions. That means you will have to work in silence, by yourself and not disturb other people taking the test. Nor will you be allowed to take any notes into the room with you. Between each period when you work on the test, your teacher will lock away the work you are doing, which means that you can't do anything to your paper outside of the special times when the test takes place.

What makes the test most different from a traditional exam, though, is that you will have the chance to see the paper before you actually start taking the test. The paper will be given to you on or soon after 1st May. You can then spend the time before the first test period doing research and preparing for it. Of course,

you can also work on ideas for the test in between the times when you are actually sitting it. There is nothing to stop you improving part of the test you have already done, next time you work on it. It therefore makes sense for you to use this time to make sure that you find out as much appropriate information as you can and to work on the ideas and issues that come up in the test.

The topic area for the controlled test is published in the syllabus over two years before the test itself. Each year it is different. Your teacher will obviously do some work on the topic area to prepare you for the test, but you won't be allowed to submit any assignment coursework that covers that particular topic.

The controlled test will, of course, be concerned with the same key concepts that you have read about earlier in this book – the same ones that you have been working on as part of your course, including your coursework assignments. You can take an educated guess, therefore, that the test is likely to cover at least some of the following areas:

- Analysis of texts
- Promotion/marketing
- Institutional background
- Audience

- Media language – forms and conventions
- Representation

You will also be tested on the 'assessment objectives', which cover:

- Knowledge and understanding
- Analysis and interpretation
- Production skills

So what does this mean in practice? Well, to some extent it determines the kind of task that you will be given. For example, one possible approach is the 'simulation'. In this you will be asked to play a role, or possibly a number of roles, in order to complete the tasks set. This might involve you undertaking a situation comedy, identifying the main elements of the sitcom, suggesting possible settings/characters, designing trailers and presenting ideas for promoting the show. Obviously a wide range of skills is called for here.

Examiners like to make the roles you are asked to play realistic, by choosing something that you might reasonably be asked to do at some point early in a career in media production. On some occasions, therefore, a simulation would be inappropriate; the test might then ask direct questions, such as 'What characteristics do you expect to find in the majority of Westerns?'

It is unlikely that you would be expected to take on the role of a Hollywood film director.

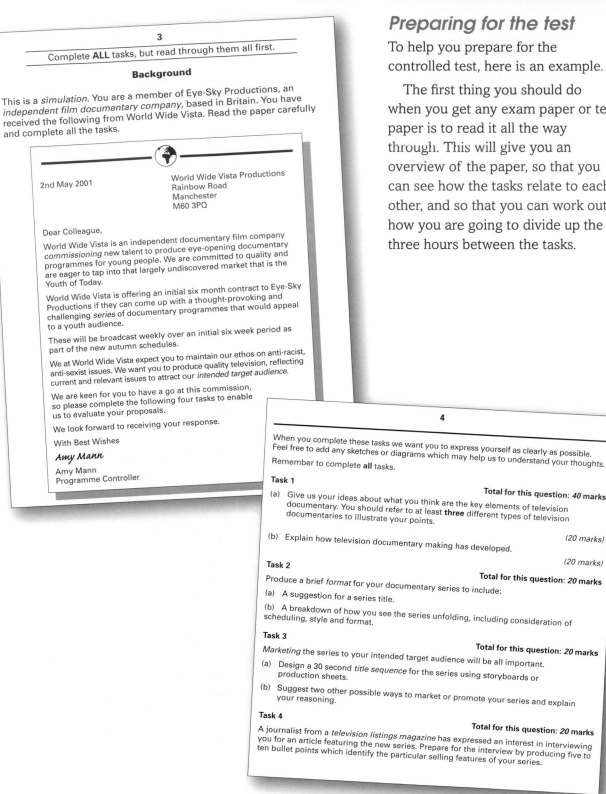

3

Complete **ALL** tasks, but read through them all first.

Background

This is a *simulation*. You are a member of Eye-Sky Productions, an *independent film documentary company*, based in Britain. You have received the following from World Wide Vista. Read the paper carefully and complete all the tasks.

2nd May 2001

World Wide Vista Productions
Rainbow Road
Manchester
M60 3PQ

Dear Colleague,

World Wide Vista is an independent documentary film company *commissioning* new talent to produce eye-opening documentary programmes for young people. We are committed to quality and are eager to tap into that largely undiscovered market that is the Youth of Today.

World Wide Vista is offering an initial six month contract to Eye-Sky Productions if they can come up with a thought-provoking and challenging *series* of documentary programmes that would appeal to a youth audience.

These will be broadcast weekly over an initial six week period as part of the new autumn schedules.

We at World Wide Vista expect you to maintain our ethos on anti-racist, anti-sexist issues. We want you to produce quality television, reflecting current and relevant issues to attract our *intended target audience*.

We are keen for you to have a go at this commission, so please complete the following four tasks to enable us to evaluate your proposals.

We look forward to receiving your response.

With Best Wishes

Amy Mann

Amy Mann
Programme Controller

4

When you complete these tasks we want you to express yourself as clearly as possible. Feel free to add any sketches or diagrams which may help us to understand your thoughts. Remember to complete **all** tasks.

Task 1

Total for this question: **40 marks**

(a) Give us your ideas about what you think are the key elements of television documentary. You should refer to at least **three** different types of television documentaries to illustrate your points.

(20 marks)

(b) Explain how television documentary making has developed.

(20 marks)

Task 2

Total for this question: **20 marks**

Produce a brief *format* for your documentary series to include:

(a) A suggestion for a series title.

(b) A breakdown of how you see the series unfolding, including consideration of scheduling, style and format.

Task 3

Total for this question: **20 marks**

Marketing the series to your intended target audience will be all important.

(a) Design a 30 second *title sequence* for the series using storyboards or production sheets.

(b) Suggest two other possible ways to market or promote your series and explain your reasoning.

Task 4

Total for this question: **20 marks**

A journalist from a *television listings magazine* has expressed an interest in interviewing you for an article featuring the new series. Prepare for the interview by producing five to ten bullet points which identify the particular selling features of your series.

Preparing for the test

To help you prepare for the controlled test, here is an example.

The first thing you should do when you get any exam paper or test paper is to read it all the way through. This will give you an overview of the paper, so that you can see how the tasks relate to each other, and so that you can work out how you are going to divide up the three hours between the tasks.

An important clue in deciding how much time to spend on each task is the mark scheme. Note in the example that the tasks break down as follows:

Task 1	40 marks
Task 2	20 marks
Task 3	20 marks
Task 4	20 marks

Rather than simply spending an hour on each question it would obviously make sense to spend more time on the first task, which is worth more than any other questions. So you might decide to spend 70 minutes on task one and 35 minutes on each of the other tasks. This will leave you with a spare 5 minutes for checking your work.

You will have some time between seeing the test paper and the first session when you start work on it. Use this time intelligently to some preparatory work. It is a good idea to make some fairly detailed notes: even though you aren't allowed to take notes into the exam room, they are a useful way of helping you both remember your ideas and to revise between exam sessions.

Planning First, you need to plan how you are going to approach the test. Assuming you have already planned how long to spend on each task, you must now decide in what order to have a go at the tasks. It will probably make a lot of sense to tackle them in the order they appear on the paper. The reason for this is that the tasks may well be related in such a way that you will find it easier to tackle some questions after you have completed others. For example, in the paper we are looking at,

you can see that it would be helpful to have worked through the first task to give you some ideas as a basis for the second and third tasks.

Research Secondly, you need to do some research to help you complete the tasks. Some of the marks are given for knowledge – information that you have learned or found that you use to complete the tasks. In the example, you would need to do some research into documentaries to help you with the first part. This would include work on genre, narrative, visual style, audience and representation Notice that you need to refer to at least three diffirent types of documentary. So if you have not done so already, you need to think about what example you will use to illustrate your answers. Much of this will be work you have already covered as part of your course. To complete part two of the first task, some information about the production and distribution of films would be useful.

For task 4, you are asked to respond using bullet points. This means getting your ideas down in a precise, clear and succinct fashion to be prepared for the interview with the journalist.

Production skills also play an important part in the tasks you are likely to be set in the controlled test. These are worth nearly a third of the total marks available. (Production skills are discussed in more detail on pages 211–218.) Tasks two and three show the sort of work that you are likely to undertake to cover this assessment objective. Developing your skills in writing scripts, drawing storyboards and laying out advertisements and posters are all skills you need to work on to prepare for the Controlled Test.

Your drawing skills don't need to be especially good to score marks on the more graphics-based tasks – it is your ideas that are important. A storyboard that shows a good variety of shots, an ability to construct narratives and a capacity for linking visual images to soundtracks is fine, even if you can only use drawings of matchstick people.

When you come to take the test, you will be given a special sheets for the production tasks by the examining board. These will include storyboard framesheets, production sheets and blank sheets for design and print layouts. It is a good idea to think in advance how you might make the best use of these.

You will have to hand your work in for the last time after the final session of the test. Before you do so, check it thoroughly for spelling, punctuation and grammar, and make sure that it is logical and clearly signposted, so that when it is marked the examiner will be able to work out easily what you have done and in which order.

Practising the test

It would be a good idea to practice a Controlled Test before you come to sit the real one – rather like a mock exam. Here are some suggestions for how you might approach the sample printed on page 232. Why not have a go at working through it now?

Before you begin work, be sure you have a clear idea what sort of programmes can be classified as documentaries. *Big Brother*, for example, is often considered to be a type of documentary although some people prefer to classify it as reality TV. Remember too that you are not limited to contemporary documentaries.

Task 1.

Part a) is your chance to show off what you know about the genre of television documentaries. You need to identify their 'key elements' or in other words to say what you think make documentaries distinctive from other television genres. You are also asked to illustrate your answer by referring to three different types of documentary. So obviously you need to be able to write about different types such as fly on the wall, investigative documentaries or docu-soaps. You will also need to choose some good examples of these types of documentary from those that you have seen. If possible, it is a good idea to make one of these examples a fairly recent one. This will show the examiner that you have a good up-to-date knowledge of what is happening in the media.

UNITED ARTISTS Present
"NANOOK OF THE NORTH"
Produced by ROBERT J. FLAHERTY

Nanook of the North is cited by most film historians as the first feature-length documentary.

Part b) is designed to test your awareness of documentaries over a period of time. You need to show that you understand how they have developed or changed. You may wish to start at the early beginnings of documentary last century with *Nanook of the North* for example. You may like to contrast this approach to documentary film making with more recent popular examples such as the docu-soap. In between you might like to show off your knowledge of the different styles and formats of documentary that have developed since the early days of television. However you choose to answer the question, it is a good idea to show that you understand some of the reasons behind the changes, such as the development of lightweight camera equipment.

Task 2.

Although the task is also split into two parts, it does not necessarily mean they are worth equal marks. In this example you are likely to need to write rather more for part b) as it looks to be worth more than part a).

Try to come up with a lively and imaginative title. Think of some of the titles already used for documentary series on the television and see if you can find one that is different and original. If you want to write a couple of sentences explaining you choice, then that is OK but you do not have to.

Part b) needs more detail. Not only do you need to give ideas for the content of the documentaries to be shown in the series, you also need explain when it might be broadcast, what it will look like and what sort of shape the programme will have. Don't forget that all of these aspects need to match in with the target audience identified in the brief.

Task 3.

Another two part task, although in this case each part seems to be worth about the same. For part a) remember what you have learned about creating a good storyboard or scripting a video sequence. This is the opening of the programme – a title sequence – so don't forget you need to hook your audience. You should try to grab their attention so that they will stay watching the rest of the programme. Part b) asks you for ideas for marketing the programme. You need to think about the way in which new television series are promoted, on billboards or in newspapers for example. Don't forget some of the less obvious ways of drawing attention to a new programme such as appearances on chat shows by people appearing in or involved with the programme.

Task 4.

The final task asks you to prepare for an interview with a journalist from a magazine, such as the *Radio Times*. Remember the idea is that you will be saying things that will help promote the series in the feature article the journalist is writing. So you need to make some notes, using bullet points that will present the programme as lively, upbeat and above all appealing to the target audience. There is no need to write a huge amount for this task. You are asked for five or six bullet points. Each of these could be just a couple of sentences, in note form, that will sum up and highlight the appeal of the series. Be precise and succinct in what you say and you will gain you marks in this task.

Before you finish

Now it is time to check your work through:

- Have you had a go at all the tasks?
- Is it easy to work out which answer belongs with which task?
- Does it all make sense?
- Is the spelling, punctuation and grammar as accurate as you can get it?

Once you are satisfied that everything is in order, you are ready to hand in your script.

All you can do now is wait, and hope that your result is as good as you expect – or maybe even better!

6

TASK
NUMBER

EXEMPLAR (for the guidance of the candidate)

STORYBOARD SHEET
Directions, dialogue, camera,
music, special effects (sfx)

7

EXEMPLAR (for the guidance of the candidate)

LEAVE MARGIN BLANK

PRODUCTION SHEET

TASK NUMBER

MEDIA: FILM, TELEVISION OR RADIO

Special instructions: Vision	Special instructions: Sound	Dialogue	Other information: Setting, interior, exterior, action	Timing

Contacts and Resources

A number of organisations have built up resources that can be used by teachers as part of the coursework to a specification of this type. **The British Film Institute** (21 Stephen Street, London W1T 1LN; tel. 0207 255 144; *www.bfi.org.uk/*) produces an extensive range of books, teaching packs and allied resources. **Film Education** (Alhambra House, 27-31 Charing Cross Road, London WC2H 0AU; tel. 0207 976 2291; *www.filmeducation.org/*) also organises events for teachers and students, as well as producing useful study guides and occasional video trailers of films on general release. **The English and Media Centre** (18 Compton Terrace, London N1 2UN; tel. 0207 359 8080; *www.englishandmedia.co.uk*) organises INSET support for teachers and produces stimulating materials for use in class. The **Northern Ireland Media Education Association** (NIMEA, Belvoir Primary School, Belvoir Drive, Belfast BT8 4DL; tel. 02890 491801) offers support to teachers.

Some trade organisations and bodies produce materials that can be used for particular class activities. The **Radio Authority** (Holbrook House, 14 Great Queen Street, London WC2B 5DG; tel. 0207 430 2724; *www.radioauthority.org.uk/*) publishes its codes of practice and a quarterly report on complaints it has dealt with. Similarly, the **Press Complaints Commission** (1 Salisbury Square, London EC4Y 8AE; tel. 0207 353 1248; *www.pcc.org.uk*) has materials on making a complaint and details of past adjudications. The **British Board of Film Classification** (3 Soho Square, London W1V 6HD; tel. 0207 440 1570; *www.bbfc.co.uk/*) produces a students' guide to film classification. The **Newspaper Society** (Bloomsbury House, 74-7 Great Russell Street, London WC1B 3D; tel. 0207 6367014; *www.newspapersoc.org.uk/*) is an excellent source of information on all aspects of the industry.

For teachers and students a visit to a media organisation can be worth hours of classroom study. There are a number of organisations that welcome pre-booked visits by students and provide an opportunity for them to undertake structured learning programmes on site. The **Museum of the Moving Image** (South Bank, London SE1 8XT; 0207 815 1337) and the **National Museum of Photography , Film and Television** (Pictureville, Bradford, BD1 1NQ; tel. 01274 727 488) both offer an opportunity for students to explore an interesting range of media-related exhibits and activities.

A number of useful publications are available from **AQA** (Stag Hill House, Guildford, Surrey GU2 5XJ; tel. 01483 506506; *www.aqa.org.uk*): the specification, specimen papers and mark schemes, and the Teachers Guide which offers guidance in implementing a course, explains the administrative procedures and suggests strategies for assessing coursework folders. In addition, teachers may find useful the advice concerning the controlled test and tiering.

One excellent but under-used resource is the **Teletext** service, which contains a wealth of information not only about TV itself, such as previews, programme guides and viewing figures, but also film information and details of newspaper stories. A guide for teachers on using the service is given in the education section of Teletext on Channel 4.

The **Internet** has become an effective means of keeping in touch with media education across the curriculum. Teachers using the Internet as a potential resource may find the following sites worth a visit:

The Internet Movies Database (*www.imdb.com/*) Excellent searchable site for information on cinema and the film industry.

Media UK (*www.mediauk.com/directory/*) offers useful links to TV, radio, newspaper and magazine industries.

Media Village (*www.mediavillage.co.uk/*) offers useful links to information about the media industries.

BARB (*www.barb.co.uk/*) provides access to TV audience figures.

Glossary

Italic text indicates that the word is defined elsewhere in the glossary.

KEY

F   **Film**

M **Music**

P   **Print (newspapers and magazines)**

R   **Radio**

TV **Television and video**

Academy ratio [F] The standard frame Aspect ratio adopted by Hollywood of 44.3, or 1.33:1, width to height.

Actuality [R] Sound, recorded or transmitted, of real events that are taking place outside the real events that are taking place outside the studio, such as an interview.

Advertising radio [P] The proportion of a newspaper or magazine taken up by adverts, as opposed to stories and pictures.

Advertorial [P] An advertising feature about products, written like a news story and usually accompanied by pictures.

AM (Amplitude modulation) [R] Long and medium wave frequencies on which radio stations are received.

Anamorphic lens [F] A projection lens used to produce Widescreen images at the cinema.

Anchor [TV] The presenter of a programme, so-called he or she holds the show together.

Anchorage [P TV] The use of words in a caption or commentary to hold or limit the meaning of an image.

Animation [F] Method of making drawings or models move on screen, by shooting still images a few frames at a time.

A&R (Artists and repertoire) [M] The department of a music company responsible for discovering new acts and looking after musicians.

Aspect ratio [F TV] The relationship between the width and height of a film or TV image. See Academy ratio and Widescreen.

Astra [TV] The satellite positioned at 19.2 degrees east that carries all the Sky channels.

Audience participation [F M P R TV] Getting the audience involved in the media.

Audience positioning [F M P R TV] The relationship between the audience and the media product. How the media tries to determine the response of an audience to its products.

Audience segmentation [F M P R TV] The identification and splitting off of particular audiences by media products.

Audio [F M R TV] Sound, either as part of a Broadcast or as a Soundtrack.

Auteur [F] The author of a film. The person who gives a film its special identity of style.

Autocue [TV] A screen that displays what the presenter has to say during the broadcast.

Back announcement [R] Information about an item given by a presenter after it has been broadcast.

Backlighting [F TV] Lighting placed behind a subject to create a silhouette.

BARB (Broadcasters' Audience Research Board) [TV] The organization that collects and publishes weekly audience figures or ratings.

Best boy [F] The assistant to the *Gaffer*.

Big close-up (BCU) [F TV] A shot that shows the face filling a frame, good for expressing strong emotions.

Bollywood [F] The nickname of the Indian film industry (a mixture of 'Bombay' and 'Hollywood').

Boom [F R TV] A long pole on which a microphone is placed in order to pick up sound.

British Board of Film Classification (BBFC) [F] The organisation that issues certificates to films and videos, stating whether they are suitable for children or young people to watch.

Broadcasting Standards Commission [R TV] The organisation set up by Parliament to investigate complaints about taste and decency on TV, video and radio.

Broadsheet [P] A newspaper printed on sheets of paper 116.83 × 81.28 cm (46 × 32 inches). See also *Tabloid*.

Bulletin controller [R TV] the person responsible for the film reports and still photographs needed for the broadcast.

Bulletin producer [R TV] The person who makes sure that the bulletins run exactly to time.

Bulletin script [TV] A typed script of the words that appear on the Autocue, along with other information about the bulletin.

By-line [P] Information giving the name of the person who wrote an article.

Camera script [F TV] A script on which camera angels and shots have been planned.

Cardioid [F R TV] A radio that picks up sound from directly in front and to the sides.

Cart machine [R] A machine that records and plays short sound recordings such as Jingles and Trails.

Cassette tape [R] A tape system in which the tape is enclosed in a plastic cover and played on a cassette player.

Catch-line [P R] A word used to identify a story.

Cathode ray tube [TV A tube in a TV set that produces the picture on screen.

CB radio (Citizen's band radio [R] System used by amateurs to communicate with each other.

CD (Compact disc) [M R TV] Musical or video recording in digital form impresses onto a plastic disc.

CD-Rom (Compact Disc-Read Only Memory) Information in the form of video, sound or text, stored on a CD that is read by a computer using a laser.

Censorship [F M P R TV] The control of what the media reproduces, by governments or other agencies, on either moral or political grounds.

Channel [TV] A fixed band of frequencies on which transmission can be made.

Chief sub-editor [P] A senior journalist with design and layout skills. He or she decides which stories will go on each *Page scheme*.

Chroma key [TV] a device that allows an image to be filmed in front of a background that has been produced elsewhere.

CinemaScope [F] a *Widescreen* film image.

Cinerama [F] A *Widescreen* process using three projectors to produce an image on a curved screen.

Circulation [P] the number of copies that a newspaper or magazine sells.

Clapperboard [F TV] A board on which details of each *Take* are given, and which is clapped in order to synchronize sound and vision.

Classified adverts [P] Small adverts in columns, arranged into categories, e.g. Situations Vacant, usually placed in newspapers by individuals.

Cliff-hanger [P R TV] A situation that keeps the audience guessing what will happen in the next episode of a programme or story.

Close-up (CU) [F TV] A shot in which only a subject's head and shoulders are shown.

Colour separation [P] A printing process where pages are printed using only four colours: black, yellow, red (or magenta) and blue (or cyan). All the colours needed to produce a full-colour photograph are made by mixing different sized dots of these four basic colours.

Code [F M P R TV] An element of convention through which the media communicates meaning to us because we have learned how to read it.

Community radio [R] A station serving a small community, e.g. a university campus.

Connotation [F P R TV] The secondary, associated or additional meaning that a *Sign* carries in addition to its everyday meaning. See also *Denotation*.

Context [F M P R TV] Where we consume media products.

Continuity [F TV] ensuring that each shot in a film or TV programme has details that match.

Convention [F M P R TV] the accepted, or apparently natural way of constructing a media text, which familiarity will have made an audience come to expect.

Copy [P] 1. A story written by a journalist. 2. Words written by an advertising agency to sell a product.

Crane [F TV] A shot from above, using a device of the same name.

Crash edit [TV] Editing footage on domestic VHS machines by using the pause facilities.

Credits [F M R TV] Details of the people involved in the making of the media product.

Crop [P] To cut down a photographic image, usually to get rid of unwanted detail.

Crosshead [P] A word used to separate paragraphs in a newspaper or magazine story.

Cross-over artist [M] An artist who appeals to music consumers of several types.

Cue [R TV] to find the beginning of a piece of music, film or tape and prepare it for transmission.

Cue sheet [R] an introduction to a *Package*, which is written by the reporter for the presenter of a radio programme to read out.

Cut 1. [F TV] an edit in which two segments are joined together by simply switching from one to the other 2. [F] The edited version of a film. 3. [P] To reduce the length of a story.

Cut-away [F TV] A shot inserted into a scene that shows action taking place somewhere else.

DAT (Digital audio tape) [M R] Tape used to store digital recordings of a high quality.

Deep focus [F] A cinematic technique whereby objects are kept in focus in both foreground and background.

Delay system [R] A system to prevent obscenities being broadcast on live radio, by delaying transmission by several seconds.

Denotation [F M P R TV] The everyday or commonsense meaning of a *Sign*. See also *Connotation*.

Depth of field [F TV] The distance in an image over which images remain in sharp focus.

Desk-top publishing (DTP) [P] Software packages that enable print publications of a professional quality to be designed on a personal computer.

Digital broadcasting [R TV] A technique of transmitting signals digitally to produce better reception and to allow greater use of capacity by transmitters.

Digital recording [M] A form of recording that changes sound into a signal of on and off electrical impulses. It produces better sound quality than traditional recording techniques.

Direct inputting [P] Using a computer terminal to key in *Copy* ready for subbing and typesetting.

Director [F TV] The person responsible for the artistic interpretation of a film or programme.

Display advert [P] An advert for a product, with photographs and graphics, that is places in a newspaper or magazine by a business.

Dissolve [F TV] An editing technique in which one image or scene fades into another.

Dolby [F R TV] A technique in sound recording that helps cut out background noise and distortion.

Dolby Surround [F R TV] A type of *Surround sound*.

Dolly [F TV] A wheel on which a camera can be mounted to allow it to move around a set.

Double heading [R TV] The use of two presenters on a programme such as a news bulletin.

Dual keying [P] A system in which *Copy* was first typed by a journalist and then typed again into a linotype machine by a compositor.

Dub [R TV] To copy from one tape to another.

Editor 1. [P R TV] The person ultimately responsible for the content of a newspaper, magazine or news programme. 2. [F TV] The person who puts together a film or TV programme from the footage shot.

Elaboration [P] The paragraphs that follow the *Intro* of a story, which tells readers more about it.

E.N.G. (Electronic news gathering) [TV] A report from the scene on video.

Establishing shot [F TV] A shot that shows the characters in a location, to let the audience know where they are and how they are situated.

Establishing two shot See *Two shot*.

Event movie [F] Blockbuster film that is accompanied by a large amount of *Hype*.

Exciter lamp [F] A light in a projector that enables the optical soundtrack to be read.

Exposure [F TV] The amount of light allowed to enter by a camera.

Fade [F TV] An editing technique in which an image disappears gradually, leaving the screen blank.

Fader [R] A slider on a radio desk that alters the volume of a microphone or other sound device.

Fading up [F TV] A technique in which an image slowly appears from a blank screen.

Fanzine [P] A low-budget publication produced by enthusiasts about their particular area of interest, such as a band or a football team.

Feature [P] An article that takes an in-depth look at a topic or issue.

Feature film [F] A full-length film, often the main film, usually fictional.

Feed [R TV] Transmission of a programme or information, usually to or from headquarters.

Feedback 1. [M R TV] A high-pitched sound created by placing a mike too close to a speaker. 2. [P R TV] Responses from an audience about an issue or programme.

Fibre optic [R TV] Transmission of a *Signal* down a thin cable by means of light beams.

Fill [P] A story of no more than one or two paragraphs, used to fill a gap on a page.

Film gauge [F] The size or width of film, e.g. 35 mm or 16 mm.

Final cut [F] The last version of an edited film prior to release. See *Cut*.

First run [F] The first showing of a film, usually in selected London cinemas.

Flashback [F TV] A narrative device in which a character thinks back to a previous event, which is shown on screen.

Flat pan [P] A plan of a magazine that shows every page and what will appear on it.

Floppy disc [P R TV] A means by which information from a computer can be stored in a portable form.

FM (Frequency modulation) [R] A system of transmitting high frequency signals to give good quality sound reproduction.

Focus [F P TV] To make sure that the important images are sharp.

Focus puller [F] An assistant camera operator, part of whose job is to operate the focus on the camera.

Footage [F TV] Film or video tape that has been shot.

Footprint [R TV] The area over which a satellite transmission can be received.

Format [R TV] The way in which a programme is put together or constructed, e.g. as a studio discussion.

Fps (Frames per second) [F] The unit of measurement of the speed at which a film is projected or shot.

Fragmentation [F M P R TV] See *Market fragmentation* and *Audience segmentation*.

Frame [F TV] The way the camera is used to place an image within its field of view.

Freeze-frame [F TV] Stopping the action and creating a still image, e.g. when athletes cross the winning line.

Frequency [R] The position on the dial of a radio station on a scale that uses units called hertz to measure the cycles per second at which the station is broadcast.

Gaffer [F TV] The person in charge of the electrics and lighting on a film set.

Gate [F] The part of a camera or projector in front of the lens, through which the film passes.

Gauge [F] The size or width of celluloid on which a film is shot, e.g. 35 mm.

General release [F] The *Exhibition* of a film that is shown in cinemas across the country.

Generation [TV] The number of times a tape has been copied.

Genre [F M P R TV] The type of category of a film, programme or other media text. See *Sub-genre*.

Gold (Classic gold) [R TV] A type of broadcast in which music or programmes from a previous era are featured.

Grip [F] Stagehand. See also *Key grip*.

Gross [F] The total revenue of a film from *Box office* and *Spin-offs*.

Hammocking [TV] Placing a new or less appealing programme between two successful shows in order to attract an audience.

Hand-held [F TV] Using a camera without a tripod.

Hard news [P R TV] News that is important and needs to be reported immediately.

High angle [F TV] A shot taken from above the subject.

Highlight [R TV] Part of an event or programme considered worthy of special attention, e.g. highlights of a football match.

Home pages Documents containing information on the *Internet*.

Hot-metal printing [P] A kind of printing that was used in the 1960s. Ink was placed onto movable metal type and newsprint was then run over the top of the plates.

Hypodermic model [F M P R TV] The idea that the media injects its consumers with messages and meanings it chooses and that the audience has no real power to resist.

Ideal viewer/reader [F M P R TV] Someone who is typical of the audience for a particular product.

Identity [R] The identity of a radio station, established, for example, by the use of jingles.

Image [TV P] A visual representation of something.

Image analysis [F M P TV] The study of how images are put together, and how the audience takes meaning from them.

Index [F M P R TV] A sign that works by having a link with the concept it represents, e.g. a thermometer is often shown to imply extreme heat or cold.

Industry [F M P R TV] The organisation that produces media products, e.g. a Hollywood studio or a newspaper proprietor.

Insert [F TV] A shot that is put into a sequence to give a more complete view of what is going on, e.g. someone's reaction to an event or comment.

Institution [F M P R TV] An organization that produces media products. It has a system of values, usually apparent in the way in which texts are produced.

Intercut (Cross cut) [F R TV] To present action from two different scenes by shifting from one to the other, to suggest they are happening simultaneously.

Internet A world-wide system of communication between individuals through the use of personal computers.

Intro [P] The first paragraph of a story.

Iris [F TV] A device on a camera that determines how much light passes through the lens.

Item [R TV] A single news story in a bulletin.

Jump cut [F TV] An edit in which action appears to jump in an illogical way.

Key grip [F] Person in charge of the *Grips*.

Key light [F TV] The main light used to illuminate a scene.

Laser disc [F TV] A high-quality means of reproducing a film on a TV screen, whereby video and sound signals are encoded on reflective discs and read by laser.

Leader 1. [] The beginning of a piece of recording tape. 2. [P] The main editorial in a broadsheet newspaper.

Letterbox [TV] A technique whereby *Widescreen* films are shown on TV, leaving black spaces at the top and bottom of the screen.

Libel [F P R TV] A law aimed at preventing false and damaging statements about people being published in a permanent form in print and broadcast products.

Library shot [TV] Footage shot by a TV camera crew, which is then stored in a library to be used as illustration for a news or current affairs story.

Linotype [P] A machine used for composing blocks of text in newspapers, magazines and books.

Lip mike [R TV] A microphone that is held close to the lips to cut out most of the background noise, e.g. at a football match.

Lip sync [F TV] Keeping the sound and the movement of the actors' lips in time with one another.

Live action [F TV] Film or television that involves people as opposed to *Animation*

Long shot [F TV] A shot that shows the characters in the distance, with details of their surroundings, before they are seen in *Close-up*.

Macro lens [F TV] A lens that allows very close-up detail.

Market fragmentation [F M P R TV] The breaking down of the market for media products into small units.

Market saturation [F M P R TV] When a particular part of the market is seen to be completely catered for by products. See also *Gap in the market*.

Masthead [P] The title of a newspaper on the front page.

Media language [F M P R TV] The means by which the media communicates to us and the forms and conventions by which it does so.

Mediation [F P R TV] The process by which the media represents an event or issue, by intervening and selecting information for the audience.

Medium shot (MS) [F TV] A shot between *Close-up* and *Long shot* that gives the character and the surroundings roughly equal amounts of the frame.

Megahertz [R] A measurement of wavelength that stands for one million cycles per second.

Minority audience [F M P R TV] A small audience with an interest in a subject not regarded as popular or widespread.

Mix [F M P R TV] To put together sound or images from different sources, e.g. the visuals on a TV programme or the sounds on a record. See also *Remixing*.

Monitor [F TV] A TV that allows someone to watch action that is being recorded on screen, to ensure that it looks as it should.

Mono (Monaural, monophonic) [R TV] Sound that is produced through just one channel or speaker. See also *Stereo*.

Montage [F P TV] The putting together of visual images to form a sequence.

Multi-media Computer technology that allows text, sound, graphic and video images to be combined into one programme.

Multi-plex [F] A cinema with several screens.

Nag (News at a glance) [P] A short summary that gives the main points of the news.

Nagra [F] A sound recording machine used in film-making.

Narrative [F M P R TV] The telling of a story or unfolding of a plot that is common to most media texts.

Narrative code [F P R TV] A way of describing the conventions or elements that the audience has come to expect to be included in a story.

Narrowcast [P R TV] Sending a message of information to a small and defined audience, as opposed to broadcasting to a mass audience.

Needle-time [M R] The time used in playing records that a radio station must pay for.

Negative [F P] An image that has been shot onto film from which a *Print* or *Positive* is taken.

News agency [P R TV] A private company that sells stories to the news media. See *Wire Service*.

News agenda [P R TV] A list, made by the *News editor*, of stories that should be followed up.

News bulletin [R TV] A short summary of the current main news stories.

News editor [P R TV] Person who assesses the value of news coming in and gives it to reporters.

News list [P R TV] A list with information on events and stories.

News sense [P R TV] A word used by journalists to describe a gut feeling about what makes a good story that will interest readers.

News values [P R TV] Factors that influence whether a story will be selected for coverage.

Nib (News in brief) [P] A one- or two-paragraph story that gives only the basic facts.

Nicam stereo (Near-Instantaneous Companding System) [TV] A technique that allows TVs to broadcast programmes in *Stereo* sound.

Nine-o'clock watershed [TV] An agreement not to show explicit sex or violence before 9.00 pm, so that parents will know that it is safe to allow their children to watch TV before this time.

OB (Outside broadcast) [R TV] A broadcast from outside the studio, usually of an important news or sporting event.

Offset [P] A system of printing in which the image is transferred to a roller before being printed on to the newsprint itself.

Optical soundtrack [F] A way of putting sound on to a film so that it can be read by a photoelectric cell.

Out-take [F TV] A scene that is unsuitable because of technical problems or errors in it.

Overexpose [F] To allow too much light on to a film, spoiling the image.

Package [R TV] A pre-recorded news item or feature provided by a reporter for a programme.

Page lead [P] The main story on a newspaper page, usually the longest story with the biggest headline.

Page scheme [P] A plan of the news pages, drawn up by the advertising department to show where adverts that have been sold on the page are placed.

Pan and scan [F TV] Technique of selecting part of a *Widescreen* image to make it fit onto a standard TV screen.

Pan shot [F TV] A shot in which the camera moves horizontally, either following a piece of action or shifting across from one image to another, as though making a survey of a scene.

Parallel action [F TV] A technique in which the action is edited to show two separate events taking place at the same time.

Pay-per-view [TV] A system used by subscription channels in which the audience pays to see specific programmes, such as films or sport.

Phototypesetting [P] A technique in which stories are typed on computers and then printed onto bromide paper. This paper is then cut to size and pasted onto page plans, which are photographed.

Pirate radio (Free radio) [R] Stations that are not licensed.

Playlist [M R] A list of records that the radio station is committed to playing.

Point-of-view shot [F TV] A shot that shows the audience exactly what a particular character sees.

Positive [F P] Photographic image or film that has the colours and tones of the original.

Post-production [F TV] The editing of film or TV programme.

Pre-production [F TV] The planning stage of a film or TV programme.

Press Association (PA) [P R TV] An agency that supplies news to organizations such as newspapers.

Prime time [TV] Peak viewing time, usually the evening.

Print [F] A *Positive* copy of a film.

Producer 1. [F TV] the person responsible for initiating, organizing and financing a venture. 2. [R] the person responsible for the production of a radio programme. 3. [M] Someone who oversees a recording in the recording studio and gives it a particular 'feel'.

Product placement [F TV] A form of *Sponsorship* in which advertisers pay the producers of films to have characters use their products.

Profit margin [F M P R TV] The difference between what a media product costs to produce and what it costs to buy.

PRS (Performing Rights Society) [M] Organisation that looks after the interests of musicians and artists and collects royalties for work that is broadcast.

Public service broadcasting (PSB) [R TV] Broadcasting that is funded by the taxpayer, as opposed to commercial broadcasting, which relies on advertising revenue.

Qualitative data [F M P R TV] Information of people's opinions about media products, e.g. whether they like them and why.

Quantative data [F M P R TV] Information in the form of numbers, such as how many people watched a particular programme or read a specific magazine.

Quintrophonic sound [F] Sound system amplified through five speakers, three in front of the audience and two behind.

Rate card [P] A list of the advertising fees charged by the publication.

Ratings [R TV] The number of viewers or listeners that a programme attracts.

RDS (Radio Data System) [R] A tuning system that allows the station that is playing on radio to be identified by showing its name on a digital display.

Reaction shot [F TV] An image showing a character's response to a piece of dialogue or dialogue.

Reader [F M P R TV] A member of the audience, especially someone who is actively responding to the Media text.

Rear projection [F] A technique of filming and image projected behind another image to suggest that action is happening on location.

Reel-to-reel [R] An open-reel tape recorder/player, as opposed to a cassette player.

Remixing [M] Combining the separate tracks of a recording in a different way to produce a different sound to the original *Mix*.

Representation [F M P R TV] The act of communicating by using symbols to stand for things.

Rolling news station [TV] A channel that broadcasts nothing but news 24 hours a day.

Rotary press [P] A means of printing newspapers and magazines by using a cylindrical drum.

Royalties [M] Fees paid to an artist if one of their songs is broadcast or recorded by another artist.

Running order [R TV] A sheet that lists each news item in the order in which it will appear in the *Broadcast*.

Run-of-paper advertising [P] An advert in a newspaper, whose position is left to the newspaper.

Rushes [F] The film shot in one day.

Sampling [M] A technique in which sounds from existing recordings are used to make new ones.

Satellite broadcasting [TV] The use of satellites to bounce a signal back to earth to be received by a dish.

Scale [P] To reduce the size of an image without cutting out any detail.

Scan [P] To make an electronic copy of an image.

Screenplay [F] The script for a film.

Serial drama [TV] The technical name for *Soap opera*.

Sexism [F M P R TV] Prejudice against a person based on their gender.

SFX [F TV] Special effects or devices used to create particular visual illusions, e.g. battles in space or animated characters talking to actors.

Short 1. [F] A film of less than feature length. 2. [P] A story usually between three and eight paragraphs in length.

Shot [TV] A single image taken by a camera. See also *Long shot*, *Medium shot*, *Close up*, *Big close up*, *Point-of-view shot*, *Pan shot* and *Zoom*.

Showcase concert [M] A gig intended to show record companies the quality of a band.

Shutter [F TV] A mechanism that opens and closes as film moves behind the camera's lens.

Sign [F M P R TV] A word or image that is used to represent an object or idea.

Signal [R TV] An electronically coded message that is sent out from a source, such as a radio transmitter, to be picked up by a receiver, such as a radio.

Sitcom [TV] A *Genre* of programme that relies for its comedy on a particular situation, e.g. students living together in a flat.

Slide [TV] A still photograph of a person, symbol or scene.

Slot [R TV] A time period on a TV or radio schedule.

Soap opera [R TV] A *Serial drama* that is broadcast in frequent episodes.

Soft focus [F TV] The device of shooting the subject a little out of focus to create a specific effect, usually to do with nostalgia, an attractive female star or dreams.

Soundbite [R TV] A phrase that is memorable and can be easily absorbed into a news report. Much favoured by politicians.

Sound effects [F R TV] Additional sounds other than dialogue or music, designed to add atmosphere and realism to a piece.

Sound engineer [M] A technician who sets up and operates the recording studio.

Soundtrack [F TV] The *Audio*, as opposed to the visual, element of a film or programme, which is usually a mix of dialogue, music and effects.

Splash [P] The main story on the front page of a newspaper or magazine.

Splice [F R] To join two pieces of film or tape.

Split screen [F TV] A technique in which two or more images are shown at once on a screen.

Sponsorship [F M P R TV] A form of advertising in which advertisers pay to have their name shown or read in association with a media report.

Staff writer [P] A journalist who is employed to work on one particular newspaper or magazine.

Steadicam [F TV] A device that allows a camera operator to move with the camera without jolting or shaking it.

Stereo (Stereophonic) [F R TV] Sound reproduction simultaneously through two separate channels. See also *Mono*.

Stereotyping [F P R TV] Representation of people or groups of people by a few characters.

Still [F TV] A static image.

Storyboard [F TV] A mock-up of how a sequence will look when it has been filmed.

Style mag [P] A magazine dealing with fashion in things such as dress, interior design or motoring.

Sun-editor [P] A person responsible for checking a journalist's copy, deciding its position in a newspaper or magazine and designing the page on which it will appear.

Sub-genre [F M P R TV] A *Genre* within a genre.

Support [P] Usually the second longest story on a newspaper page, 'supporting' the main story.

Surround sound [F R TV] A technique using a number of speakers to improve the sound quality of films and radio and TV programmes.

Sync [F TV] When sound and image are linked properly together in time.

Tabloid [P] A newspaper with half the size of a *Broadsheet*, with pages measuring 58.42 × 40.64 cm (23 × 16 inches).

Tail [F TV] The end of a piece of tape.

Take [F TV] A single recording or filming of a scene. Several takes my be needed to get the scene right.

Talkback [R TV] A system of communication used off-air between the studio and the production team.

Talking head [TV] A shot of a person talking to the camera.

Technical code [F M P R TV] The conventions of producing media text that are determined by the equipment used and what it is capable of doing, e.g. different camera angles or zooms.

Teletext [TV] A film and information service broadcast as a separate signal on TV channels, which can be received by a TV set with a special decoder.

Terrestrial television [TV] Television stations whose signals are transmitted and received without the use of satellite technology.

Tilt [F TV] Camera movement in a vertical direction.

Time lapse [F TV] A technique of filming single frames of action at delayed intervals and replaying them at normal speed, to speed up dramatically an action or event.

Track [F TV] To move the camera alongside a piece of action.

Trail/trailer [F R TV] An edited version of a film or programme designed to interest an audience in the text itself.

Transmission area [R] The part of the country to which a radio station broadcasts.

Transponder [R TV] An individual channel of communication from a satellite.

Travelogue [R TV] A programme about travel.

Treatment [F TV] A preliminary script showing how a film or programme might be put together.

Two shot/Establishing two shot [TV] A shot in which two people are shown in the frame together, often used an as *Establishing* shot at the opening of an interview or some dialogue.

Typography 1. [P] The design of lettering in printing. 2. The process of typesetting.

Underground [F P] An alternative publication or film, which often attacks or ridicules the mainstream.

Unidirectional [F R TV] A microphone that picks up sound from the direction in which it is pointed.

Uses and gratifications approach [F M P R TV] The study of how people use media products and what they get out of them.

VCR [TV] Video cassette recorder.

VHS (Video home system) [TV] The standard system used for domestic video recording.

Viewfinder [F TV] The part of a camera in which the operator can see and frame an image.

Vision mixer [TV] Equipment for linking together two camera images on the screen.

Voice over [F TV] Off-screen voice that usually tells the story, explains the action, or comments on it.

Vox pop [R TV] A collection of comments from members of the public.

Web site A publication of the *Internet*, named after the World Wide Web, which organises the information.

Whip pan [F] A very fast movement of the camera along a horizontal plane.

Widescreen [F TV] An *Aspect ratio* in which the width of the image is much greater than its height.

Wildtrack [F R TV] A recording of background or atmospheric noise that can be used at the editing stage.

Wipe [F TV] An edit in which one image moves across the screen to replace another by apparently wiping it off.

Wire service [P R TV] A *News agency* that provides national and international news to a media organization.

Zoo format [R] A radio programme that includes other voices besides that of the presenter.

Zoom 1. [F TV] Device on a camera that allows movement towards or away from an image or piece of action. 2. A shot in which the camera zooms in from a *Long shot* to a *Big close-up*.

The Modern P

Coppa, Frank J.

The modern Papacy since 1789

LONGMAN HIST

General Editor: A.I

This ambitious new
medieval times thro
written by a leadin
students and genera

The first volume to

The Modern Papacy
Frank J. Coppa